ART DIRECTION AND PRODUCTION DESIGN

BEHIND THE SILVER SCREEN

BEHIND THE SILVER SCREEN

When we take a larger view of a film's "life" from development through exhibition, we find a variety of artists, technicians, and craftspeople in front of and behind the camera. Writers write. Actors, who are costumed and made-up, speak the words and perform the actions described in the script. Art directors and set designers develop the look of the film. The cinematographer decides upon a lighting scheme. Dialogue, sound effects, and music are recorded, mixed, and edited by sound engineers. The images, final sound mix, and special visual effects are assembled by editors to form a final cut. Moviemaking is the product of the efforts of these men and women, yet few film histories focus much on their labor.

Behind the Silver Screen calls attention to the work of filmmaking. When complete, the series will comprise ten volumes, one each on ten significant tasks in front of or behind the camera, on the set or in the postproduction studio. The goal is to examine closely the various collaborative aspects of film production, one at a time and one per volume, and then to offer a chronology that allows the editors and contributors to explore the changes in each of these endeavors during six eras in film history: the silent screen (1895–1927), classical Hollywood (1928–1946), postwar Hollywood (1947–1967), the Auteur Renaissance (1968–1980), the New Hollywood (1981–1999), and the Modern Entertainment

Marketplace (2000–present). *Behind the Silver Screen* promises a look at who does what in the making of a movie; it promises a history of filmmaking, not just a history of films.

Jon Lewis, Series Editor

1. **ACTING** (Claudia Springer and Julie Levinson, eds.)
2. **ANIMATION** (Scott Curtis, ed.)
3. **CINEMATOGRAPHY** (Patrick Keating, ed.)
4. **COSTUME, MAKEUP, AND HAIR** (Adrienne McLean, ed.)
5. **DIRECTING** (Virginia Wright Wexman, ed.)
6. **EDITING AND SPECIAL VISUAL EFFECTS** (Charlie Keil and Kristen Whissel, eds.)
7. **PRODUCING** (Jon Lewis, ed.)
8. **SCREENWRITING** (Andrew Horton and Julian Hoxter, eds.)
9. **ART DIRECTION AND PRODUCTION DESIGN** (Lucy Fischer, ed.)
10. **SOUND: DIALOGUE, MUSIC, AND EFFECTS** (Kathryn Kalinak, ed.)

ART DIRECTION AND PRODUCTION DESIGN

Edited by Lucy Fischer

RUTGERS UNIVERSITY PRESS
New Brunswick, New Jersey

Dedicated with love and admiration to David and Brandi with wishes for a happy and fulfilling life together

Library of Congress Cataloging-in-Publication Data
Art direction and production design / edited by Lucy Fischer.
pages cm — (Behind the silver screen series ; 9)
Includes bibliographical references and index.
ISBN 978-0-8135-6436-4 (hardback) — ISBN 978-0-8135-6435-7 (pbk.) —
ISBN 978-0-8135-6437-1 (e-book)
1. Motion pictures—Art direction. 2. Motion pictures—Setting and scenery.
I. Fischer, Lucy, editor
PN1995.9.A74A78 2015
791.4302'5—dc23
2014017490

Visit our website: http://rutgerspress.rutgers.edu
Manufactured in the United States of America

CONTENTS

ACKNOWLEDGMENTS

I would like to thank Jon Lewis for inviting me to edit this volume as well as assisting with it, and all the contributors to the book who did an excellent job with a difficult task. I have also appreciated the assistance of several people at Rutgers University Press: Leslie Mitchner, Marilyn Campbell, and Lisa Boyajian. At the University of Pittsburgh, staffer Jen Florian helped me with many tasks, as did several graduate research assistants: Jonathon Vander Woode, Sara Button, and Matthew Carlin. I also appreciate the travel funds awarded me by Dean John Cooper (Arts and Sciences) and Ronald Linden (European Union Center of Excellence). As always I am grateful to Mark Wicclair for support that goes well beyond the boundaries of any scholarly project.

ART DIRECTION AND PRODUCTION DESIGN

INTRODUCTION Lucy Fischer

Production design will always be silent, unsung, and one of the most important aspects of filmmaking.

—*Polly Platt*

While generally unknown and uncelebrated, the cinema's true unsung heroes are production designers and their talented teams of art directors and set decorators. They are the architects of illusion; they are tasked with taking a blank soundstage or location and producing a visually convincing, functional, and appealing setting for the screen. In short, they are visionaries designing cinematic dreams.

—*Cathy Whitlock*

As is clear from the epigraphs above (the first by a practitioner, the other by a scholar), art direction is a poorly recognized and undervalued component of film production. In fact, one might claim that it is invisible to the general public, ironic for a craft that emphasizes the pictorial. Charles and Mirella Jona Affron have remarked that art direction rarely receives any attention in film advertising and publicity, which generally stress what is deemed most saleable in a movie.[1]

This omission has led Juan Antonio Ramirez to protest: "No longer may the historian treat movie architecture, itself the inanimate vehicle of symbolic cultural messages, as something of only marginal or secondary interest."[2] This book answers this challenge by placing the practice of cinematic art direction, most appropriately, center stage.

Behind the Scenes

One of the reasons the craft has received minimal attention is that its definition is complex and confusing. Among the laundry list of tasks potentially bracketed by production design are the following: art direction, set design, painting, storyboarding, decoration, construction and budgeting, technical drawing, location hunting, color design, and special effects. The craft's purpose is a comprehensive one: to produce an overall pictorial "vision" for the work. What is clear from this wide-ranging definition is the fact that, unlike some other elements of production, which relate to only one stage of the process (e.g., editing, which follows shooting), production design spans the entire filmmaking progression. Furthermore, as Thomas Walsh, a former president of the Art Directors Guild, notes, the practice "is a corner of the central triangle that unites the director, the cinematographer, and the designer in a creative and interdependent partnership."[3] But often that very connection leaves critics and viewers confused about who is responsible for elements of a film's look.

Beyond comprising a huge number of tasks, the very term by which the practice is known has been up for debate throughout cinema history (like "film studies" itself). Of course, before there was a title at all, the job of fashioning sets generally fell to a carpenter. But, as the Affrons have shown, in the early years of American filmmaking terms such as "technical director" or "interior decorator" were employed until "art director" supplanted them, apparently gaining wide currency in the 1930s.[4] In fact, the term has been traced back as far as a *Photoplay* article from August 1916.[5] It wasn't until 1939, however, during the making of *Gone with the Wind*, that producer David Selznick dubbed William Cameron Menzies as "production designer"—a title that is still in use. In Europe, by contrast, the terms were sometimes different: in Germany "architect," in France "architect-decorator," and in the Soviet Union "painter-artist."[6] Clearly, these diverse monikers also reflect the varied ways in which the job was viewed—whether as a branch of construction or the visual arts. Whatever the term, it is clear that, over the years, the practice has advanced from a trade to a craft and finally to an art form.[7] Despite this evolution, it has often remained under the radar, in part because for most of Hollywood history sets were largely designed to be unobtrusive (like classical cinema's "invisible editing")—examples of what Leon Barsacq has called "impersonal technical perfection.[8]

Like the declaration of all "firsts" in film history, there are disagreements over who the "original" art director was (an evaluation made more difficult by the confusion of terminology). Some point to Wilfred Buckland (the set designer for theatrical impresario David Belasco in New York) who, as early as 1914, worked as art director on Cecil B. DeMille's *The Squaw Man* (1914), as well as on *Brewster's Millions* (1914), *The Call of the North* (1914), and *The Virginian* (1914).[9] They also point to individuals associated with D. W. Griffith's early masterpieces: Frank Wortman, who worked on *The Birth of a Nation* (1915), and Walter L. Hall, who was employed on *Intolerance* (1916).[10] Interestingly, the Internet Movie Database list of credits for the former contain all of the following individuals as part of the Art Department, giving us a sense of the unwieldy range of the craft: Frank Wortman (set designer), Shorty English (carpenter/uncredited), Jim Newman (assistant carpenter/uncredited), Cash Shockey (set painter/uncredited), Hal Sullivan (assistant property master/uncredited), and Joseph Stringer (set builder/uncredited).[11]

But a closer look at film history reveals individuals engaged preliminarily with art direction in the inital years of the medium's development. Charles Musser, for instance, in his book on Edwin Porter and the Edison Company, mentions Richard Murphy's being hired as a set designer in September 1907. As he notes, "Richard Murphy would later follow Porter to Rex and Famous Players. In 1919, when he went to the British Famous Players–Lasky Studio, he was accompanied by his assistant William Cameron Menzies."[12] So we can draw a through-line from art direction in early cinema to *Gone with the Wind*. Evidently some critics of the early film era already appreciated art direction. As one from 1908 stated: "Edison pictures are noted for elaborate scenic productions and the artistic beauty of the scenes, whether natural or painted interiors."[13] Ramirez also notes that Anton Grot worked for the Lubin Company after coming to the United States in 1913,[14] with the first film for which he received art direction credit being *The Light at Dusk* (1916). Whatever the case for "firsts," it is already clear (from the gender association of the names amassed so far) that, in the early years (and through the classical era), art direction was a male-dominated enterprise.[15]

The craft seems to have reached a certain plateau in 1924 when a group of sixty-three practitioners formed the Cinemagundi Club, a networking society whose name was a variation on the Salmagundi Club, an arts organization in New York City founded in 1871.[16] First led by Leo "K" Kuter as its president, the members met in a clubhouse on Beechwood Drive.[17] During the first Academy Awards presentation, honors for art direction were given to films made in 1927 and 1928 (Rochus Gliese for *Sunrise* [1927], William Cameron Menzies for *The Dove* [1927] and *Tempest* [1928], and Harry Oliver for *7th Heaven* [1927]). Files in the Margaret Herrick Library of the Academy of Motion Picture Arts and Sciences refer to the existence of a League of Art Directors and Associates that included such myriad subdivisions as art director, assistant art director, set designer, draftsman, technical draftsman, set dresser, draper, process technician, pictorial painter, title technician, miniature technician, and sculptor. In a meeting on 9 December 1929 (after resisting affiliating with a labor union), the League decided to join United Scenic Artists Local Union 235. Thus, it became a "true craft guild" whose goal was to improve the wages and working conditions of its members. Its efforts, however, were stymied by the Depression. Finally on 6 May 1937, the Society of Motion Picture Art Directors was organized by fifty-nine practitioners at a meeting at the Hollywood Roosevelt Hotel. Later, its name was changed to the Art Directors Guild with Stephen Goosson as its first president. The group had three purposes: (1) to assure collective bargaining; (2) to establish educational, recreational, social, and charitable activities; and (3) to purchase a building to function as a center. The organization's initial board included such notables as Van Nest Polglase, Cedric Gibbons, Richard Day, and Willy Pogany. The Guild has seen many changes since then. In 1949, television art directors were included in their membership, and in 1967 the term "television" was added to its name. In 2003, the purview of the group was expanded further as it also took on Scenic, Title, and Graphic Art. Finally, in 2005, the Guild purchased its own building in Studio City.[18]

The personnel involved in art direction have from the first features, like *The Birth of a Nation*, been many and have generally been organized in a hierarchal fashion. In the studio era there was a supervising art director—the first ones being Cedric Gibbons at MGM (who served from 1924 to 1952) and Hans Drier at Paramount (who served from 1927 to 1948).[19] These men assigned specific films to a unit art director (for instance, Richard Day at MGM or Earl Hedrick at Paramount). Given the strong role of the supervisor, various studios were known for creating a particular onscreen "look"—be it the opulent glamour of MGM, the European elegance of Paramount, the Art Deco modernity of RKO, or the urban grit of Warner Bros. In general, however, Hollywood film evinced a rather eclectic style that blended tradition and the modern.[20]

In the studio era, several spaces onsite were particularly important in relation to art direction. One was the back lot, where sets from earlier films were stored for possible reuse. Ramirez describes these locales eloquently as comprising a "multitude of fragmentary buildings, half-constructed and half-ruined, in a perpetual process of transformation, representing something like a biological cycle of birth, maturity, fertility, decay and death."[21] He sees a parallel between the ephemeral nature of studio sets and real-life architecture—both of which are often razed and available to us only as a photographic record.[22] As film scholars, we often run into this lacuna when the only evidence we have of lost films and their mise-en-scène are production stills. We confront it as well when we attempt to plumb the history of picture palaces and learn that jewels (like New York's Fiftieth Street Roxy, which opened in 1927 and seated around six thousand people) are no longer with us (the Roxy was destroyed in 1960).[23] But, as Ramirez points out, there are major differences between film sets and quotidian décor. He lists six primary features of the former: (1) they are fragmentary; (2) they have different proportions and sizes than their real prototypes; (3) they are rarely rectangular; (4) they are generally exaggerated; (5) they are elastic and mobile; and (6) they are valued for speedy execution and potential reuse.[24]

As for the fragmentary nature of sets, we need only think of the missing "fourth wall" that allows the viewer to see what is going on in a scene. Furthermore, many sets have no ceilings in order to allow for the placement of lighting and microphone equipment. In fact, when Orson Welles asked for ceilings to be included in the set for *The Magnificent Ambersons* (1942), it was regarded as unusual.[25] As for sets being exaggerated, one need only think of certain extreme examples from German Expressionism—be it *The Cabinet of Dr. Caligari* (1920), in which all the painted flats are done in false perspective, or *Sunrise* (1927), in which shots of the City Woman's vacation cabin are foreshortened through the use of slanted floors and objects as well as oversized items in the frame (figure 1). One thinks as well of the huge room in *Citizen Kane*'s (1941) Xanadu (far more cavernous than any real one we can imagine) in which Susan Kane executes a jigsaw puzzle. As for rectilinear construction, Ramirez asserts that most film sets follow a trapezoidal model and illustrates the point with a production still from *Jezebel* (1938).[26] As for mobility, one thinks of the curvilinear sets for Busby Berkeley's 1930s musicals that move around in space as the spectacle

FIGURE 1: Forced perspective (e.g., huge light fixture, slanted table) in sets gives *Sunrise* (F. W. Murnau, 1927, art dir. Rochus Gliese) an Expressionist feel.

and camera require. Finally, as for repurposing, one thinks of how elements of the MGM Art Deco interior sets (envisioned by Cedric Gibbons) reappeared in numerous films, or how the opera set built for *The Phantom of the Opera* (1925) was reused each time a film required theatrical box seating.[27] More recently, a Vatican meeting room from *Angels and Demons* (2009) reappeared as a bar in the vampire film *Priest* (2011).[28]

Today the notion of recycling movie sets has taken on a new cast as structures and props are routinely repurposed.[29] The art director Eva Radke, for example, notes that, while generally "a handful of grips and a couple of production assistants were ripping everything up and throwing it into Dumpsters, I spent much of my time trying to find homes for everything." Whether that was "on Craig's List, between friends or giving it away in stages," she felt, "no matter what, there was still an incredible amount of waste all the time. It was just unconscionable." This led her to form FilmBizRecycling, which now has a warehouse in Brooklyn where, for instance, workers might be found "deconstructing a set and putting it back together as a high-end coffee table."[30]

Today, without a plethora of studio back lots, production teams often rent sets. Airline Film & TV Promotions (founded in 1974 and located in the San Fernando Valley), for instance, is a company that specializes in providing cinema and television with aeronautical sets. Included in their inventory are a first-class section of a 747, an airport ticket counter, a baggage carousel, and the inside of a DC-10.[31] Like film costumes (some of which are now housed in the Smithsonian or the Metropolitan Museum of Art), a few film sets have achieved a lofty status. Some of those used in filming *Mandela: Long Walk to Freedom* (a 2013 film version of Nelson Mandela's autobiography [art dir. Willie Botha]) were slated to be donated to the Nelson Mandela Foundation for a satellite museum in Qunu. Producer Anant Singh said that they "would allow people to be transported through time and enable them to experience places that had great significance in Mandela's history."[32]

Though the studio era is long gone, its organizational model for production design continues to influence the contemporary era of independent filmmaking. As Whitlock notes, the individual in charge

> oversees a staff of talented designers and decorators. . . . The art director reports to the production designer. The art director oversees [such things as] . . . the preparation of blueprints, models, and storyboards to scheduling and managing the busy department. Also reporting to the production designer are set decorators, the people who oversee set dressers and support personnel (upholsterers, drapery workrooms, etc.); set designers, whose duties can include design and preparation or architectural drawings and elevations; as well as the various support departments of construction, property, location manager and scenic artists.[33]

Today many traditional scenic painters have been replaced by computer designers as technology impacts the profession. Numerous recent Academy Awards in Production Design have gone to movies in which computer-generated imagery (CGI) is crucial, such as *Avatar* (2009), *Alice in Wonderland* (2010), and *Hugo* (2012) (see plate 1). Despite this shift, Patrizia von Brandenstein claims that production design "is still a handmade business. The decisions get made with a pencil. Computers are just 'tools.'"[34] Computer graphics is not the only technology that has affected art direction over the years. Rather, developments like the Schüfftan Process (reportedly devised in 1927 for the production of Fritz Lang's *Metropolis*) changed the way that models were utilized by allowing their mirror reflection to create the illusion of performers interacting with miniatures. Similarly, the coming of color and sound required changes in set construction and design, all of which are examined in the chapters of this book.

Thus far, we have been discussing art direction as though it largely involved work upon a stage of some kind—whether in the primitive Edison Black Maria studio of the 1890s or on a modern soundstage. But production design also involves the choice of shooting location—a fact not always recognized. In the earliest years of cinema, when filmmaking was largely an East Coast affair, this meant, for instance, selecting the best part of New Jersey to represent the Wild West. As the feature film developed, it involved the choice of California locations for the epic battle scenes in *The Birth of a Nation* (1915) or the Vermont locale for

FIGURE 2: A stagecoach in the foreground is dwarfed by the majestic and sculptural Monument Valley buttes in *Stagecoach* (John Ford, 1939, art dir. Alexander Toluboff) that become "stars" of the film.

the dramatic ice floe sequence of *Way Down East* (1920). Perhaps no other director was to be more associated with a landscape than John Ford with Monument Valley, Utah (figure 2). While Ford has claimed that he knew of the location from his travels, others say he was introduced to it by the location manager on *Stagecoach* (1939), Danny Keith.[35]

In the post–World War II era, the use of location (versus soundstage shooting) was expanded with the availability of lighter-weight cameras (technology again influencing production design) and the influence of such European movements as Italian Neorealism and the French New Wave— which developed in countries where the war had ravaged production facilities or in which a set of cinematic rebels sought to oppose stodgy "quality cinema." If we consider the list of films for which landscape (whether urban, pastoral, or exotic) has been a factor in their being honored with an Academy Award for Art Direction, we find many that foreground location shooting: *On the Waterfront* (1954, art dir. Richard Day); *Lawrence of Arabia* (1962, prod. des. John Stall and John Box); *Gandhi* (1982, prod. des. Stuart Craig, supervising art dir. Bob Laing); *Out of Africa* (1985, prod. des. Stephen Grimes); and *Memoirs of a Geisha* (2005, prod. des. John Myhre).

Over the history of American cinema, production designers have had a variety of training and backgrounds that prepared them for the job. Originally, most were simply carpenters. Later, individuals (like Cedric Gibbons, Michael Corenblith, or Anne Siebel) were often architects. Others (like Vincent Korda) were painters and still others (like Harry Horner, Polly Platt, and Patrizia von Brandenstein) came from the world of theater. What has also been true is that, like film directors, American production designers have been an international group—with renowned practitioners moving to Hollywood from abroad (for instance, Eugène Lourié [from Russia, via Paris] or Alexander Golitzen [from Russia]). So the field has had a transnational cast to it almost from the start.

Art direction (like fashion in film) has also had a broad influence, offscreen, on the appearance of the American home. In the classical era, it led to the everyday use of certain innovative materials like chrome or plastic (especially Bakelite) in interior design.[36] Moreover, it resulted in the popularization of certain design styles (like Art Deco).[37] In that vein, an article from 1964 talks of how the sets from a movie of that year (*The Unsinkable Molly Brown*) were to be exhibited at Home and Decorator shows.[38] A more recent piece, "From Film Sets to Interiors," in the *Weekend Australian* reports that the style of production designer Catherine Marshall (who worked on Baz Luhrmann's *Romeo + Juliet* [1996] and *Moulin Rouge!* [2001]) has "slipped from the silver screen into Australian homes with collections of wallpaper and rugs, and . . . fabric."[39] Today one also finds numerous websites in which filmgoers register their fantasies of living in or acquiring domestic screen spaces. One such website catalogs (along with detailed production credits) "20 Unforgettable Movie Interiors."[40] Among them are those from *Auntie Mame* (1958, prod. des. Malcolm C. Bert [uncredited], art dir. Malcolm C. Bert,

FIGURE 3: Many viewers imagined living in the fabulous mid-century modern home inhabited by George (Colin Firth) in *A Single Man* (Tom Ford, 2009, prod. des. Dan Bishop, art dir. Ian Phillips, set dec. Amy Wells), with its high-tech kitchen, muted tones, and minimalist shelving.

set dec. George James Hopkins); *The Fountainhead* (1949, art dir. Edward Carrere, set dec. William L. Kuehl); and *A Single Man* (2009, prod. des. Dan Bishop, art dir. Ian Phillips, set dec. Amy Wells) (figure 3). Another website called "15 Apartments on Film That We Wished We Owned" mentions Barbara Novak's in *Down with Love* (2003); Alice and William Harford's in *Eyes Wide Shut* (1999); and Patrick Bateman's in *American Psycho* (2000).[41] A third website, "The 20 Houses from the Movies We'd Actually Want to Live In," cites the doctor's residence in *Sleeper* (1973), the Frye residence in *Ferris Bueller's Day Off* (1986), and the Carver residence in *The Ice Storm* (1973).[42]

Step-by-Step

In her book *Production Design: Architects of the Screen*, Jane Barnwell defines and examines each stage or element of production.[43] The list of tasks below, partially borrowed from Barnwell, is arranged in a manner that suggests chronology. In practice, the order is not always maintained, and there is great variation in how the steps of the process are engaged by individual designers.

Pre-Production

Most art directors agree that work on a film starts long before shooting begins. Drew Boughton, who worked on *Unstoppable* (2010), was involved with the project some three to four months before cinematography commenced. Indie production designer Erin Muldoon Stetson finds a similar situation: "Most of my work is done in pre-production, but that's also the most fun part, because that's where you come up with your grandiose ideas of perfection. It's not until later that you have to make compromises." Anne Siebel (production designer for *Midnight in Paris* [2011]) says that the official pre-production period for the film lasted seven weeks but that she was already at work months earlier.[44]

Script

The job of most production designers begins when they are given a script for an upcoming movie, since this allows them to understand its basic plot, setting, narrative, theme, and characters. Alternately, some, like Joe Alves, who worked on *Jaws* (1975), received galleys of the Peter Benchley novel even before Steven Spielberg had signed on to the project as director.[45] Polly Platt claims that production designers can even detect problems in a screenplay: "When I don't get any ideas about a set, I know there's something wrong with the scene." Apropos, she convinced Peter Bogdanovich to change the setting of *What's Up, Doc?* (1972) from Chicago to San Francisco.[46]

Shooting Script

This is critical to production designers because it alerts them to what aspects of the broad setting of the film will actually be photographed; it thereby helps them to comprehend how the camera and actors will navigate and to build sets accordingly. The producer of *Ransom* (1996) says of Michael Corenblith's set for the film: "In a sense, the camera is the client, because the set has to be designed so the camera can flow easily and dynamically through the space." Director Ron Howard agrees: "The shape of the floor plan [of Corenblith's set] really lent itself to the Steadicam work I had in mind. There's a lot of room for the camera to roam." Corenblith also eliminated harsh edges by curving the walls and corners because, as Howard notes, "rounding the shapes is good for framing and staging too, and gave us opportunities to do things with a wide-angle lens." Howard also remarks that the glass doors on the set "slide into the walls when I need a larger space or have to crank up the intensity of the story through camera movement."[47]

Budget

Production designers have to calculate the cost of the work that they will supervise and this must conform to the budget proposed by the film's producer. According to Barnwell, that figure generally represents about 10 percent of total production costs.[48] While some films allocate very large budgets to the art department (e.g., *Titanic* [1997]), others do not (figure 4). In working on *Midnight in Paris* (2011), Siebel was told by the director Woody Allen that there would be "no construction, as Woody does not spend more than 10 million dollars per movie. With such a small budget for an art department it was a challenge to do this movie in France."[49]

FIGURE 4: Set on a huge ocean liner in the opulent Gilded Age, *Titanic* (James Cameron, 1997, prod. des. Peter Lamont, art dirs. Martin Laing, Charles Dwight Lee, set dec. Michael Ford) was a film for which a large portion of the budget was spent on set design.

Kristi Zea says "knowing how much things cost" is crucial. "You have to be responsible for the money." She claims that Lawrence Kasdan said he would hire her for every movie "if [she could] stick to a budget." As an example, for one film, she chose reproduction Ethan Allen furniture rather than antique early American pieces.[50]

Research

This aspect of the job parallels the work of historians of culture, art, or cinema. After establishing the period (or periods) in which a film is set and whether it involves realistic or fantastic spaces, the designer must come up with the relevant "look" for sets that need to be constructed or "dressed." Of working on the historical film *Marie Antoinette* (2006), Siebel says:

> I did a lot of research, and had a real thrill doing all the construction. It was such a pleasure to go into the smallest details reproducing Versailles, to see how it was done—a really good way of learning history, better than at school. It was fantastic to go to Versailles, to meet the people who maintain the gardens and to talk with historians. I met this completely mad woman who is collecting everything about Marie Antoinette, and it was really incredible to see some of the pieces. It's a really interesting part of our job to do the research, to put yourself in a different period.[51]

Some films involve more pedestrian research. For *The Last Picture Show* (1971)—set in Texas in the 1950s—Platt looked at photo albums, yearbooks, and *Life* magazine articles.[52] For creating her "wildest fantasy of a kid's room" in *Raising Arizona* (1987), Jane Musky examined children's storybooks for mysterious, "horrific" illustrations.[53]

FIGURE 5: In *Amadeus* (Milos Forman, 1984, prod. des. Patrizia von Brandenstein, art dir. Karel Cerný), the set design was motivated by Mozart's music, "tingling like crystal," and care was taken to make the scores (seen in the lower left corner) appear accurate for the eighteenth century.

Concept

Determining the overall concept for the visuals of a work is the production designer's first task and one that relates to the film's narrative. Corenblith, for instance, states: "I try to find a visual key that unlocks the story; I look for a compelling and slightly offbeat visual take and try to create relationships that buttress the story dramatically."[54] For *Goldfinger* (1964), Ken Adam had to configure a scene taking place at Fort Knox. Initially, the producers rejected his design, saying "it looked like a prison." Adam explained that "it was supposed to; I liked the idea of the gold stacked up behind bars."[55] Eventually, he convinced them. When presented with the galleys of *Jaws* (1983), Alves imagined how he wanted the picture to look. His idea was to use a life-size mechanical shark placed in a real ocean. He also wanted the seaside New England beach town to appear idyllic—with cabanas and a gazebo.[56] Patrizia von Brandenstein describes the concept for *Amadeus* (1984): "Mozart's world was reflective, bright, silvery, pastel, brilliant, tingling like crystal, faceted like his music. It was the music that drove the design" (figure 5).[57] Patrick Tatopoulos recalls that when he was asked to build a futuristic city for *Total Recall* (1990), "We found this incredible factory just around the corner, and we went there to look [at it] as a place to build some of our sets." Though it was deemed inappropriate for that purpose, it "became the focal point [of his design], the idea of a concrete slab with water in between to define the world in some ways."[58]

Location Scouting

For films that will use real-life settings, the search to find them begins early on. Musky says that usually she first talks to the director, then goes out with the location scout and manager. On a Scorsese film, however, the script is already annotated with pencil figures and shot lists that dictate what locations need to be found.[59] For Tony Scott's *Unstoppable*, about a runaway train, Drew Boughton notes: "We shot in existing locations primarily which were stunning." Of course, such spaces are often transformed for a film. As he remarks: "The things we brought to the locations were all of our trains which were painted by us. We painted all the principal locomotives and train cars specifically to the instructions of . . . Scott and Production Designer Chris Seagers."[60] Even a realistic film like *The Last Picture Show* required changes to its West Texas locale. As Platt recalls, "I changed the whole street which had the movie theater on it. We put in the marquee. I changed the facades on at least three buildings."[61] For *Midnight in Paris*, Siebel had to find places that could stand in for 1920s locales. As she recalls:

> We had a task . . . within the budget restrictions, to find a solution that makes the viewer believe that it is a location from that period. 'Moulin Rouge' was a particular challenge for me, my art director, and my construction manager. The original building from the beginning of the 20th century does not exist anymore, and there are very few concert halls or theaters that could be used to reproduce the original structure. We found one concert hall . . . with a balcony running around it, and I took [the cinematographer] there to show him the space that I will transform with false wooden floor, built balustrades, drapes, and period lights. I chose this place and studied a few visual elements that would attract the audience's eye—light bulbs . . . table, railings—particular pieces that I found in the period references from my initial research. We managed to achieve the look we wanted with the mood and lighting . . . and if you look at the references, it's the same feel.[62]

Sometimes location shooting is combined with special effects. For scenes in *Diamonds Are Forever* (1971) that are set in Las Vegas, Ken Adam recalls: "I was not thrilled with the architecture in Vegas. So I chose the most modern building there, then increased it twice in height with a matte painting, working very closely with a great and legendary matte artist named Albert Whitlock."[63] For *GoldenEye* (1995), which took place in St. Petersburg, Russia, the crew shot some of the film on location; but for other scenes, Martin Campbell reconstructed the city in a British studio.[64] For *A Chorus Line* (1985), von Brandenstein transformed the Mark Hellinger Theater: "We regilded everything we could lay our hands on. We put in the decorate [*sic*] proscenium—which had all that wonderful, mad, Beaux Arts architecture."[65]

Sequence/Chronology

Following the selection of locations, some production designers pin up photographs of the locations they have chosen in sequence, in order to get a sense of the overall flow of location design.

Color Palette

As we know, until the mid-1930s, color photography was not widely used in film. It did appear in short sequences of spectacles and, throughout the silent era, footage was often tinted, toned, or stenciled in various hues. Beginning in 1940 (after the release of *Gone with the Wind*), Academy Awards for Best Art Direction were given in two categories: black-and-white and color. With the exception of two years (1957 and 1958), this practice lasted through 1966.

In a color film, the choice of hues is critical. Owen Paterson, who worked on *The Matrix* (1999), a film that depicts a variety of "worlds," says that parts of the movie were given "a predominance of green. . . . Wherever it was possible and practicable we took the blue out, we even took it out of the sky of the translight in the government building." Alternately, in sections depicting "the real world we tried to push blue as much as possible, so there is a blue base to everything; the Nebuchadnezzar [hovercraft] has a blue base. There are other colors used in the film, but it is a relatively monochromatic palette that we have used throughout, with small hints of other colors for definition."[66] For *Midnight in Paris*, Siebel states that scenes taking place in the twenties used colors "of the period—brown, maroon and beige"—whereas "brighter colors [were used] for contemporary [scenes], to give a sense of passing from one period to another."[67] Decisions regarding coloration also come up in films shot in black and white. To get the look she wanted for *The Last Picture Show*, Platt needed to paint the bricks of buildings a darker tone and to dry brush white objects to enhance their appearance. On *Silkwood* (1983) von Brandenstein "kept the colors industrial. . . . There was an absence of color except for the danger colors: red stop green go." Alternately, for *Married to the Mob* (1988), Musky wanted the coloration of a "comic book."[68]

Painting

There are many ways in which painting can function in relation to set design. On a basic level, sets are painted according to the tone and color scheme of a film, or to create a *trompe l'oeil* effect. On a more advanced level, the history of painting can be invoked as an inspiration for the look of a film. Many people felt that Stanley Kubrick was influenced by eighteenth-century painting in making *Barry Lyndon* (1975), which was set in that era. Furthermore, in biopics about known artists (e.g., *Klimt* [2006]) the visuals are often marked by the pictorial style of the film's subject, for instance, Art Nouveau (see plate 2). Additionally, art works can be required for set decoration. The producers of *Ransom* determined that the protagonist (a rich man) would have a substantial painting collection. Known paintings could not be borrowed due to security and lighting issues, so "scenic artists who were painting the set made copies of characteristic works by [Edward] Hopper, [Winslow] Homer, John Storrs, Arthur Dove, Thomas Hart

FIGURE 6: Many of the most spectacular shots in *Citizen Kane* (Orson Welles, 1941, prod. des. Van Nest Polglase, set dec. Darrell Silvera), like this one of an elderly Charles Foster Kane reflected in a *mise-en-abyme*, depend in part on matte painting.

Benton, Raphael Soyer, John White Alexander, and Guy Pène du Bois."[69] For a section of *New York Stories* (1989) about an artist, Musky had to locate a real painter (Chuck Connelly) whose style was right and whose hands could be used for close-up shots of the painting process.[70] Finally, matte painting (by which a scene is painted on a large glass plate allowing it to be seamlessly integrated into a shot) has played a role in production design, though now it has largely been replaced by CGI. A contemporary website, however, applauds "The 50 Best Matte Paintings of All Time," among them those occurring in *Citizen Kane* (figure 6), *Black Narcissus* (1947), *Quo Vadis* (1951), and *Superman* (1978).[71]

Characters

Decisions about set design are made not only in relation to a film's narrative and location but its characters. As producer Brian Grazer says: "With a movie set, so much time and effort go into something that is ultimately secondary to the development of the characters' lives and emotions, yet it has to be absolutely right. If it's not absolutely right, when things don't ring true, they undercut the characters' integrity."[72] For *Targets* (1968), says Platt, she "was trying to design a home that might create a murderer."[73] For *Raising Arizona*, since the protagonist loved the Southwest, Musky used lots of raw wood for his house.[74] For *Ransom*, Corenblith had to envision how an affluent New Yorker would live. To accomplish this, he visited numerous Upper East Side apartments, but, in his film set, "many of the original wall partitions had been removed, and the wide sweep of space was broken up only by an occasional group of furniture or island of wood paneling." Corenblith also sought inspiration in the work of Frank Lloyd Wright and Eliel Saarinen, "favoring their organic flow of space, natural materials and the play of wood tones against other surfaces." A sense of intimacy in the apartment was also required, notes director Ron Howard, "so Michael came up with translucent glass doors to divide the spaces if necessary." They provided "a lot of latitude, and they're much more visually interesting than solid doors because we can have shapes and silhouettes moving behind them."[75]

Polarization

Film narratives often revolve around oppositions that reveal themselves in set design—whether it be the one between a working girl's apartment and a department store magnate's estate in *Our Blushing Brides* (1930), or between Kansas and Oz in *The Wizard of Oz* (1939). For *Ransom*, Corenblith had to contrast the poor and rich worlds of Manhattan. As he notes: "I had to convey the conflict of high and low society. For that high world, we wanted lavish expanses of space, because, especially in an urban situation, space denotes power. I also used natural, muted tones and textures and a palette of precious-metal hues—the color of money. For the low world, we chose harsh, glaring paint and built a warren of angles and dark rooms that would make the audience feel hemmed in."[76]

Lighting

In creating a set, the designer needs to think about the nature of the light source implicit in the scene—whether it be natural light through windows or artificial light (by gas, candle, or electric bulb). As *Ransom*'s executive producer Todd Hallowell states: "Lighting and windows are a paramount concern." In the film's Upper East Side Manhattan apartment set they "had to make the windows and placement of the terrace believable. If you're going to have light falling on someone's face, you have to show the audience where it's coming from."[77] After finishing *Midnight in Paris*, Siebel recalls that another director of photography called her "asking how we managed to achieve this unity of lighting—and it's because we worked together from the beginning on . . . [such things as] the vibration of the bulbs and [the] dim[ness] of the lights."[78]

Sketch

Sketches of sets give the director an idea of what the production designer envisions. For *Jaws*, Joe Alves provided the production team with drawings of "shark activity," and for *The Man with the Golden Gun* (1974) Peter Murton sketched a reactor set and the villain Francisco Scaramanga's (Christopher Lee) maze, which appear in Laurent Bouzereau's book *The Art of Bond*.[79] Often, sketches are produced not by the production designer but by art department illustrators. One such individual is Karl Shefelman, who maintains a website in which he posts drawings from such films as *It's Complicated* (2009) and *Addicted to Love* (1997). As for his craft, he says: "I work in a variety of formats and styles, depending upon the job. Most of my illustrations are hand-drawn but I can also work with Photoshop. Often there is only time for quick sketches but occasionally I have the opportunity to further flesh out renderings."[80]

Storyboard

This is a panel or series of panels of rough sketches outlining the scene sequence and major changes of action or plot in a film production. As Tom and Heidi Lüdi (the authors of *Movie Worlds: Production Design in Film*) state, "In the difficult moment where the black letters of the text rise from the white page to form the first visual images, the production designer makes illustrations based upon the script and specific research and also the first location scouting."[81] Some directors (like Brian DePalma on *The Untouchables* [1987]) create it themselves, while others (such as Joel and Ethan Coen), according to Musky, "don't storyboard the way a set's going to look."[82] Often, the production designer will create the storyboard. Bouzereau's *The Art of Bond* includes detailed storyboards for a tank chase scene in *GoldenEye* and a helicopter attack in *The World Is Not Enough* (1999), by Peter Lamont and Robert Wade, respectively.[83] There are also dedicated storyboard artists, such as Todd Anderson (*Raising Arizona*).[84] Storyboard artist Shefelman posts samples of his work from *The Departed* (2006), *My Super Ex-Girlfriend* (2006), *Mr. Popper's Penguins* (2011), *American Gangster* (2007), *Hide and Seek* (2005), *The Smurfs* (2011), and *Did You Hear About the Morgans?* (2009) on his website.[85] Another site mentions that "for the first time, the Museum für Film und Fernsehen, in cooperation with the Kunsthalle Emden, is showing storyboards for films of the last 80 years to a wide audience. The spectrum spans from delicate, monochrome works in graphite and India ink to tremendous bursts of color carried out in colored pencils, crayons or felt-tip pens, chalk and watercolor."[86]

Technical Drawings

When a set needs to be built, technical drawings must to be prepared (based on an artist's rough sketch) as a blueprint for the builders. Here, production design meets architectural methodology. J. W. Rinzler has recently published *Star Wars: The Blueprints*, in which numerous technical drawings for the film series are included.[87]

Models

There are two senses of the term "model" that are relevant to production design. On one level, it can refer to an architectural model of the set, which is prepared so that the director and cinematographer have a three-dimensional prototype of the space to experiment with prior to full-scale construction. For example, a photo in Ramirez's *Architecture for the Screen* shows Jack Warner and other studio executives surveying a model of the set for *The Silver Chalice* (1955).[88] On a second level, the term can refer to the miniatures that are often prepared for filming certain settings that are impractical or impossible to shoot in any other way. This could mean a model of a fictional monster (like the ape designed by Willis O'Brien for *King Kong* [1933]), a huge mansion, or the buildings of New York City as seen from the sky. Although Platt primarily used location shooting for a scene at a drive-in in *Targets*, for some of the shots she used a miniature.[89] Of course, these days much of this work is done through CGI, but models continue to play an important role in scenic design. A March 2, 2012, article in the *Daily Mail*, for instance, discusses the model representing Hogwarts Castle that has appeared in every Harry Potter film. Designed by Jose Granell, it is "50 feet across . . . [and] has more than 2,500 fibre optic lights to simulate lantern torches and students passing through hallways. It even has miniature owls in the Owlery and hinges on the doors." The building took its inspiration from real structures: Durham Cathedral and Alnwick Castle. The model is slated to go on display as part of "The Making of Harry Potter" studio tour at Leavesden Studios, near Watford, England.[90]

Construction

Obviously, after technical drawings for a set have been completed and approved, the set must be built. Designer Owen Paterson has described the construction of the set for the hovercraft Nebuchadnezzar in *The Matrix*. As he notes:

> That took about two and a half months, I think. . . . All those pieces were pre-built. All of those elements were made separately and brought in as units. Because it was for visual and special effects, it meant that the set had to be built from the core out, all the flooring had to be done, the walls and the ceiling had to be able to float. The first thing that was put into place was the ceiling; we put it on chain motors and took it up to the ceiling, built the set around it and then lowered the ceiling into it. It was an immense set, a very complex object.[91]

Set Decorating and Dressing

Once a set has been constructed or a location found, it is still an empty shell that must be populated with décor and objects. Wherever possible in ornamenting rooms, set decorator Katie Spencer likes to use "authentic furniture, dressing and small props . . . because there is something very exact about them as they bring their own histories and stories. Also you're going to see them—a pen or a wallet—on the big screen in the cinema at ten times its real size, and authenticity then is invaluable." However, "sometimes [authentic objects] just don't exist or aren't available anymore and that's when they become expensive prop makes." Even when you can find the requisite objects (e.g., drapes or furniture), you may "want to make [them] anyway because you can't get them in the color or fabric scheme that you need." When working on historical films, Spencer feels that "you have a duty to be as accurate as possible." For the Dunkirk beach sequence in *Atonement* (2007), she and production designer Sarah Greenwood went to Dunkirk to see the town and its history for themselves. "Back in the UK we spoke to the veterans, and researched the war museums—portraying a story that is very near history comes with the responsibility to be authentic."[92] Susan Bode was in charge of dressing the ritzy Manhattan apartment set used in *Ransom*. As she remarks, "It's hard to do 'rich' on a budget, particularly an opulent contemporary interior. If your look is traditional, you can finesse it by using reproductions." She spent days at the Decorating and Design building in New York looking for materials. She also scoured antique stores for the kind of collectibles the fictional residents might have acquired. "The set has to be consistent with the characters," she says, "so I pretend I'm them when I'm buying things. The finished set should play like a waltz from room to room."[93]

Props

While props can simply be elements of set decoration, they often have a major role in the action of a film. Alves calls the shark in *Jaws* just a "big prop." He was given a tight production schedule and it proved difficult to find someone who could quickly build the monster; but eventually he succeeded.[94] Von Brandenstein speaks of how for *Amadeus* the prop man had to create a music manuscript in the eighteenth-century style.[95] Paterson has spoken in detail about a prop that was required for *The Matrix*. As he recalls,

> Our chief model maker, Tom Davies and his guys . . . made something called a bug extractor, which had to perform a lot of tasks. It had to be able to be manipulated by the actress and made to look like it was doing something: [for example] . . . extracting a bug out of Neo's stomach. It had to be able to both pump as well as have a relatively dramatic movement as it shoots down and the bug comes out. It had to be able to extract an object from the prosthetic stomach, as well as fire a second prosthetic into a little glass tube which you could then see wriggle about, all the time seeing an image that looks like a futuristic

ultrasound. There were hundreds and hundreds of hours spent making that object.[96]

Production

Erin Muldoon Stetson points out that traditionally "someone from the art department has [had] to be on set at all times in case there [were] any last minute changes or prop problems."[97] In the era of CGI and set creation, however, the role of the production designer has expanded greatly during filming itself, since often compositing and "virtual" art direction need to be considered while a film is being shot.

Post-Production

While, according to Boughton, the work of a production designer "generally ends after all principal photography is done," there have always been times when his or her work extended into the post-production period, especially when photographic processing and optical printing were involved (e.g., combining live-action footage with matte paintings).[98] Clearly, in the digital era, when many film sequences are shot against greenscreen or bluescreen, a production designer's vision only comes to fruition in the post-production stage.

The Essays

Although following a chronological structure, the chapters in this volume also enact a variety of approaches to chronicle the state of art direction in the American film industry from its inception until today. Thus, the essays collectively raise questions about such diverse issues as the careers of particular art directors, the influence of specific design styles, the import of individual studios or films, the effect of technological changes, and the role of shifts in industrial modes of organization.

In chapter 1, I survey the development of production design between 1895 (when the movies were born) and 1927 (the peak of the silent era). In so doing I focus on the shift from primitive art direction in the early films of Thomas Edison to more sophisticated settings in works by Edwin Porter. I then chronicle the relocation of the movie industry from the East Coast to the West Coast in the 1910s, with the epic film (e.g., *Intolerance*) becoming popular and necessitating grandiose mise-en-scène. Finally I discuss the influence of the European art film and aesthetic movements of the 1920s on American set design—specifically Art Nouveau (in *The Thief of Bagdad* [1924], art dir. William Cameron Menzies) and Expressionism (in *Phantom of the Opera* [1925], art dir. Ben Carré). The chapter also contrasts independent and studio production in the era.

In chapter 2, Mark Shiel takes a very broad approach to examining art direction during the height of the studio era, 1928–1946, drawing on interviews, news articles, and magazine pieces. The period saw the major technological change of the coming of sound, which necessitated shifts in set building and design, and attempts were made to fabricate the "real" rather than to "find" it. It also saw the unfolding of World War II, with its attendant shortage of production materials—leading to more location shooting. In surveying work in this era, Shiel discusses such stellar practitioners as Cedric Gibbons and Anton Grot, as well as major productions such as *Gone with the Wind*.

In chapter 3, Merrill Schleier examines American production design in the "post-classical" or "transition" era (1947–1967) when the studio system was in decline and film attendance revenues decreased in the wake of television and suburbanization. While many production designers continued to work for studios and have success, there was a move toward director autonomy in choosing collaborators. Thus, as part of the "Freed Unit" at MGM, Vincente Minnelli had a say in working with art director Preston Ames. However, the trend was toward art directors becoming free agents working on independent productions. Here, Schleier concentrates on the case of Russian émigré Boris Leven and his work on the film *Giant* (1956, produced and directed by George Stevens).

In chapter 4, "The Auteur Renaissance," Charles Tashiro examines Hollywood between the years of 1968 and 1980, when the notion of the film director as artist took hold—drawing upon French theory and production. On the one hand, the promotion of the director to prominence tended to minimize the public's sense of his or her collaborators (including the art director). On the other hand, since auteurism was often associated with a unique visual style, production design became more important. Tashiro then goes on to discuss the move toward realism and location shooting in the era whereby an art director's role displayed a tension between naturalism and expressiveness (as in Robert Altman's films *Nashville* [1975] and *McCabe & Mrs. Miller* [1971], with art direction in both by Leon Ericksen). Tashiro ends his chapter by concentrating on the career of Dean Tavoularis, who worked on major films directed by Arthur Penn, Roman Polanski, and Michelangelo Antonioni—some of which not only present images of the time periods in which they are set but also (in a meta-cinematic move) of the design style of earlier movies.

In chapter 5, "The New Hollywood," J. D. Connor turns his attention to art direction between 1981 and 1999, focusing on the tension between design's function in supporting a film's narrative versus design elements that draw attention to themselves (which duly elevates the role of the craftsperson). The latter trend was visible in the era's production of "high-concept" mainstream action films like *Top Gun* (1986) or fantasies like *Dick Tracy* (1990) and *Batman* (1989). Connor is also interested in the extra-filmic aspects of production design that manifested themselves in the publication of books on "the making" of particular movies or in the creation of theme park rides (e.g., from *Jurassic Park* [1993]). Finally, Connor examines the list of Academy Awards given in the era in order to note the kinds of films that won and those that did not, as well as to investigate the shape of certain design careers.

In chapter 6, Stephen Prince confronts "Hollywood's Digital Back Lot" from 2000 until the present—a timespan in which great technological change took place through the popularization of CGI in movie production. While focusing on the changes wrought by new methods (HDRI [high dynamic range imagery]) and programs (Autodesk Maya), Prince emphasizes how important physical sets and props remain in filmmaking. Furthermore, he describes how through the process of "photogrammetry," art directors can base synthetic sets on photographs of real locales. In general, Prince sees techniques of CGI as an extension of the kinds of special effects that have always embellished films; and most movies today evince a combination of studio or location shooting with computer compositing to create a new "digital environment."

1

THE SILENT SCREEN, 1895–1927 Lucy Fischer

This chapter considers American production design during the major years of the silent era. However, before starting, the first thing that must be acknowledged is that currently we have only a fraction of the films produced at our disposal. As a recent Library of Congress survey indicates, "Of the nearly 11,000 silent feature films made in America between 1912–30 . . . only 14 percent still exist in their original format." Of those, about 11 percent take the form of "foreign versions or . . . lower-quality formats." Despite this handicap, enough films are in circulation to allow us to outline the broad configurations of the period, starting with the birth of cinema in 1896.[1]

Early Production Design: The East Coast and the Edison Manufacturing Company

To call the creation of scenery for the first films made by U.S. companies "art direction" (or perhaps even to use the term mise-en-scène) would be to invest the enterprise with delusions of grandeur. For the most part, few records exist documenting how such sets were fashioned or by whom; and, clearly, in the early years, the film sets were minimal, functional, and unremarkable—to the extent that they existed at all. Furthermore, the films themselves did not yet include credits for art direction or many other production tasks.[2]

As we know, the first "studio" was that of Thomas Alva Edison and was called the Black Maria (allegedly because it looked like a police patrol wagon of that name). It was built in 1892 on the grounds of Edison's research laboratory in West Orange, New Jersey, founded in 1887.[3] Construction of the Black Maria cost a total of $637.67. It was fifty feet long and thirteen feet wide and its walls were covered in black tarpaper.[4] It had a roof that could be opened to admit daylight for illumination, and the entire structure revolved so as to gain access to the sun as it shifted in the sky. Given the historic and originary role of Edison in early film history, his company's production serves as a case study for this era.

The first films shot in the Black Maria were deposited for copyright at the Library of Congress in August 1893 by W.K.L. Dickson (Edison's assistant and the man who produced or shot many of his early films). Originally, the films (photographed by Edison's Kinetograph camera) were made for his Kinetoscope (a peep-show machine) but later for his Vitascope projector. The earliest film for which there is documentation is *Record of a Sneeze* (1894) "performed" by an Edison employee, Fred Ott. All told, Dickson and cameraman William Heise filmed over seventy-five motion pictures during the year 1894.

Given that we have very little by way of "production history" for these films (aside from Charles Musser's masterful and encyclopedic *Before the Nickelodeon: Edwin Porter and the Edison Manufacturing Company*), we often have to glean information from the cinematic texts themselves. Like many other one-minute works from the Black Maria, *Record of a Sneeze* is shot against a black background (presumably the walls of the studio). This is also the case for *Sandow* (1894), depicting a strongman, and *Carmencita* (1894), depicting a Spanish dancer. *Fatima* (1897) varies the mise-en-scène a bit by having its subject perform against a backdrop of painted scenery. Some films of this period were hand-colored—like *Annabelle Serpentine Dance* (1895), decorated with patches of yellow. This clearly adds a post-production element to filmic design. Certainly, even from an early stage, the image of Woman in film was associated with ornamentation.

Interestingly, in *A Morning Bath* (1896), depicting (according to the Edison catalog) a "mammy" washing her "little pickaninny," instead of the standard dark background, there is a white one—a change that must have been made in order to ensure that the black woman would be seen.[5] A similar strategy was employed for *Watermelon Eating Contest* (1896), featuring a competition between two black men. These remain rare exceptions to the dark background "rule"; but, of course, few people of color were photographed in this period.

There were films shot at the Black Maria that had a minimal degree of "scenery." For *Annie Oakley* (1894), for instance, a target is hung on the wall so we can see the results of her marksmanship (as disks fall to the ground). In *Chinese Laundry Scene* (1895), an unconvincing theatrical "flat" (with doors that open and close) serves as the site of a chase between a cop and a Chinese man. In *Seminary Girls* (1897), we view the semblance of a more three-dimensional room (which includes several beds, a nightstand with a wash basin and water pitcher) in which young women in nightgowns have a pillow fight. More elaborate scenery is involved in *What Demoralized the Barber Shop* (1898), which not only reproduces a basement salon (with haircutting chairs, cabinets, wall signs, and shaving tools) but includes a flight of stairs with a window above through which we can see the legs of several passing women—a sight that throws the male shop customers into paroxysms. Finally, scenery is used in a film that stars Edison himself. In *Mr. Edison at Work in His Chemical Laboratory* (1897), the inventor is shown amid shelves of jars, puttering with some beakers at a table. According to the Edison catalog (which wrongly implies that Edison was simply "caught in the act"):

> This film is remarkable in several respects. In the first place, it is full life-size. Secondly, it is the only accurate recent portrait of the great inventor. The scene is an actual one, showing Mr. Edison in working dress engaged in an interesting chemical experiment in his great Laboratory. There is sufficient movement to lead the spectator through the several processes of mixing, pouring, testing, etc. as if he were side by side with the principal. The lights and shadows are vivid, and the apparatus and other accessories complete a startling picture that will appeal to every beholder.

While many films were shot in the Black Maria, others were photographed outdoors. *The Burglar on the Roof* (1898) appears to be shot atop an actual building. Here, Edison incorporates the location shooting he honed in actualities such as *Herald Square* (1896), *American Falls from Above, American Side* (1896), *Stanford University, California* (1897), or *Freight Train* (1898) into his short fiction works.

The Work of Edwin Porter

According to Musser, Edison decided as early as 1900 that he needed a more advanced studio in order to be competitive in the growing industry. He rented space at 41 East Twenty-first Street (in New York's entertainment district) and, by February 1901, opened a glass-enclosed rooftop studio that provided more protection from the weather than had the Black Maria (which was then closed). The new location gave Edison Studio an advantage over Biograph and Vitagraph, which still maintained open-air facilities. Edwin Porter, Edison's major director (who was hired in 1900), bragged that he had been given control of "the first skylight studio in the country."[6] It could, however, only accommodate one stage set at a time[7]—though, as Marc Wanamaker notes, a set was often only a "wood platform with cloth sun diffusers draped above . . . with the walls . . . merely painted flats propped up by braces." Much, however, could be accomplished in this fashion (including trompe l'oeil) since "everything that could be painted *was* painted—wall hangings, artworks, furniture and rugs. Every material was imitated from brick, tile, plaster and stucco to stone, wood and all sorts of paneling." As Wanamaker remarks: "Rubber could be molded and made into bricks or tiles. Resin could be used for prop making, and foam could stand in for rocks." For further effect, backdrops were frequently used to depict landscapes or city views as seen outside a window.[8] By the time that Edison's New York City studio opened, George S. Fleming had been hired as scenic designer; he started working for the company in January and earned more than Porter.[9]

Almost immediately one senses greater sophistication in the visual style of the short films produced in the new facility (under Porter's purview). In *The Old Maid Having Her Picture Taken* (1901, co-directed by Fleming),[10] we find a more three-dimensional set (including several chairs and a prop camera) as well as more set "decoration" in the form of a mirror, a clock, and a wall picture display—all of which will be destroyed in the narrative by dint of the matron's homeliness. Quite elaborate, though highly theatrical sets (reminiscent of stage melodrama) are used in *Jack and the Beanstalk* (1902, Porter, co-directed by Fleming).[11] The film opens by depicting a mill with faux water flowing. Like most of those to come, the set is somewhat three-dimensional (though a focus on this feature would not truly come into play until the advent of camera movement, which made it a necessity). After a fairy appears and Jack trades a cow (a man in comic costume) for magic beans, he plants them and a prop vine begins to grow to the top of the frame. When we next see Jack asleep in his room, we notice that the set is not completely flat but has corners. When he awakens and finds the vine outside, he climbs to a plateau where a painted background displays the tops of mountains. In a later shot, the fairy reappears (sitting on a crescent moon) and, through a special effect, a circular matte opens center frame depicting a (painted) castle. This is the abode of the ogre from whom Jack will steal a chicken and some gold. When Jack descends the vine to return home, a fairy magically transforms him into a prince and the film ends with an elaborate tableau of women posed in a wondrous fairyland. Clearly, in its look, use of a female figure, and magical actions, the work resembles the *féerie* films of Pathé and Star Films (the company of Georges Méliès). Models are employed for Spanish ships glimpsed in the background in *Sampson-Schley Controversy* (1901) and for the steamboat race between the *Natchez* and the *Robert E. Lee* in *Uncle Tom's Cabin* (1903). Miniatures are used for an animated bed in *Dream of a Rarebit Fiend* (1906) and a burning house in *Kathleen Mavourneen* (1906).[12]

A particularly interesting case of filmic design occurs in *European Rest Cure* (1904) because of its mixture of location and studio shooting. The film, which chronicles the mishaps of a man on a European vacation tour, opens with real scenes of the New York City harbor as the protagonist walks up an ocean liner's gangway. Real crowds are seen to wave our hero off. Furthermore, we view documentary shots of the New York City skyline as seen from the moving ship. But these are the last location images we get until the final shot of the film in which the man returns home (more harried and bruised than when he left) and is picked up by a horse and buggy. In between we see rather elaborate theatrical-type sets (in which he stands on a concealed stage, with foreground and background flats augmenting the space) representing such things as touring Paris (shown in a café set), climbing the pyramids (depicted with the Sphinx behind him), being robbed by thieves in Italy (shown with ruins in the background), or taking a mud bath in Germany (sitting in a real tub in a faux landscape). The contrast between the actuality shots of New York (where Edison was located) and the stagey sets of places to which his crew failed to travel is extreme and unsettling to us, but probably more palatable to the viewer of 1904.

After some six years in the new studio, Edison again decided to upgrade facilities. This time he built an indoor, glass-roofed building on Decatur Avenue and Oliver Place in the Bronx—one that also had ample glass windows to provide daylight. The production crew arrived in July of 1907.[13] In the interim there had been some staff changes. Fleming left in April 1903 and was replaced by scenic painter William Martinetti, who earned as much as Porter.[14] However, a few months after moving to the Bronx studio Martinetti was replaced by set designer Richard Murphy.[15] It is after this that the *New York Dramatic Mirror* stated that "Edison pictures are noted for elaborate scenic productions and the artistic beauty of the scenes, whether natural or painted interiors."[16]

A visitor to the Edison facility writing in the *Film Index* talked about its having a property room (supervised by W. J. Gilroy), which included "18 Springfield rifles and a small armory of other weapons, toys, Roman togas, fairy costumes" and "figures, eagles, and so on." As for the sets, the author writes:

> The scenes painted under Mr. Stevens' direction by the scenic artists, are in distemper—that is, they use only blacks, browns and whites, with the varying shades of these, as photographs do not take color as color, but only suggest it. Houses or block scenery are built up and the stands and wings constructed as in a theatre, only with much more attention to details and naturalness. For the camera, unlike the eye, can not be easily deceived. "Staginess" is avoided and realism is in every case given place over "effect." Scenes indoors can be taken at any time, now that the new and wonderful artificial daylight has been introduced at the studio.[17]

The author raves about the lighting effects (devised by Porter) as well as the sophisticated stage that could handle diverse narrative settings:

> A water scene? Certainly; and the mystery is explained when we examine the floor of the stage. This floor, 55 x 35 feet, is built in square sections, which can be lifted away, one by one. Beneath is discovered a great tank, the full size of the stage and 8 feet deep. The floor and beams are so arranged as to render the formation of a pond, a fountain or lake, or even the seashore, easy according to the number of sections of floor taken up.[18]

Interestingly, Porter's *The Rivals* (shot in September 1907), which concerns a comic competition between two men for the hand of a young woman, did not take advantage of the new studio but was filmed entirely outdoors (in cars, horse buggies, a park, a graveyard, a beach, and steps of a house, etc.). On the other hand, his *House of Cards* (1909)—which takes place in the West (an ostensible opportunity for landscape)—uses sets exclusively. *Thirty Days at Hard Labor* (1912), made by Oscar C. Apfel (three years after Porter left the Edison Company), reveals a significant (though perhaps obvious) truth about set design—that far more detail and attention is given to sets in movies about the rich than in those about the poor. The film concerns a wealthy young gentleman who wishes to marry the daughter of a self-made man who requires that the youth work with his hands for a month before the wedding. The set of the bride-to-be's living room is quite elaborate and includes drapes framing the window (which reveals a painted scene outside), a decorative fireplace with mantel and clock, flowers in vases, a desk with inkwell, lamp, books and bookends, a statue on a pedestal, bookshelves, wall sconces, and upholstered chairs. When the couple steps out on a balcony (the railing draped with fabrics), the set (which twinkles) gives us the sense of water flowing below. Equally detailed is the set for a German restaurant at which the suitor eventually works (which is decorated with coats of arms, leaded glass windows, tablecloths, and candles). These sets, however, contrast sharply with the scenes shot in real exteriors of the prospective groom doing manual labor: digging ditches, breaking stones, or shoveling coal.

One finds a similar ornateness in other films with wealthy settings. *The Passerby* (made by Apfel in 1912) tells the tale of a group of men who take a bridegroom out to dinner. When one of their group sends his regrets, they invite a stranger (apparently down on his luck) to the meal and he tells a tale of woe. The set for the opening scene, perhaps representing a fancy men's club (and executed in three-dimensional fashion), includes wooden tables, upholstered chairs, a fireplace mantel (with candles and a metal plate), potted palms, a statue of a woman, and fancy window treatments. The dining room to which they retreat is amply decorated as well with another fireplace (with intricate candelabras on the mantel) and an elaborately framed portrait above of a woman. As the guest recalls his past life, numerous other well-decorated sets appear: a restaurant, the stock exchange, a drawing room, a club, an office, a betting joint, etc. Interestingly, numerous interior sets include fireplaces—and each is done in a different style and adorned with diverse objects. When windows are shown, they reveal a variety of urban scenes outside. Only in two shots, however, do we ever get location images of the street. Interior walls show moldings, paneling, and wallpaper borders; often chandeliers hang from the (invisible) ceiling. Clearly, the Victorian style of interior furnishing (with its penchant for spaces cluttered with bric-a-brac) gave designers a great opportunity to ornament their sets.

It is clear how far the Edison Company has come in set design in the years between the tarpaper-walled Black Maria and 1912—moving from the absence of sets, to painted flats, to theatrical staging, to sophisticated three-dimensional mise-en-scène (intermixed with location shooting)—all occurring at the same time the movies shifted from one-shot films to edited narratives. Furthermore, a man slated to be among the greatest production designers in Hollywood history, Cedric Gibbons, joined his studio in 1915.[19] However, by March 1918, Edison had closed his Bronx facility and retreated from filmmaking entirely—not a surprise for a man who had always been more interested in equipment than the objects it produced.

While Edison's was perhaps the first studio built on the East Coast (and the only one we have space to describe in detail), there were others in this era that existed alongside his. Kalem set up shop in 1907 and Biograph built an electrically lit rooftop studio in New York in 1903 that remained there until 1913.[20] Other studios were located across the river in Fort Lee, New Jersey (among them Solax, headed by French émigrés Herbert and Alice Guy Blaché). An article by Hugh Hoffman appearing in *Moving Picture World* on November 14, 1912, provides one of the best descriptions of an early film studio (Solax), especially the shops involved in production design—so it is quoted at length:

> The studio proper is constructed of structural iron and glass. The floor . . . is large enough to accommodate five ordinary stage settings at once or three extra deep settings. The glass frames surrounding the studio are so constructed as to be easily removable, allowing a full flood of sunlight to enter the place. This arrangement is valuable also for natural backgrounds to interior settings that have windows. The camera, by this means, can record a studio interior with a genuine landscape as a vista.[21]

Touring the various departments of the studio, Hoffman writes:

> The property room is at one end and next to it is the paper-mache working department. The third room is a property room, containing the more solid and unbreakable articles in great profusion. Fourth along the line is the large scene-room where many, many flats are stacked close together. At the extreme right end the carpenter shop is located, and its connection with the scene painting department just above is ingenious. . . . The scenic artists work directly above the carpenters and at either side of their room

> is a wide slot through which a sliding frame raises or lowers the scene. . . . Next to the scenic room is another property room for the storing of the more delicate articles, such as bric-a-brac and crockery.[22]

There were also major East Coast companies located outside of New York. Lubin Manufacturing Company produced films in Philadelphia between 1897 and 1916. Its glass studio, built at Twentieth and Indiana Streets in 1910, was a state-of-the-art operation and took up a city block.[23] Essanay and Selig Polyscope Company (1907–1915) were located in Chicago.[24] A 1909 article raves about the latter's carpenter shop and property rooms in which "one can find almost any kind of article for use in adding to the realism of a scene, whether oriental or occidental." The author also talks of a trick bridge to be used in an upcoming film "in which a horse and his rider will be seen galloping across a bridge, high above the water, when suddenly the structure will collapse in the middle and precipitate both into the flood. The scenic artist and the carpenter combine to produce these effects."[25]

Production Design and the West Coast: The 1910s and the Epic

Though originally based on the East Coast and in the Midwest, American film production was always peripatetic, and films were often shot in warmer, brighter, and more exotic climes (e.g., Florida, Cuba, the West Indies, or Bermuda).[26] Within the United States, however, the favored locale soon became California—desirable not only for its plentiful daylight and hospitable temperatures, but because it offered a variety of scenery—urban, pastoral, desert, seaside, and mountainous (both sunlit and snow-covered). According to Eileen Bowser, by the winter of 1910–1911 nearly all the major companies had arrived there, and by 1911 a newspaper article heralded Los Angeles as a film "producing center."[27] Soon thereafter, competition erupted between American and European cinema industries around the latter's production of grand epic films. Giovanni Pastrone's *Cabiria* was released in the United States in June of 1914 and added another reason to prefer California over other locales—its wide-open, expansive spaces appropriate for shooting scenes of mass spectacle.

One of the individuals who began working on the West Coast was D. W. Griffith and, according to Beverly Heisner: "As with many other elements of film design in America, it was [he] who pioneered the elaboration of sets and costumes in his longer films." She also notes that Griffith had been interested in décor even while making shorts for the Biograph Company: "He grew tired of the backgrounds painted by one Eddie Shulter and hired the architecturally trained Harry McClelland, an Englishman, to design and paint his sets. Encouraged by Griffith, McClelland colored his settings light grey, rather than the earlier 'Biograph brown' which Shulter had preferred. . . . Lighting could be varied more effectively with the new color scheme."[28] *Judith of Bethulia* was shot in 1913 and released in March 1914, actually before *Cabiria* opened in the United States. It was the director's first feature film for Biograph, where he had worked since 1908. Exteriors were shot in Chatsworth, California, and interiors in New York. Seen as a direct response to the growing European "threat," its narrative derived from the biblical Book of Judith and concerned a siege of a Jewish city by the Assyrians. It was the studio's most expensive film to date at $36,000 and required some 1,000 people and 300 horses for its production.[29] According to a contemporary review, sets and props were created specifically for the film and included "a replica of the ancient city of Bethulia; a faithful reproduction of the ancient army camps embodying all their barbaric dances; chariots, battering rams, scaling ladders, archer towers, and other special war paraphernalia of the period."[30] The magnitude of the enterprise was also referenced in the piece:

> Between two mountains was the location chosen for the great wall against which Holofernes hurls his cohorts in vain attacks. Eighteen hundred feet long, and broad enough to permit of the defenders being massed upon it, the wall rose slowly until it was a giant's causeway connecting the crags on either side. Within, a city sprang up, in whose streets take place some of the most thrilling scenes in the pictures. Beyond it, in the valley, was pitched the great armed camp of the Assyrians. In the chieftains' tent alone were hangings and rugs costing thousands of dollars.[31]

After completing the film, Griffith left Biograph and permanently moved his company to California.[32]

His next film was the famous and infamous *The Birth of a Nation* (1915), a Civil War epic in which the director paid minute attention to creating sets marked by historical accuracy. This was crucial to Griffith's method. As he wrote: "In dealing with an historical subject . . . which is placed in a certain distant period of history, months and sometimes years of research work of a regular department is given to obtaining the correct idea of the manners, customs, costumes, and settings of the period in which you are placing your story." An intertitle for one scene in the film, for instance, tells us that the setting we are about to see is "AN HISTORICAL FACSIMILE of the State House of Representatives of South Carolina as it was in 1870" and cites a specific photograph as source. But, for Griffith, sets needed not only to convey "the atmosphere of the period but they must be made beautiful."[33]

From a production design perspective, the more impressive work was his next film, *Intolerance: Love's Struggle Throughout the Ages* (1916), a tripartite narrative bracketing 2,500 years and three historical periods: the Fall of Babylon, the crucifixion of Christ, and the Saint Bartholomew's Day Massacre of 1572. Promotional materials for the film deemed it a "colossal spectacle."[34] Of the totality of sets, that for the Babylonian era (sixth century B.C.) is especially remarkable. Created by British theatrical designer Walter L. Hall and built over six months by master carpenter Frank Wortman and staff, it consisted of multiple levels, was some 150 feet long and 90 feet high, and rose above Sunset Boulevard.[35] For influences, Hall drew on ancient Persian, Egyptian, and Roman art. Griffith photographer Karl Brown recalls Hall as follows:

> He could draw with superlative skill and paint better, or at least more accurately than anyone I had ever seen work with paint and brush. . . . Hall combined the gift of an imaginative creative artist with the needlepoint accuracy of a fine architect. His preliminary drawings were all done with pencil on specially surfaced heavy cardboard, like title cards. . . . There was no tentative fiddling around; a bold stroke here, and half an arch was on the board; another stroke, and the entire arch was there, hard and clear and firm.[36]

Certainly, production design involves a great deal of research, and to accomplish this for the Babylonian sequence Griffith and Hall studied the following sources, compiling notes and scrapbook illustrations: works by John Layard, Archibald Sayce, and Morris Jastrow Jr., as well as *Ancient Times: A History of the Early World* (1916) by James H. Breasted and the two-volume *A History of Art in Chaldea and Assyria* (1884) by Georges Perrot and Charles Chipiez. In the program booklet for initial screenings of the film, congratulations by both Sayce and Jastrow appeared. As the former wrote: "The Babylonian scenes are magnificent, as well as true to the facts. I was much impressed by the attention that had been paid to accuracy in detail." In keeping with this (as in *The Birth of a Nation*), some of the film's intertitles tout the veracity of the film's settings (e.g., "Replica of Babylon's encircling walls . . . broad enough for the passing of chariots"). In the same program booklet, historian Jastrow wrote: "You [Griffith] have succeeded in conveying to the audience a remarkably vivid picture of the art [and architecture]. . . . I was amazed to see how carefully you reproduced our knowledge of the enormous walls of the city, with their battlements and gates, the palace, the battle towers, the battering-rams and other instruments of ancient warfare."[37] Finally, according to Bernard Hanson, the design team was also influenced in their shot composition by the following paintings: *The Fall of Babylon* by Georges Rochegrosse (1891), *Belshazzar's Feast* by John Martin (1821), and *The Babylonian Marriage Market* by Edwin Long (1875).

There are many extraordinary sets in the Babylonian sections of *Intolerance*, the most famous being the stepped gate, decorated with columns, statuary (elephants and humans), and pictorial friezes, its splendor emphasized by a crane shot that draws nearer to it. Equally impressive are the huge walls of the city with their parapets, carved doors, and sculptures. Noteworthy as well are the quarters of the Princess Beloved—cluttered spaces embellished with curtains, carved moldings, statuary, rugs, draped fabric, and furniture. In addition to three-dimensional sets, some sequences utilized painted backgrounds (as in the recurrent shot of the city as seen from a balcony). Finally, sophisticated props had to be fashioned, including moving towers (used by the approaching army) and huge chariots.

The Twenties: Two Styles, Modes of Production, and Designers

William Cameron Menzies: Fantasy, Art Nouveau, and Independent Production

Though forged in the teens, the epic film (an obvious showcase for production design) continued to be produced in the 1920s—one of the most extravagant being Cecil B. DeMille's *The Ten Commandments* (1923) with art direction by Paul Iribe (a French émigré). According to Robert Sennett, upon completion of the film, DeMille decided it would be easier to bury the set (with gates 120 feet high and nearly 800 feet wide) in the sand rather than to drag it back to Los Angeles, one hundred miles to the south.[38] Evidently, some sixty years later, an oil company digging in the Guadalupe Dunes discovered it and now two filmmakers, Bruce Cardozo and Peter Brosnan, are trying to restore it and are making a movie about it. There is now a visitor's center at the Dunes where one can see a short film about the set's unearthing.[39]

But it is an epic of another sort—fantasy—that is, perhaps, most inspiring in this era; and its exemplar is *The Thief of Bagdad* (1924), directed by Raoul Walsh, with production design by William Cameron Menzies. As a sign of the film's importance, Cathy Whitlock says it "marks the pinnacle of the silent era epic"; likewise, Sennett asserts that it signals "the birth of film design as star."[40]

Perhaps one reason for its artistic excellence had to do with the competition Hollywood felt from the European art film. In 1924, writing in the *New York Times*, George McAdam refers to "a flurry, almost a panic, among American photoplay producers . . . because of a threatened invasion of the home market by European producers."[41] Of course, in general, Hollywood had nothing to worry about, economically, in relation to European cinema (despite Germany's status as its greatest rival). In fact, throughout the 1920s the European film-producing nations tried to fight U.S. hegemony in order to survive. In 1926, for instance, Martha Greuning writes in the *Times* about their organizing a "revolt against our films."[42]

But it was perhaps a slight to the pride of American producers that their films were viewed more as commerce than as art. In 1922 Benjamin De Casseres writes pejoratively in the *Times* of how the "two outstanding features of the American motion picture have been . . . [the] total absence of epical and poetic imagination," concluding that "the American mind is not imaginative." Moreover, he sees

American film as entirely formulaic. Speaking of the artistry of *The Cabinet of Dr. Caligari* (1920), he notes how "this astounding product of motion picture has jolted the average American motion picture mind more than all the other foreign pictures combined." He continues: "No American producer would have dared it. But its influence is already apparent in some of the pictures we are making."[43]

While not beholden to *Caligari*, *The Thief of Bagdad* was influenced by a European design movement—Art Nouveau (though this was never mentioned in reviews of the film). The sense of *Thief* as an American art film is evident in a review by poet Carl Sandburg, who wrote: "Probably no one photoplay since the motion picture business and art got going has been greeted so enthusiastically in the circles known as highbrow and lowbrow. . . . In *The Thief of Bagdad* . . . there is both intelligence and fine art quality."[44] In achieving this standard, *Thief* realized the dream of French critic Louis Aragon, who argued, in 1918, that cinematic "*décor* [is] the adequate setting of modern beauty." As he continued: "It is vital that cinema has a place in the artistic avant-garde's preoccupations. They have designers, painters, sculptors. Appeal must be made to them if one wants to bring some purity to the art of movement and light."[45]

Significantly, Menzies saw the movies as consonant with a growing respect for aesthetics in the broader culture. As he said: "The pictorial beauty of the modern photoplay is an indication of the more general appreciation and the greater demand for beauty that is characteristic of modern life." Furthermore, he believed that "good art is good business" and called misguided "the idea . . . that the artistic picture is destined to be unpopular."[46] In the case of *Thief*, he was right. (As testament to this, some eighty-four years after the film's production, the American Film Institute deemed it the ninth best fantasy film ever made.)[47]

While aware of the European tradition, Menzies was a home-grown talent, born in Connecticut in 1896 (during the first years of film history). He was to become one of the premier production designers in cinema history—his work spanning both silent and sound eras. He is probably best known for his work on *Gone with the Wind* (1939), for which he was the first to receive the title of Production Designer. He was also among the few in his craft to become a film director (most famous for *Things to Come* [1936]). Educated at Yale and New York City's Art Students League, he first worked in advertising and then as an illustrator of children's books. His introduction to cinema came through the mentorship of art director Anton Grot. Menzies saw production design as entailing wide-ranging skills, once having said (in a 1929 lecture delivered at the University of Southern California) that the practitioner "must have a knowledge of architecture of all periods and nationalities. He must be able to picturize and make interesting a tenement or a prison. He must be a cartoonist, a costumier, a marine painter, a designer of ships, an interior decorator, a landscape painter, a dramatist, an inventor, [and] a historical . . . expert." Menzies also saw cinema as primarily a visual art—"a series of pictures" or "fixed and moving patterns."[48]

Thief was a star vehicle for Douglas Fairbanks Sr., who served as its producer; thus, like *Intolerance*, it was an independent production. Reputedly he spent some two million dollars on the project—most of that for design.[49] Shot in some thirty-five days,[50] the film necessitated massive sets, which were built on six acres on North Formosa Street in Los Angeles.[51] To assist him, Menzies brought in Grot as an associate artist.[52] According to the recollections of his wife, Menzies (about twenty-eight years old at the time) landed the commission in the following way:

> Doug [Fairbanks] saw Billy [Menzies] and said he was too young for the job. So he came back and made a real show of what he could do. He worked and worked on these paintings day and night, then he asked for another appointment. He went over carrying all these drawings on his head because they were heavy, and he walked into Douglas Fairbanks's office with these boards balanced on his head and said he'd come to show him that he wasn't too young. He got the job.[53]

This remembrance is contradicted by Sennett, who claims that Grot did many of the charcoal drawings for the film.[54] The catalog for a 1980 exhibition on art direction at London's Victoria and Albert Museum compares the styles of the two designers. It states: "Menzies' canvas was broader [than Grot's] and his brush more daring. He was an imaginative inventor of complete cinematic ideas, and it was perhaps inevitable that he should become a film director in his own right."[55] Evidently, for Menzies, creation of the storyboard was as central to a film's design as the set:

> [He] would start with rough thumbnail sketches in his notebook and develop them, or have them developed by others, into detailed colour artwork. Often on later films these sketches would be propped next to the camera or carried as constant references. The sketches showed every scene including its set, props, lighting, style, camera angle and the disposition of the actors. The method has since become a commonplace of production design.[56]

Thief is an adaptation of the classic *A Thousand and One Nights*, a collection of West and South Asian folk tales compiled in Arabic during the Islamic Golden Age. Its first English translation appeared in 1706 under the title *Arabian Nights*. The film adaptation tells the story of a Bagdad thief who scales the palace walls to steal jewels, but, in the process, becomes enamored of the princess. After being jettisoned from the palace, he vows to return, posing as one of many princely suitors competing to win the princess's hand. He steals a horse and fancy clothing and returns as "Ahmed, Prince of the Isles of the Seas" and the princess chooses him to wed; but a Mongol prince reveals that the thief is a fraud. The caliph (the princess's father) orders the thief flogged, but he escapes. When the caliph asks the princess to choose another mate, she stalls, asking each suitor to bring her a treasure. Hearing this, the thief vows to find bounty of his own and, after getting advice from a wise man, goes in search of a magic chest. This quest leads to many adventures in dangerous and supernatural locales: the Cavern of Enchanted Trees, the Valley of Fire, the Valley of the Monsters, the Abode of the Winged Horse, the Citadel of the Moon, and the realm of the Old Man of the Midnight Sea. Eventually, the thief returns to the castle and uses his magic to battle the forces of the Mongol prince, who is attempting to force the princess to marry him. The thief's tricks work and he wins her coveted hand.

It is clear how this narrative offers an art director a plethora of opportunities, and Menzies took them all. First, of course, there is the story's exotic setting. In his book *Architecture for the Screen*, Juan Antonio Ramirez claims that the film—with its "resonances of Islamic art from Iran and North India casually rub[bing] shoulders with the Alhambra Palace in Granada"—opened the doors to Hollywood Orientalism.[57] But we had already seen evidence of this trend in *Intolerance*'s depiction of Babylonia. Furthermore, this nod to the East is characteristic of Art Nouveau (as in the work of painter Gustav Klimt, or architect Antonio Gaudí).

To fully analyze the sets of *Thief*, it is necessary to divide them into various locales. First there is the city of Bagdad itself—outside the palace walls or within. The sets for the streets are majestic and massive, creating a bold contrast between the scale of edifices and people (as do such oversized objects as vases, stairways,

FIGURE 7: The thief in *The Thief of Bagdad* (Raoul Walsh, 1924, prod. des. and art dir. William Cameron Menzies) poses against a background of "whiplash curves."

and windows). The walls of the palace (which loom over the city) have many minarets and towers and are decorated in tile (with repetitive geometric shapes characteristic of Islamic style). Furthermore, some objects (for instance a gong) are inscribed with Arabic calligraphy.

The city, overall, has numerous arabesque arches—also typical of Islamic architecture. In some shots, however, sections of the wall look almost glass-like (rather than opaque) and are done in an Art Deco style. The arabesque motif is also carried out in the walls of the interior palatial court. Inside the palace, the look is quite different and characterized by more of an Art Nouveau aesthetic. Here, the rectilinear, chevron panels found outside the palace become more circular and curvilinear, though they still maintain some of the Deco feel. This is not surprising as many elements of Art Nouveau were repurposed in the later movement (which "debuted" at a Paris world exposition in 1925).

Given that Art Nouveau was often seen as a "feminine" style, it is not surprising that it is in the princess's quarters that we find its most emphatic use—for instance, in the curving sweep of her bedroom staircase with its scroll-like form. This motif is repeated on numerous screens and grilles throughout the palace—some of which sport the style's famous "whiplash curve" (figure 7). Art Nouveau was also known for its organic imagery, favoring (among other things) floral designs. Again, the props and latticework in *Thief* are consonant with this sensibility (figure 8).

A decorative sense is also attached to the most evil figure in the film, the Mongol prince, and critics have noted how ornament (which is frequently disparaged in Western culture) is often associated with women and the Other. His palace is

FIGURE 8: Floral/organic motifs (characteristic of Art Nouveau) appear in props, screens, and window grilles.

FIGURE 9: The gorgeous, ornate, Art Nouveau-inspired palace of the evil Mongol Prince.

incredibly ornate and beautiful, and a sword with which he has had someone poisoned is tipped with an elaborate, curvilinear globe (figure 9).

The film's Arab setting is resonant with Art Nouveau iconography, which drew upon Islamic architecture and design. For instance, the canopied gate that served as entrance to the Paris Exposition of 1900 (at which the style "debuted") took the form of a baldachin, with open latticework executed in an Islamic mode. The Souvenir Program Booklet for *Thief* even talked of burning incense in the movie theater—another homage to the East.

Menzies's art direction had to emphasize the narrative's dreamlike, ethereal aura, and, again, this squares with Art Nouveau's focus on fantasy. Thus, for instance, he utilized highly polished black reflective floors, special lighting techniques, gauze as a light diffuser, and buildings lit from below.[58] Gauze is also a design element in the princess's bedroom—used as a means to hide the thief and, of course, in the princess's facial veiling. Here we should recall that the figure of the Arab woman was popular in the period of Art Nouveau, as in the painting *Salomé Dancing* (1874–1876) by Gustave Moreau and the sculpture *Salaambô chez Matho* (1900) by Théodore Rivière.

But the truly fantastic elements of the plot erupt in the thief's magical adventures in pursuit of a treasure for the princess. And it is here that Menzies marries production design with special effects. As the film's Souvenir Program Booklet states, Fairbanks "conscripted all the artistic, mechanical and imaginative talents of many people" to achieve the outcome he desired. Perhaps the most spectacular

FIGURE 10: The Realm of the Old Man of the Midnight Sea—a "Lalique wonderland."

setting is the realm of the Old Man of the Midnight Sea that members of the Art Department created, spending months blowing ornate glass.[59] Here, we recall that delicate, clear glass decorative objects were the signature product of Art Nouveau designer René Lalique—so this scene appears to take place in a Lalique wonderland (figure 10).

Menzies discusses how other aspects of the sequence were accomplished:

> We took a set and cut seaweeds out of buckram, and had a series of them hanging down in several places. A wind machine was put on so the seaweeds flapped but as the scene was taken in slow motion, they undulated when shown on the screen. The camera had a marine disk over the lens and was turned over. Mr. Fairbanks was let down into the scene and went through the motions of swimming under water. The scene had the appearance of water.[60]

Miniatures (often combined with process shots) were used for other fantasy sites (for instance, the Valley of Fire, the Valley of Monsters, and the Abode of the Winged Horse). Models were combined with process shots to render the Cloak of Invisibility,[61] and live action and process shots were used for the thief's ride through the sky. Contrary to these, the flying carpet effect was created in quite a material fashion—by securing a three-quarter-inch-thick piece of steel rigged by sixteen piano wires anchored to the top of a crane.[62] The crew also had to arrange for a moving camera (which Menzies asserts "is another thing the art director is involved in"), and "a platform [was] built for the cameraman which travelled with the crane."[63]

Menzies used the tinting and toning of footage in various sections to augment the movie's sense of whimsy. As the Souvenir Program Booklet asserts: "A roseate glow [was used] for the romantic moments; a garish green where the terrifying monsters appear; a soft uranium sepia where the beautiful golden haze glows about the dream city of Bagdad and throughout all the fantasy a rich Maxfield Parrish blue" (color plate 3). As for the reference to Parrish, his style has been claimed by aficionados of both Art Nouveau and Art Deco. Interestingly, while the Souvenir Program does not mention Menzies in its text, it does cite the film's poster artists—Anton Grot and Willy Pogany. The latter was a book illustrator who specialized in creating Art Nouveau plates for works of myth and legend, for instance, *The Rubáiyát of Omar Khayyám*. He also executed posters for the Ballets Russes, a company whose costumes and sets were rife with Art Nouveau elements.

Ben Carré, Expressionism, and the Studio System

By the mid-twenties, the studio system was in full swing. One of the major players was Universal, founded and led by Carl Laemmle. He had purchased a 230-acre ranch in North Hollywood for $165,000 and created Universal City (simultaneously a film factory and a town), which opened on March 15, 1915.[64] According to Phillip J. Riley, by 1924, Universal "was a magical land that existed outside of reality." As he continues:

> It had its own mayor and city council, fire departments, post offices, power plants, street department, chicken ranch, mountains, rivers, a miniature desert, drill grounds big enough for 10,000 troops, rocky western backgrounds, and many acres of sound stages and backlot sets. . . . The front lot had five large "Electrified" stages with a few of the glass stages left over from the earlier days. . . . Around the stages were fifty-one buildings which housed dressing rooms, carpentry shops, mills, plaster shops and all the other trades necessary to make movies. . . . There were also one hundred horses, stabled for their Westerns. . . . The backlot had . . . European villages, The Five Corners, Western Town and over 500 prop buildings.[65]

In Richard Koszarski's view, except for producing works like Erich von Stroheim's *Foolish Wives* (1922) (known as studio "jewels"), "artistic quality was not necessarily at a premium" at Universal in this era.[66] In 1923, however, the studio aimed high with *The Hunchback of Notre Dame*, directed by Wallace Worsley and starring Lon Chaney—a film that earned a popular and critical success. In particular, the movie was noted for its majestic replica of the famous French cathedral. Laemmle was looking for another property of equal grandeur as a follow-up picture for Chaney (whose performance in *Hunchback* had been extolled).

Evidently, during the time that Irving Thalberg was at Universal (before leaving for MGM in 1923), he was interested in adapting Gaston LeRoux's novel *The Phantom of the Opera* (1910) for the screen; but the project had been dropped.[67] In 1923, after visiting Paris and meeting LeRoux, Laemmle resuscitated the venture and the first treatment of the script was submitted on 12 October. In the checkered career of the film's production, there would be numerous additional versions, rewrites, and edits before the film's New York City premiere in September of 1925.[68] The story (of a deformed, insane man dwelling in the cellars of the Paris Opera House who tutors, falls in love with, and eventually abducts a beautiful young singer) combined mystery, perverse romance, and horror. It was the latter two features that gave the tale an Expressionist feel—and could draw upon another European art and film movement.

For the most part, the horror genre at this time was associated with German cinema and such works as *The Student of Prague* (1913), *The Cabinet of Dr. Caligari*, *The Golem* (1920), and *Nosferatu* (1922). There had been some fledgling American horror films (like various versions of *Frankenstein*),[69] but none had achieved the kind of acclaim associated with their Continental counterparts. Significantly, when it came time to publicize Universal's *Phantom*, words like "weird," "eerie," and "devilish" were used in its advertising materials.[70] Evidently, the original script also included grim graveyard scenes that were later eliminated.

The film was directed by New Zealand émigré Rupert Julian (though he was eventually replaced by Edward Sedgwick, who was credited for "supplementary direction"). Three art directors worked on the film: E. E. Sheeley (the set designer for *Hunchback*), his assistant, Sidney Ullman, and Ben Carré (who was listed first as Art Director and then as Consulting Artist). Archer Havelock Hall (brother of famous designer Charles Hall) was the Technical Director who supervised set construction. According to Phillip J. Riley's book on the making of the film, "The amazing atmosphere of the real Opera house which . . . made the film a classic was the creation of Ben Carré. It was he who designed the underground and backstage sequences for the film."[71]

Carré was born in Paris in 1883 and left school at thirteen to apprentice as a house painter. Soon, however, he was offered a job as a scenic painter at the Amable Studios and, after that, obtained employment as a backdrop painter at the Paris Opera, the Comédie Française, and Covent Garden. This work won him an offer from Gaumont Studios in 1906. While there, he worked on production design, which by then had expanded to include three-dimensional sets and furnishings, as well as special effects. In 1912, he was invited to join Éclair Studios in Fort Lee, New Jersey, and, by 1914, had forged a close working relationship with

French director Maurice Tourneur. When, in 1919, Tourneur was offered his own studio in Culver City, Carré accompanied him to California.[72]

The main reason that Universal turned to Carré for art direction in *Phantom* was that the film's narrative required the studio to build a life-size facsimile of the Paris Opera House. While Universal had access to the original blueprints for the building, Carré had actually worked there, and knew the theater more intimately than anyone else at the studio (especially the Opera's backstage and storage areas). According to Carré, he was hired to produce sketches of areas of the Opera that did not appear on the blueprints, among them the scene docks, the underground lake, and the animal ramps. He produced twenty-four illustrations, which were mounted in a large book measuring some four feet by five feet. While he was familiar with many areas of the Opera, some that appear in the film he conceived "right out of [his] imagination."[73] After submitting the sketches, Carré departed, expecting that he would be called back to supervise set construction; but he was not (since he was in Europe at the time).[74] Years later, when he saw the finished film, he stated: "They did not [only] use my sketches as a basis to design the sets—they copied them exactly; to the point where people are still searching the real Opera house for the rooms that came out of my imagination."[75] His view is supported by notes on the script that say such things as "Carré is working out the details."[76]

Two aspects of production design for *Phantom* are noteworthy. One relates to questions of spectacle and historical accuracy. Here, fittingly, Carl Sandburg opined that the film gave "new meaning to the word 'sensational.'"[77] Ultimately, it is the scale reproduction of the Paris Opera House that is impressive, as supervised by Hall. As we know, as early as Griffith's *The Birth of a Nation*, subtitles informed viewers that certain scenes were precise replicas of important historical sites from the Civil War and Reconstruction. And, of course, already with *The Hunchback of Notre Dame*, Universal had faced the problem of staging scenes in another ersatz famous Paris building. In this regard, most striking in *Phantom* are the sequences that occur either in the Opera lobby (with its grand staircase) or its auditorium (with its huge seating area, orchestra pit, and tiers of balconies and boxes).

Clearly, the studio wished to sell the film as an extravaganza and in publicity used adjectives like "mammoth," "massive," and "gigantic," calling the work a "superfilm," a "super-thriller,"[78] and a "super jewel."[79] The press book for the film gives exhibitors copy to plant in newspapers in order to stress the film's epic proportions:

> The famous Paris Opera House was built in a specially constructed building [Stage 28, which was 360 feet by 145 feet] as no studio was large enough to contain these sets. The auditorium, with five tiers of balconies, boxes and full size stage; the grand staircase and foyer, the salon

> de danse, dressing rooms, orchestra pit, fly gallery and numerous other features . . . were reproduced in exact size and detail.[80]

An opening title proudly notes that what follows was "produced in its entirety at Universal City." Publicity releases assert that the film's sets were "the first [ones of] all-steel" built "in the history of the industry" (since traditional wood sets would not have supported the crowds), and involved the "largest interior set ever constructed."[81] Press materials also speak of the task of decorating the opera house:

> The foyer, staircase, and boxes are elaborately sculptured and carved. There are also numerous paintings and sculptures in the original building which were reproduced with amazing cleverness. It is said to have taken eleven sculptors and scenic artists six weeks to duplicate an idea of the frescoes, sculptures, and decorations for the film's settings.[82]

One of the most memorable scenes in the film takes place on the roof of the Opera as Christine (Mary Philbin) and her lover, Raoul de Chagny (Norman Kerry), talk beneath a giant statue of Apollo on which the Phantom secretly perches, his cape flying in the wind. Significantly, a press article (accompanied by a photo) is headed, "This Colossal Statue which Ornaments the Opera House is a Small Detail of the Massive Set."[83] Like the rest of the Opera set, it was built to scale. In order to show the skyline of Paris from the rooftop, a glass painting of it was mounted before the camera.[84] The press release also gives statistics about the army of technicians involved in the film's production (for instance, 300 stagehands and electricians) as well as the staggering amount of wood trucked in for the project ("the largest shipload of lumber in the history of Los Angeles").[85]

Of course, the storyline of *The Phantom* is famous for a particular prop—the chandelier that the Phantom releases to drop on the opera audience. (In actuality, there was an accident with a light fixture at the Paris Opera in 1896.)[86] Again, press materials for the film tout the chandelier's extraordinary features: it "weighs 16,000 pounds" and falls "over a hundred feet upon the frightened people below."[87] For other set decorations, according to Scott MacQueen, "studio manager Julius Bernheim sent scouting parties to Europe to procure fin-de-siècle furnishings and operatic props."[88]

Certain scenes (shot when Sedgwick took over) involve the flight of the Phantom into the streets of Paris, chased by a mob (not part of LeRoux's original novel). According to George Perry, some of the sets formerly used for *Hunchback* were repurposed here. Since the scene took place at night, the medieval character of the buildings would not be noticed.[89] Finally, the sequences occurring in the public areas of the Opera are important for another reason—an early use of natural color—later to become a crucial aspect of production design. Clearly, color was chosen in order to make the film even more sensational than it already was. Although originally Laemmle was going to use Prizma color, the episodes in question (the ballet, the opera *Faust*, and the masked ball) were, ultimately, shot in two-color Technicolor (favoring red and green)—with a special consultant on hand. A different color process was used in the scene of the Phantom atop the statue and dressed for the masked ball, wearing a skull mask and a flowing red cape (color plate 4). Here, the color was transferred to the release print utilizing the Handschiegl process.[90] Many other scenes in the film were colored through toning and tinting, as was usual for works of this era.

The film's uncanny, Expressionist, and "Freudian" tone is evinced in the scenes that occur backstage at the Opera as well as those that take place in the sinister underground cellars, passages, chambers, and waterways that constitute the Phantom's cavernous domain (figure 11).[91] (Here intertitles refer to an "intricate maze" or to a "dismal haunt of creeping things.") Aside from the influence of German horror films, some have seen the imprint of works like the *Imaginary Prisons* series by artist Giovani Battista Piranesi.[92]

There is evidently some historical truth to the existence of cryptic subterranean spaces in the actual Opera building. Its labyrinthine, multilevel basements were once used as a temporary government site for the Communards during

FIGURE 11: The cavernous underground realm of the Opera—the home of the Phantom in *The Phantom of the Opera*.

Louis Napoleon's reign. Years later, people found rotted bodies of soldiers and prisoners who had died in the building's dungeons. Because of this, rumors circulated that the Opera was haunted by ghosts.[93] Furthermore, while the building was under construction in 1861, the crew unearthed a buried stream, which they later used for hydraulic power to operate theater equipment.[94]

To create this strange, grotesque, hidden universe, as illustrations in Riley's detailed study of the film make clear, Carré sketched dark, tiered, arched, descending, underground ramps that connect one level of the basement to another. He also pictured in detail the large, rough stone bricks that form the denizen's walls. He populated the backstage areas with frightening props (an open-mouthed snake head, a human skull, a gargantuan statue, a decapitated head, a huge-faced dragon) as well as menacing hanging ropes (for curtains and counterweights). Furthermore, this area (and the Phantom's lair) had a series of unsettling trapdoors. Carré also drew the underground lake and entrance to the Phantom's abode, supported by arched pillars. A final sketch reveals the area behind Christine's dressing room, which is magically accessed by walking through a mirror (a scene that MacQueen sees as important to later works by Jean Cocteau).[95] Ominous weights, pulleys, and wheels punctuate the stark space. As Carré has indicated, all of these images were meticulously copied in the film—where dim lighting, shadows on the wall, and the horrific appearance of the Phantom (his countenance first masked, then revealed as dreadful through Chaney's brilliant makeup and prostheses) augment the Expressionist atmosphere (figure 12).

FIGURE 12: The Phantom's dark shadow helps create a horrific and unsettling atmosphere in the Opera's backstage recesses.

Again, Universal's publicity machine cranked out copy that hyped the film's grotesque underground sets. One touted the "Chamber of Mystery"—a place for "ingenious tortures." Here, they are referencing a secret room (five stories beneath the underground lake) in which the Phantom traps Raoul and his brother Philippe (John Sainpolis), who are searching for Christine. The article continues: "The chamber consists of a large room in hexagonal shapes, the walls of which are great mirrors. By a series of multiple reflections, the room may be made to appear, to those inside it, an African jungle, filled with ferocious beasts, a pleasant forest filled with shade-trees, or any other kind of landscape." For the lake on which the Phantom sails with Christine, in which he swims, and which later floods the "mystery chamber," Universal allegedly built "ten 700,000 gallon tanks." Furthermore, the studio boasted that "the construction and staging of this flood scene is one of the biggest engineering feats ever attempted in motion pictures" and necessitated the supervision of mining engineers.[96]

One aspect of the Phantom's hideout not envisioned by Carré was a piece of furniture used for Christine's bedroom. It was found on the European hunt for decorative objects. It was "a fanciful and wholly surreal bed, like a gilded gondola or slipper" that once belonged to entertainer Gaby Deslys.[97] Eventually, it was used again for Norma Desmond's boudoir in *Sunset Blvd.* (1950)—another film with a nod to Expressionism.[98] Clearly, it was too precious not to save and recycle in other productions. Similarly, the huge stage on which *Phantom* was shot is still in use on the Universal lot. Equally noteworthy is the Phantom's bed (which resembles a coffin and is adorned with candles)—an object that shocks Christine when she first perceives it. Here, connections are made between the Phantom and a vampire (the "undead")—another stock figure of the horror film.

Finally, perhaps the most interesting aspect of *Phantom* from the perspective of production design is the self-reflexivity implicit in its storyline. After all, it is a backstage drama set at the opera—a theatrical form known for its striking mise-en-scène. Since much of the action occurs either onstage or behind the scenes, there is ample opportunity for us to view "sets-within-sets," as it were—in the opera being performed as well as in the backdrops and props stored for other performances. Furthermore, we get a peek at the machinery necessary for spectacle to be realized—cranks, ropes, pulleys, curtains, and trapdoors.

Conclusion

With the construction first of a Manhattan rooftop studio in 1901 and then an electrically powered facility in the Bronx in 1907, art direction became more sophisticated, especially in films directed by Edwin Porter—with three-dimensional, cornered sets and more elaborate furnishings (particularly in dramas that focused on the wealthy). A mixture of location and studio shooting characterized works of this era as well as the roots of model use and special effects. Nonetheless, set design at this time still had its origin in theatrical melodrama and was only later to discover its full cinematic possibilities.

With the move of many film companies to the West Coast (and competition from the European epic), production design became more refined and impressive. Especially remarkable in the 1910s and early 1920s were such spectacles as Griffith's and DeMille's biblical narratives—*Judith of Bethulia* and *The Ten Commandments*—with their monumentally proportioned sets and lavish decorative details. In this period, we also begin to see the kind of research into historical accuracy that would mark much production design in the future.

Among the most notable aspects of American art direction in the mid-1920s was the influence upon it of certain European design movements, due, perhaps, to competition from the Continental art film. In the ornate settings and furnishings of the independently produced *The Thief of Bagdad*, we glean the mark of Art Nouveau. In the dark and horrific look of Universal's *The Phantom of the Opera*, we sense the shadow of Expressionism—in a film that self-reflexively concerns the theatrical world and the role of production design within it.

2

CLASSICAL HOLLYWOOD, 1928–1946 Mark Shiel

> *Of all the assaults leveled at Hollywood's movie makers, few concern the technical quality of their products. In the fifty years since the motion picture was invented, its technicians have turned out an ever more convincing series of illusions. This ability to make its audiences believe that they are looking at a real Sahara or a real battle has done much to place Hollywood in its pre-eminent position over its British, French, and Russian rivals. As a consequence no group of men is more important nor more respected in Hollywood than the illusion makers. They must understand lighting and electronics and know the crafts of carpentry and plumbing and painting. They must be engineers and artists, fully aware of the problems of stress and color and perspective. And finally they must be able to organize quickly, and fairly cheaply, the myriad details which go into the manufacture of a German town, an Alaska tundra, or a fake submarine. For all these versatile abilities they are very highly paid.*
>
> —Life, *7 August 1944*

The decade and a half preceding *Life* magazine's special feature on the "illusion makers" was a high point in the history of art direction in American motion pictures. Especially at the Hollywood majors, the art department became the embodiment of Hollywood cinema's constitutive tension between creativity and manufacturing as the trained architects or artists it employed worked in an industrial setting but often displayed distinctive artistic vision by means of craftsmanship and manual skills. While usually keeping a low profile in designing and making sets and décor, the art department was responsible for much, if not most, of the content of the images appearing in any given feature film and played a role in selecting and preparing locations, costumes, lighting, and even cinematography. It also helped to ensure the seemingly natural conventions of narrative space in classical Hollywood cinema—most sets were built according to principles of linear perspective, staging in depth, and narrative continuity, and most art directors prioritized verisimilitude in designing detailed and architecturally plausible three-dimensional environments to aid the evocation of a fictional world by the cast and crew during shooting. The scenery depicted was varied, but interiors generally prevailed over the great outdoors, both in the settings of films and because they were mostly filmed within the confined space of the closed, indoor, concrete, and soundproof shooting stages that dominated feature film production. These enormous spaces and the myriad sets they contained made art direction and set design a matter not only of imagination but of complex logistics and business management in a mass production regime.

Most of the available literature on the subject evinces a biographical approach. What follows interprets the variety of art direction in the period in question, as an activity and in finished films, in terms of the large cultural, technological, and economic processes by which urban and rural space were modernized in the early twentieth century and the crises of those processes during the Great Depression and World War II.

Art Direction and the Coming of Sound

The Hollywood studio system achieved global renown during a period of massive and prolonged capital investment in the late 1910s and 1920s, in which the majors concentrated their efforts in fixed-site studio production, mostly in Los Angeles; large shooting stages and technical workshops; Fordist principles of mass production; and Taylorist principles of scientific management, by which large numbers of specialized employees were organized hierarchically.[1] In this context, art direction had begun to emerge as a discipline in its own right, although the major studios' reliance on it was intensified by the coming of sound and the Wall Street crash. In the mid-1930s, total employment in the studio system stabilized at around 30,000; each of the majors produced about fifty to sixty-five feature films per year; and average budgets ranged from about $200,000 at RKO to about $500,000 at MGM.[2] The variety of studios and films from prestige pictures to Poverty Row programmers, the coexistence of A- and B-features, and the numerous individuals involved guaranteed diversity in set design, even within individual studios, although that diversity was somewhat constrained by the formulaic nature of genre-based filmmaking and by fluctuating economic pressures.

Not all feature films relied on sets to attract spectators. For example, Tino Balio points out that most of the numerous films of Shirley Temple, who was the number-one box office star from 1934 to 1938, were cheap to make, with "simple stories, few sets, mostly indoor, and small shooting companies."[3] And something similar might be said of the tremendously successful films made by Laurel and Hardy for Hal Roach Studios. Indeed, numerically speaking, B-movies accounted for as much as 75 percent of all feature films in the 1930s, the majors making B's on a budget of $50,000–$100,000 each while small independent firms spent $5,000–$20,000 per picture.[4] Some of these were very creative despite a lack of resources—for example, the expressionist horror film *Dracula* (Tod Browning, 1931), designed by Charles D. Hall for Universal. But most B's were less innovative and extravagant than A's in mise-en-scène; many used sets with poor build quality and detail, sometimes disguised by low lighting; some reused sets from other films; and some (for example, western serials) used location filming as a way to save money. At the majors, however, set construction was always one of the most important expenditures in a film's budget, and usually the most expensive after the screenplay and salaries of director and stars. For example, the star-studded high society drama *Dinner at Eight* (George Cukor, 1933, MGM) had a $500,000 budget, of which sets cost $150,000 while $123,000 was spent on the script and $85,000 on the actors.[5]

The art director of *Dinner at Eight*, Cedric Gibbons, told the public in 1929 that "greater pictorial beauty will be assured in sound pictures by more elaborate sets."[6] The following year, James L. Davis, real estate editor of the *Los Angeles Times*, estimated that the coming of sound had required an investment of $110 million in new and upgraded studio buildings.[7] Since the foundation of the first movie studios in Los Angeles, in the early 1910s, there had been a constant trend toward more and larger studio buildings, in keeping with growth in the number and average length of films produced, and leading to an increase in the number and ambition of sets.[8] For example, the Triangle studios in Culver City, the future home of MGM, had opened in 1916 with five stages of 8,000 square feet each on an 11.5-acre lot.[9] In 1928, William Fox opened new studios on 108 acres in Westwood, whose four stages drew on innovations in steel and concrete engineering to cover 35,000 square feet apiece.[10] The next year, RKO commissioned a new stage for its Hollywood studios, 100,000 square feet in area and 90 feet in height, which was said to be the largest in the world and could be used either as one space or subdivided in four.[11] Moreover, some studios operated several sites—for example, Warner Bros. managed twenty-eight stages at three facilities in Hollywood and Burbank, and a 1,100-acre ranch for outdoor locations as well.[12]

The *Los Angeles Times* evoked the rapid evolution of the industry by contrasting a past in which sets were "shell-like, panel-board structures, painted and braced behind . . . with a minimum effort [and] demolished almost immediately after each scene" and a new era in which "larger and still larger interiors are being constructed daily for talking pictures. Outside locations, while still used more or less effectively, seem to be gradually relegated to the background, and the magnificently constructed settings are becoming more and more prevalent."[13] Boris Leven, who shared an Oscar nomination with Bernard Herzbrun for the art direction of the musical *Alexander's Ragtime Band* (Henry King, 1938, Twentieth Century–Fox), was somewhat ambivalent about this centralization: "The joy and the curse of working as an art director was that everything was *right there*. You almost never went on location; everything was shot in the studio, or on the back lot."[14]

The late silent comedy *Show People* (King Vidor, 1928, art dir. Cedric Gibbons, MGM) is notable for liberally mixing indoor sets and exterior locations around Los Angeles while presenting the romance of a lowly slapstick comedian and an egotistical actress who stars in high-class costume dramas. One of the film's themes is the loss of honesty and naturalism that comes from over-reliance on studio fakery, although, in retrospect, we can say that it is precisely the lack of sound that allowed the film successfully to represent the city beyond the studio's walls. In 1929, new soundstages were built at MGM that would be central to its subsequent industrial dominance, and whose construction was intended to create a cocoon from the outside world. Their eight-inch-thick concrete and steel walls and roofs were lined with inner acoustic plaster walls, with an air gap in between to create a soundproof vacuum, all resting on sixteen feet of foundations buried in sand and a floor sixteen inches thick, comprising six inches of sand, four inches of concrete, three inches of cork, and two layers of timber boards.[15] In such places, art direction was defined in its heyday as an art of replication and simulation, and perhaps even the improvement of nature and the built environment. Indeed, the coming of sound required art direction to adapt to other engineering innovations as well. Gibbons explained that the walls of sets for sound could not be built facing each other or at right angles, which would create echoes, while "building sets of proper acoustic material . . . costs about twice as much as building ordinary sets."[16] Homer Tasker, president of the Society of Motion Picture Engineers, reported from a tour of Warner Bros. in 1935 a "trend toward mechanizing almost everything involved," including "camera cranes" and "motorized sets," which "perform in almost human fashion, their movements synchronized by . . . interlocking motors."[17] RKO's largest stage included an overhead monorail system for the efficient movement of sets.[18]

The increasing ambition of sets was encouraged by tendencies in cinematography and staging that made sets more visible. While most early silent films, whether shot on location or in studio, relied on one portable tripod-mounted camera in a fixed position at a distance from the subject, in the later silent era films were often made with multiple cameras and traveling shots, while studio settings became somewhat more common than locations.[19] But the coming of sound suddenly restricted camera movement to the soundstage's soundproof booth, forcing filmmakers to relearn camera placement and movement, although by the early 1940s they had done so decisively with an array of tracking, panning, tilt, zoom, and crane shots. Meanwhile, there was a move away from the diffused lighting and soft focusing of the silent era toward a crisp and more illuminated image. Film stocks became more sensitive to light, giving greater definition and clarity, and lenses became more refined and variable, giving more flexibility and accuracy in focusing and encouraging staging in depth, in pictures from *Bulldog Drummond* (F. Richard Jones, 1929, art dir. William Cameron Menzies, Samuel Goldwyn/United Artists) to *Citizen Kane* (Orson Welles, 1941, art dir. Van Nest Polglase, Mercury Productions/RKO).

Sound also prompted a reconfiguration of film genres. American frontier settings continued to have importance and were often clearly indebted in their art direction to traditions of landscape painting, from *Cimarron* (Wesley Ruggles, 1931, art dir. Max Rée, RKO) to *My Darling Clementine* (John Ford, 1946, art dirs. James Basevi and Lyle Wheeler, Twentieth Century–Fox); most westerns, however, were produced in low-budget series by Poverty Row studios such as Monogram and Republic. Exotic ancient settings were less prevalent than in the silent era, though medieval epics such as *The Adventures of Robin Hood* (Michael Curtiz, 1938, art dir. Carl Jules Weyl, Warner Bros.) and Elizabethan swashbucklers such as *The Sea Hawk* (Curtiz, 1940, art dir. Anton Grot, Warner Bros.) achieved acclaim for their lavish and romantic locales. The rise of the gangster film, musical, and screwball comedy was predicated on a new sense of the authentic vernacular of everyday life during the Great Depression and New Deal era, proliferating modern urban settings or rapidly modernizing rural ones, from pool halls and speakeasies in *The Public Enemy* (William Wellman, 1931, art dir. Max Parker, Warner Bros.) to grand hotels and Broadway theaters in *42nd Street* (Lloyd Bacon, 1933, art dir. Jack Okey, Warner Bros.) and roadside diners and motels in *It Happened One Night* (Frank Capra, 1934, art dir. Stephen Goosson, Columbia).

Many pioneering art directors of the silent era did all, or the best of, their work prior to the coming of sound—for example, Wilfred Buckland, Ben Carré, Harold Grieve, and Joseph Urban. William Fox had an art department from 1922 and by the end of the decade the art department was among the most important on any studio lot.[20] In 1938, Gibbons, who ran MGM's art department from 1924 to 1956, wryly reflected that the painted backdrops of early cinema "were probably of more value in hiding the technicians and visitors walking around behind the scenes than in enriching the story itself."[21] Subsequently, he thought, sets had become too prominent and cluttered with furniture until, with the coming of sound, art direction achieved a happy medium, "subduing the sets to the story and action."[22] Stephen Watts, the editor of *Behind the Screen: How the Films Are Made* (1938), stressed that art directors like Gibbons aimed for "magnificence," "skilful illusion," and "painstakingly authentic detail," through "planning and hard work"—what Gibbons enthusiastically called the challenge of "tackling fresh and undreamt-of problems every day."[23] But even at the end of the 1920s some older artists, trained in theater, looked down on cinematic staging. F. W. Murnau, whose *Sunrise* (art dir. Rochus Gliese, 1927, Twentieth Century–Fox) stunned audiences with its presentation of the modern metropolis, explained to the theatrical producer Max Reinhardt that "stage and pictures must be definitely divorced from each other for the good of the latter. Stage production must be no longer made over into pictures. . . . Sets must be built by men who learn their craft in the studios and not behind theater curtains. . . . Pictures are now in their maturity and film producing is an art old enough to have its own traditions."[24] Art direction also served an economic rationale: in July 1933, an article in the *Los Angeles Times* entitled "Art Directors Would Show Films How to Save Money" explained that many movie sets were not efficiently constructed because the art director was brought into the creative process secondarily to the producer, writer, and director; hence, a new group had been established within the Academy of Motion Picture Arts and Sciences, which would promote the art director as "a trained architect and draughtsman, a mine of historical information, a specialist in the actinic and sound values of materials and paints, a practical engineer, and a financial estimator all rolled into one."[25]

Working Methods

Notwithstanding his various skills, the art director occupied just one level in a complex hierarchy. By the 1930s, the art departments of the majors had grown so much that the function of "supervising art director" was instituted to provide artistic oversight of all of a studio's productions at once, approving sketches, models, plans, technical drawings, and construction budgets and schedules proposed by each individual "unit art director," many of whom specialized in one or another genre of film. The supervising art director usually received more prominent billing in a film's credits—indeed, Gibbons was famous for having a contract that explicitly required that he get top billing. In 1931, he managed a department of forty staff members, which included six unit art directors, each working on one or two pictures at a time and each picture requiring about ten weeks' work, and these staffers collaborated directly with each film's director, assistant director, writer, associate producer, cinematographer, and sound engineer.[26] Gibbons's approach seems to have been relatively managerial—the *New York Times* used a military metaphor: "He sits in sole command of his forces in spacious quarters on the second floor of one of the executive buildings on the crowded Metro lot."[27]

Van Nest Polglase, who became supervising art director at RKO in 1932, is said to have been relatively hands-off—Ellen Spiegel suggests he "got the first and last words, but seldom stayed in between"—while Hans Dreier at Paramount allowed unit art directors greater freedom than either Polglase or Gibbons.[28] But Gibbons was especially prominent because MGM was the most commercially successful of the majors, because he was more frequently quoted in the press, not only on art direction but on architecture and interior design, and because of his famous wife, the actress Dolores Del Rio.[29] In 1936, he was also the only art director to appear in the U.S. Treasury's annual list of the most highly paid individuals in the nation.[30]

Most art directors preferred a low profile and commentators frequently expressed the view that success in the job required modesty and self-control. Stephen Watts explained that the art director "gets no glory outside the studio, except on those rare occasions when the public seizes on some spectacular effect or piece of brilliant trickery. But that is the least of his job and he rarely wishes to talk about it."[31] The *New York Times* opined that "while the screen's performers . . . usually lean more toward the flamboyant and obvious—there is one actor in Hollywood [the movie set] who must remain motionless and speechless and still participate liberally in the proceedings."[32] In a rare interview, Polglase argued that the sets in the historical romance *The Scarlet Empress* (Josef von Sternberg, 1934, art dir. Hans Dreier, Paramount) were so noticeably decorative that they detracted from Marlene Dietrich's performance, although in his own *Mary of Scotland* (John Ford, 1936, art dirs. Polglase and Carroll Clark, RKO) he felt it was right to design a royal court set to dwarf Mary, Queen of Scots (Katharine Hepburn) to indicate her helplessness during her trial for treason.

Studio publicity and the press presented art direction as a large-scale and logical creative process relying on precise calculations of financial and space and time requirements. The studio's board and chairman would determine the studio's total budget for the year ahead, setting out the number, type, and costs of each film to be made, with individual budgets then presented to each assistant director. That person then managed the "script breakdown" in which the producer, director, studio production head, supervising art director, and unit art director would read through the script in detail, estimating the number and type of sets required for the film, and their likely cost. Each unit art director would then design the sets for the film, with strict accounting procedures governing expenditures on labor and materials while cost overruns were further avoided by an emphasis on preplanning and rehearsal of the shoot and a discouragement of multiple takes. In Gibbons's words, this meant that "when the final sets are constructed . . . no changes are ever necessary."[33]

In 1931, the *New York Times* emphasized the preparation in visualizing fictional worlds. Following the script breakdown, sketch artists would produce about thirty pictures per movie, from which final costs would be estimated, sketches refined, and then converted into miniature three-dimensional models, which could be used to plan the blocking of actors and props, lighting, and camera position and movement, before being transposed back to two dimensions in detailed blueprints on which actual construction was based. Moreover, this ensured "that the exact floor space on the various stages can be allotted the various sets a full month before the cameras get into action. These are necessary precautions in a large studio to prevent overlapping of productions and for economy of space and movement during time of production."[34] Standard practice called for shooting a film's exterior scenes (if any) while the indoor sets were being prepared. And there would be a further separation between manufacture of the set in the carpenters', plasterers', and electrical workshops and its assembly on the soundstage, with both processes frequently unfolding twenty-four hours a day, every day except Sunday (figure 13). A feature on Hollywood production methods in *Life* magazine in January 1945 evoked a sense of urgent and resourceful activity:

> All Warner Bros. sets are made right on the studio lot in a humming, 125,000 sq. ft. factory fitted out with hundreds of woodworking and machine tools, a forge and a foundry. Here carpenters, painters, and metalworkers turn out everything from submarines to period furniture with rapid and versatile craftsmanship. Working within time limits of two or three weeks for set construction they have become adept at short cuts, using cast plaster to simulate carved wood or marbleized wallpaper for

FIGURE 13: "The Mill," carpenters' workshop, MGM, 1936

> a palace floor. Rocks for outdoor scenes are made from wood framing, chicken wire, and plaster.[35]

At each of the major studios, the staff of the art department was far outnumbered by the hundreds of tradesmen and women who manned the craft departments responsible to the art director. At MGM, for example, about two thousand "artisans," also including painters and set dressers, had an even lower profile than the art directors but were also essential to materializing their vision. Indeed, *Life* magazine seemed to identify with these people more than with movie stars: "Over the years Hollywood has piled technique upon technique, added skilled worker after skilled worker until now the making of even the simplest movie requires a crew of 300 to 400. . . . Among this crowd of technicians the actors are often hard to find. More than the actors, the technicians are the real citizens of Hollywood. They live in ordinary houses, dress in ordinary clothes, go to church and picnics, stay married and raise children."[36]

Studio Sets and the Built Environment

The art department was modern and efficient, therefore, but often relied on ancient crafts and techniques. For example, art director Roland Anderson was challenged by the epic scale and archaic qualities of *The Crusades* (Cecil B. DeMille, 1935, Paramount): "A DeMille film play is always a task of the first dimensions. A whole forest is hacked down, papier-mâché factories go in for overtime. At once a hegira starts to the coast [i.e., California] of swordsmiths, armor-makers, chain-mail weavers, and other proficients in trades you thought were dead a thousand years ago."[37] Around the same time, a report in the *New York Times* explained that the Ukrainian Cubist sculptor Archipenko had recently visited Paramount Pictures, where his worry that Hollywood cinema contained too much artistic compromise was put to rest by "the vibrant watercolors of Hans Dreier" for *Desire* (Frank Borzage, 1936, art dirs. Hans Dreier and Robert Usher), which Archipenko found "'Extraordinary!'"[38] And in 1938, the British art and design monthly *The Studio* published an appreciation of the charcoal sketching techniques of the Polish-born Anton Grot, who was supervising art director at Warner Bros. from 1927 to 1948. Highlighting the informal, tactile, and expressive qualities of Grot's studies for *The King of Kings* (Cecil B. DeMille, 1927, DeMille Pictures Corporation), the magazine featured his sketch of the "Foot of the Cross," in which three cloaked women huddle beneath the feet of Christ, their sullen faces looking up at him flanked by strongly marked vertical lines. For *The Studio*, Grot's work demonstrated "a well-proportioned composition of masses and of strong values of light and shade, the emphatic use of perspective and a vigorous treatment generally. Added to this there is a

FIGURE 14: Scenic art department at Twentieth Century-Fox, 1930s.

lovely richness of draftsmanship which lends great value to this specialized form of work."[39]

Artistry was also evident among the numerous painters and illustrators who were employed by the major studios to mass-produce large-scale painted backdrops, canvases for props in the background of interior sets, and meticulous small-scale landscapes for combination with live action in the technically specialized matte shots that augmented whatever was filmed on the soundstage (figure 14). *Gone with the Wind* (Victor Fleming, 1939, art dir. Lyle Wheeler, Selznick International/MGM), the ne plus ultra of classical Hollywood spectacle, was heavily reliant for its majestic scale on one hundred matte paintings of townscapes, the countryside, and crowds. The August 1944 issue of *Life* offered glimpses into the inner workings of the technique by detailing the transformation of the real Burbank City Hall into "a swank office building in a mythical South American republic."[40] Attention to detail was also evident in the making of models—a practice known in architecture since at least the Middle Ages.[41] Those for planning full-size sets were typically made at a scale of one inch to one foot, colored, furnished, and decorated, while others were miniature sets in themselves, built at various scales to create a false sense of perspective when placed before the camera. *Life* magazine detailed the construction of "a whole complicated city," Washington, D.C., for *The Doughgirls* (James V. Kern, 1944, art dir. Hugh Reticker, Warner Bros.) in which a full-size set of the rooftop of an apartment building provided a vista onto the distant Washington Monument and Jefferson Memorial, made about four or five feet high.[42]

There had been some model-making in the silent era, but in 1930 the *Los Angeles Times* linked the increasing prominence of the craft to the studios' need to reduce expenditures because of the Depression and the higher costs of production for sound: "Setting construction is also showing marked progress along economic lines. At the Fox studio, for example, Joseph Urban is building sets for the productions with which he is associated in miniature, so that the director may have a complete conception of what it is going to look like in advance. With this advantage the director, with the assistance of the scenarist and the cameraman, can then plan out the action of the picture fully in advance—virtually mapping it in all details."[43] Hence, Hollywood art direction was an extension, and sometimes an inversion, of architectural and urban planning practices, which, like set design and construction, organized and visualized large-scale synthetic environments and were also subject to intense artistic and economic pressure. Several art directors had training in fine art and design, including William Cameron Menzies and Horace Newcombe, while some, such as Tambi Larsen, who worked at Paramount for Hans Dreier, were trained in theater. However, most art directors were trained in architecture, which was the professional background of James Basevi, Robert Boyle, Hans Dreier, Randall Duell, Stephen Goosson, Robert Haas, William Horning, Leo Kuter, Boris Leven, Arthur Lonergan, Hal Pereira, Van Nest Polglase, Carl Jules Weyl, and Lyle Wheeler. Some of those entered art direction in the 1920s because it seemed a logical deployment of their training, while those who entered in the 1930s were often motivated by a lack of opportunity in architecture due to a slowdown in construction during the Depression.[44]

Like architecture, set design was anthropomorphic and customized for different clients. For example, Laurence Irving, who assisted Menzies on the adventure *The Iron Mask* (Allan Dwan, 1929, Elton Corporation/United Artists), explained that a set in which Douglas Fairbanks was to make a twelve-foot leap from a tree to a convent window was built only after rehearsal of the leap in the gym, so that the built structure would conform to the proportions and movements of Fairbanks's physique.[45] In a more modern setting such as the Club Royal sequences of the musical *Gold Diggers of 1935* (Busby Berkeley, 1935, art dir. Grot, Warner Bros.), the grand dimensions and strong vertical and horizontal lines of the modernist set were specifically designed to display and exploit the movement of actors and dancers in graceful linear and geometric arcs, with diverse bodies and limbs in concert.[46]

Arriving at United Artists in 1927, Irving was struck by the anomalous space and structures of the studio back lot, a "vast open space . . . which from a distance appeared to be the relics of a world fair exhibiting every style and period of architecture known to man—a jumble of facades of stone, marble tiles, and brick skillfully rendered in plaster on frameworks of timber and chicken wire. . . . Though more substantial than stage settings, each was truncated to the limits of the camera's line of sight, their jagged silhouettes reminding me of a shell-torn Belgian town."[47] Irving emphasizes the combination of heterogeneity and fragility in this distinctive environment as well as a disjuncture between the mass of movie sets and their surprising lack of weight—if set design was like architecture, it used little real stone, concrete, or structural steel, and even glass posed technical challenges for cinematographers.[48] In designing *The Crusades*, Anderson relied on the typologies of buildings written by the French architectural historian Eugène-Emanuel Viollet-le-Duc (1814–1879), a devotee of the solid and durable Gothic.[49] But Irving was impressed by the speed of construction with false materials: "In the world of reality, the architect had the pleasure and often anxiety of watching the translation of his plans into bricks and mortar over a period of several months; I, in this world of make-believe, had the ecstasy of seeing the products of my drawing board grow like mushrooms to full stature as at the touch of a magician's wand in as many days."[50]

Hence, set design and construction was driven by an exaggerated form of the compression of space and time analogous to that which David Harvey has identified with the modern built environment in general.[51] This was further evident in certain productions which required that geographically diverse locales be built in close proximity and in a hurry: for example, the eighteenth-century romance *Anthony Adverse* (Mervyn LeRoy, 1936, art dir. Grot, Warner Bros.) required 131 sets representing Italy, Cuba, Africa, and Paris to be constructed in four weeks.[52] Compression was also evident in the relentlessness of the process. Jack Martin Smith, employed by MGM from 1939, recalled the regimentation of the set designer's daily life: "They had a twenty-four-hour shift: eight hours, eight hours, eight hours. When you made a working drawing, you had to put all the information on it—because while you're at home, they're building."[53]

Cedric Gibbons emphasized the scale of his tasks, the unpredictability of the production schedule, and the challenge of managing limited space and moving sets around. In November 1936, for example, he wrote to Al Lichtman, executive producer at MGM, describing the studio's stage space as "woefully inadequate" and arguing for more stages to allow "efficient operation."[54] Listing the total square footage of stages at the various studios—MGM, 306,000 square feet; Fox, 260,000 square feet; Paramount, 170,000 square feet; Warner Bros., 608,000 square feet—Gibbons explained that "an average production of today requires 30% more stage space than it did four years ago" because of an increase in the average number of sets per film and in the average size of each set.[55] His job was complicated by the fact that 75 percent of MGM's total space at that time was held up by a bottleneck of five productions—*Camille* (George Cukor, 1936), *Maytime* (Robert Z. Leonard, 1937), and *Parnell* (John M. Stahl, 1937), all period costume dramas; *Captains Courageous* (Victor Fleming, 1937), a maritime adventure; and *After the Thin Man* (W. S. Van Dyke, 1936), a detective comedy. With the remaining 25 percent of stage space set aside for B-pictures,

FIGURE 15: Exterior standing set at Paramount Pictures ranch, photographed by Margaret Bourke-White for *Life*, 1937.

shorts, and standing sets, Gibbons complained of an unsustainable predicament in which stages were continuously reorganized, sets repeatedly assembled and disassembled for shooting and retakes, and perfectly good sets demolished to make room. The additional labor and overtime required for all this work added 25 percent to the average cost of an MGM film, which could be reduced if the studio had more stages.[56]

The complex and detailed calculations that preoccupied the art director often made him a kind of urban planner, constantly envisaging new structures while weighing the fates of those at the end of their useful lives. At most studios, it appears to have been standard practice after filming that sets were "torn down and relegated to the studio incinerator," although sometimes a set from an A-feature would be reused to give a B-feature a touch of class: for example, the Poverty Row production of *The Man Called Back* (Robert Florey, 1932, Tiffany Productions) used a South Seas set built for RKO's *Bird of Paradise* (King Vidor, 1932, art dir. Carroll Clark), and a *Los Angeles Times* report in March 1933 recorded that studios had recently begun to economize by building more permanent standing sets that could be used in several pictures (figure 15).[57] In 1936, when problems of space at MGM appear to have peaked, Gibbons advocated the use of standing sets for trains, hotel suites and dining rooms, lobbies, and offices, which could be modified slightly from film to film, although a *New York Times* report that year suggested that at the majors some "directors and stars feel they are being slighted if they have to use a second-hand set."[58] By 1938, Gibbons explained that, unless they were damaged and too expensive to repair, MGM's default policy was to store sets after filming, carefully inventorying them and their elements in a searchable index for future cannibalization.[59]

Authenticity, Modernity, and Improving on Nature

The working methods of the studio art department, therefore, encompassed both a sense of ideas, artistry, and contrivance and a sense of matter, labor, and authenticity, in a rapidly evolving creative industry in which spectacle was a driving ambition but a sense of precariousness was never far away. These conditions gave rise to a complex range of attitudes toward art direction among film professionals, film critics, and the public. For example, a short but significant column in the *Los Angeles Times* in 1929 showed a wry awareness of the falsity of the movie set:

> Scattered all over America, Europe, Asia, and the South Seas are hundreds of carefully preserved buildings originally built for motion-picture settings, but now pointed to with pride as landmarks of local interest. Buses run regularly from Rome to the immense reproduction of the Coliseum built by Fred Niblo for *Ben Hur* [1925]. The entrance to Santa Maria, a pretty little California town, is guarded by two sphinxes which appeared originally in Cecil B. DeMille's *The Ten Commandments* [1923] made there. W. S. Van Dyke built a special village at Tahiti for scenes in *White Shadows in the South Seas* [1928]—and it was so comfortable that natives moved into it immediately after he left! California houses of the days of '49, built for MGM's *Tide of Empire* [1929], proved so attractive that real-estate men finished them up and they are now the principal 'bait' of a new subdivision.[60]

The reference to "natives" here reminds us that exotic movie set construction was often a vehicle for Eurocentric or colonialist thinking and representation, and that awareness of the fabricated nature of the movie set did not mean critique of its ideological basis. Instead it was mostly tongue-in-cheek, as we can see as well in the popular genre of comic or melodramatic movies about the movies that exposed the inner workings of the film industry for sentimental or humorous ends, for example, in *Show People, Movie Crazy* (Clyde Bruckman, 1932, art dirs. William MacDonald and Harry Oliver, Paramount), *What Price Hollywood?* (George Cukor, 1932, art dir. Carroll Clark, RKO), *Stand-In* (Tay Garnett, 1937, art dir. Alexander Toluboff, Walter Wanger Productions/United Artists), and *A Star Is Born* (William Wellman, 1937, art dir. Lyle Wheeler, Selznick International Pictures/United Artists).

Nevertheless, Frances Fink, writing in the *Washington Post* in 1935, detected a turn toward greater realism and less extravagance in set design following the coming of sound, although art direction generally presented "an effect of realism" rather than merely accurate reproduction of the real. With reference to his work on *Topaze* (D'Abbadie D'Arrast, 1933, RKO), a comedy drama set in 1920s Paris, Polglase explained that "talking pictures have resulted in more normal settings. Imagination is there, but it does not assume the appearance of the fantastic except where the script is a fantasy. The reason for this is that modern motion picture settings are created by architects whose desire for originality is modified by a rigid adherence to the dictates of good taste. They do not resort to sensational designs excepting where the stories require them."[61] That sets should be proportionate to narrative requirements was the art director's most frequently cited maxim, and usually agreed to by critics, although what constituted proportionality was not strictly defined. Gibbons, for example, made a claim similar to that of Polglase but with a slightly different emphasis, stating that the "guiding rule of the art director" should be to create sets that "support *and enhance*" (my emphasis) story, action, character, and star performance.[62] In the 1930s, this attitude seemed to prevail, although it did have some detractors. Bosley Crowther, the *New York Times* film critic who would become a champion of *Rome Open City* (Roberto Rossellini, 1945) and other Italian neorealist films, was already impatient with excessive art direction, especially in the costume drama: two articles in which he wrote about MGM's blockbuster *Marie Antoinette* (W. S. Van Dyke, 1938, art dir. Gibbons, MGM) were essentially mocking critiques. Crowther would later remark sardonically of the film in his memoirs that "Versailles itself was slightly tarnished alongside the palace Gibbons whipped up."[63]

Embellishment was also evident in representations of New York. In December 1944, an employee of that city's Waldorf-Astoria Hotel, Ted Saucier, was sent to Hollywood as a technical consultant for the high society comedy romance *Weekend at the Waldorf* (Robert Z. Leonard, 1945, MGM). Upon arrival he marveled at the re-creation of the hotel on MGM's back lot "with white limestone mounted on bricks made of special size just for the Waldorf, exactly as they were when he left New York. And that faint line of gray cement between the sandstone blocks was exactly right. He wondered if it wasn't painfully right, if the sharpest cameras could catch such minute details."[64] The suggestion is intriguing: that sets were sometimes so carefully designed that they might include details never recorded on film or appreciated by the audience. However, the art director, Daniel Cathcart, was reported to be primarily interested in serving the story, only straying "slightly from the literal design" in fast-paced scenes where the tempo of the action meant the camera had less time to apprehend the set. Significant, too, is the extent to which the studio copy of the hotel was comprehensive, including sets not only of the exterior, entrance, lobby, and a sample of individual bedrooms but the Waldorf-Astoria's famous real-life Astor Gallery, Peacock Alley, and Starlight Roof, legendary and exclusive places to which the film promised audiences access. Moreover, like Gibbons's Versailles, the set was slightly better than the real: the *New York Times* was impressed enough to record that the set occupied over 120,000 square feet in comparison with the actual hotel's 81,337.

Comprehensive and detailed representation in such sets was achieved by the art department in consultation with the studio's research library, which gave further professional authority to the simulation. In 1950, Louis van den Ecker reflected in *Hollywood Quarterly* on his work as a technical adviser to such films as *The Count of Monte Cristo* (Rowland V. Lee, 1934, art dir. John Ducasse Schulze, Reliance Pictures/United Artists) and *The Hunchback of Notre Dame* (William Dieterle, 1939, art dir. Polglase, RKO). He emphasized the indispensability of data on diverse places and times to art directors seeking to evoke them: "The pursuit of authenticity begins with the research libraries maintained by all the major studios. Some of these contain as many as 30,000 books and bound magazines, files of clippings, photographs, and drawings, and extensive card indexes of illustrative material appearing in periodicals. The staff of a research library includes from ten to twenty permanent employees, most of whom are trained librarians."[65] By means of its amassing and tabulation of information, the studio research library allowed art directors and their sets to (at least pretend to) transcend the present time of Los Angeles and its city limits, contributing decisively to the narrative and spatial omniscience of classical Hollywood cinema at its height.

The effort to improve upon the real world extended not only to the built environment but to the representation of nature as well, and the latter is in some ways doubly interesting to consider given the greater physical and metaphysical distance existing between the real original and the copy. In the *Los Angeles Times* in 1939, Hedda Hopper recounted case after case with amazement at the ingenuity involved. For instance, World War I battle scenes for *The Fighting 69th* (William Keighley, 1940, art dir. Ted Smith, Warner Bros.) were filmed on a set whose supposedly French soil had been carefully sifted to ensure it contained no stones or debris likely to injure actors when special effects explosions were set off during filming; for the Shirley Temple picture *The Blue Bird* (Walter Lang, 1940, art dirs. Richard Day and Wiard Ihnen, Twentieth Century–Fox), a large variety of trees were made from eucalyptus wood covered in a man-made bark created by taking plaster-cast impressions from real trees; and sets for *The Road to Singapore* (Victor Schertzinger, 1940, art dirs. Hans Dreier and Robert Odell, Paramount) had been planted with real trees from the Paramount studio nursery, said to be one of the largest in the country. Unlike Bosley Crowther, however, Hopper welcomed the contrivance in the title of her article, "Hollywood Sets Would Fool Mother Nature: Scenic Experts Make Land, Sea, and Sky Look More Realistic Than Reality."[66] Indeed, in a similar spirit, an earlier *Los Angeles Times* article had profiled Paramount's Hans Dreier, who had recently contributed to the ornate and somewhat erotically charged settings of Ernst Lubitsch's *Trouble in Paradise* (1932) and von Sternberg's *The Scarlet Empress*: for a nighttime dance scene set in Havana in the romance *Rumba* (1935), Dreier had preferred not to shoot the real moon but to make his own celestial body from hundreds of flashlight bulbs suspended in a drum from the soundstage roof, a device he could more easily control and which produced just the right illumination and effect.[67]

By contrast, art director James Basevi was said to be the most skilled at emulating Mother Nature's fury. Portrayed affectionately by the *Los Angeles Times* in 1938, Basevi was "a smartly tweeded Englishman in his forties" who "sits most of each day at a drafting board smoking a pipe."[68] But despite his genteel air, he was actually more like Zeus, a designer of "made-to-order cataclysms" responsible for some of the most spectacular sets in film history, including a re-creation of the 1906 earthquake in *San Francisco* (W. S. Van Dyke, 1936, art dir. Arnold Gillespie, MGM) and the devastation of a South Sea Island village in *The Hurricane* (John Ford, 1937, art dir. Richard Day, Samuel Goldwyn/United Artists).[69] The latter had required a beach and village set 600 feet long and a water tank for a lagoon 22,500 square feet in area, 65 feet above which was a 2,000 gallon water tank for rain, and across which blew "six huge gale creators, with giant propellers, driven by twelve-cylinder Liberty motors" (repurposed aircraft engines), making a ninety-mile-an-hour wind.[70] The hurricane cost $400,000 to simulate and took four months to shoot, producing twenty minutes of film in the final cut.

The history of Hollywood cinema in the decade and a half after the coming of sound is full of films whose art direction went to great lengths in evoking the natural world. That evocation was often particularly interesting, and sometimes problematic, when a film was adapted from a theatrical play. When Max Reinhardt set aside his mistrust of cinema to make a feature film in Los Angeles, *A Midsummer Night's Dream* (1935), the luxurious production, which he directed with the assistance of William Dieterle, marked a significant shift beyond the Depression-era austerity that had marked earlier Warner Bros. films. In keeping with the operatic extravagance of Reinhardt's theatrical productions, Anton Grot designed a mythical forest that extended across two soundstages and outside into the back lot as well. But its design and the shoot were plagued by poor acoustics, artistic disagreements, production delays, and cost overruns. Requiring seventy-two days of filming instead of the planned forty-eight and a $981,000 budget instead of the planned $459,000, the film just about broke even, but only after an exceptionally intense promotional campaign.[71]

By contrast, the following year saw the relatively low-key but warmly received release of the gangster melodrama *The Petrified Forest* (Archie Mayo, 1936, Warner Bros.), a screen adaptation of the stage play of the same name by Robert E. Sherwood, which had run for six months on Broadway in 1935 (figure 16). Called by the *New York Times* a "faithful and letter-perfect copy," the film was indebted to the Broadway version in the direct transposition of its plot, dialogue, and

FIGURE 16: Shooting of *The Petrified Forest* (Archie Mayo, 1937, art dir. John Hughes, Warner Bros.) on the studio's Stage 21.

acting (Humphrey Bogart and Leslie Howard starred in the play and film), as well as in its staging: "Static scenically the picture may be, for that was the way of the play, but it is animate and vital nevertheless."[72] Indeed, a special feature in *Life* magazine later held it up as an archetype of motion picture set design, the one and only set—a roadside diner and gas station in the Arizona desert—having been painstakingly designed by John Hughes, one of the many art directors who worked under Grot's supervision in creating the social realist authenticity for which Warner Bros. was known. Indeed, *Life* magazine's photos of the set, on the studio's vast Stage 21, present a thought-provoking contrast between synthetic and organic materials and shapes: the flat and barren concrete walls and floors of the studio, crisscrossed by electric cables and overhung by heavy steel lighting trusses in the roof, make a strange juxtaposition with the evidently hand-made and tumbledown building and outhouses of the diner, the looming amorphous mass of the hillside, and the few lonely saguaro cacti and rocks propped in the sand in front of an extensive painted backdrop of the desert and distant horizon.[73]

The variety of studio re-creations of nature demonstrates that there was a real investment not only in the soundstage as a physical structure but as an idea, a place that, despite its limited dimensions and isolation, was believed to be flexible enough, when used expertly, to allow for the depiction of any indoor or outdoor, realist or fantastical environment imaginable. And this position was held despite an awareness that other kinds of cinema were possible which had more direct relations to the real: the 1930s was a high point in the international history of documentary film, and audiences remembered that cinema before sound had been relatively immediate in using outdoor settings. In the *Los Angeles Times* in 1941, a feature entitled "All for Realism," illustrated with scenes from the biographical western *Billy the Kid* (Paul Groesse, 1941, art dir. Edwin B. Willis, MGM) and the musical comedy *Moon over Miami* (Walter Lang, 1941, art dirs. Day and Ihnen, Twentieth Century–Fox), claimed that Hollywood cinema always sought "film realism" regardless of whether a film or scene was made in a studio or on location. Contrasting this with "the artificialities that formerly prevailed on the stage," the commentator continued:

> Even today the footlight art often has to use the most devious means to compete through power of suggestion with the actualities that the camera so deftly evokes. And largely that camera has achieved its peculiar power through the primitive course it was forced to pursue in other, hardier days when most pictures were made on location. Then the stage of nature could not be altered or improved on. . . . It can still lend the masterly touch of atmosphere to many a cinema. It sets the standard, and this standard is adhered to even when backgrounds take on make-believe attributes. . . . Everything is done for reality, whether in studio or beyond its portals.[74]

The dichotomy between natural and synthetic settings was arguably nowhere more evident, nor more thematically meaningful, than in *Lost Horizon* (Frank Capra, 1937, art dir. Stephen Goosson, Columbia), whose art direction proposed a potentially perfect harmony between nature and architecture in the Eden-like mountain refuge in Tibet known as Shangri-La, the set for which cost $235,000 (figure 17).[75] The film recounts the exploits of high-flying British diplomat Robert Conway (Ronald Colman), whose aircraft is hijacked and crashes in the Himalayas en route from a humanitarian crisis in China (*Lost Horizon* was released in March 1937, four months before the outbreak of the Second Sino-Japanese War). Shangri-La, where Conway and companions find safety, is a calm and productive

FIGURE 15: The lamasery of Shangri-La set from *Lost Horizon* (Frank Capra, 1937, art dir. Stephen Goosson, Columbia).

pastoral idyll, mysteriously secluded in a valley from the snowbound mountains and howling winds that surround it on all sides. Hence, Goosson's sets have great topographical and climatological variety, and the natural harmony of Shangri-La appears to be an extension of the simplicity and purity of form of the streamlined modern-style lamasery building that benevolently overlooks it, appearing for all the world like one of the many monumental pavilions that national governments built in 1937 for the politically charged Exposition Internationale des Arts et Techniques dans la Vie Moderne in Paris.[76]

But the image of Shangri-La, viewed today, together with the intense dependence of art direction upon capital and technology at this time, also serves as a reminder that the relationship between nature and the built environment was one of the key themes of intellectual debate, artistic expression, and political and economic life in general in the late 1920s and 1930s. It had been so in previous years, but key events—including the inauguration of the first and second Five Year Economic Plans in the USSR, the onset of the Great Depression, the Dust Bowl, and the New Deal in the United States, and the flight of the Bauhaus from Nazi Germany—placed the theme at the forefront of a growing international sense of crisis.[77] Against that backdrop, the studio-bound art direction of the day seems like a hyperactive illusion of urbanization, practiced as if in defiance of objective social and economic conditions.

Something similar can be said of the Art Deco and streamlined modern styles that became prominent in art direction because of their close connection to current practice in architecture and design.[78] Projecting a sense of affluence, luxury, and modernity, they dominated studio renderings of nightclubs, restaurants, apartments, and executive suites—especially those supposedly located in New York but actually re-created in Los Angeles.[79] As in other areas, Gibbons played a leading role, having attended the 1925 Exposition Internationale des Arts Décoratifs et Industriels Modernes in Paris and implementing some of what he saw there in such films as *Our Dancing Daughters* (Harry Beaumont, 1928, MGM) and *Grand Hotel* (Edmund Goulding, 1932, MGM). The designs of Hans Dreier for *Design for Living* (Ernst Lubitsch, 1933, Paramount), Jack Okey for *Female* (Michael Curtiz, 1933, First National), and Richard Day for *Dodsworth* (William Wyler, 1936, Samuel Goldwyn/United Artists) demonstrated comparable innovation at other studios, although it is generally considered that modernist set design reached its apogee in the distinctively open, light, and choreographed settings devised by Van Nest Polglase at RKO. His conviction that sets must be "pleasing to the eye" was evident in Fred Astaire and Ginger Rogers musicals such as *The Gay Divorcee* (Mark Sandrich, 1934), *Top Hat* (Mark Sandrich, 1935), and *Swing Time* (George Stevens, 1936) in which Polglase became known for favoring new materials in set construction (e.g., Bakelite for reflective dance floors) and Art Deco motifs such as thin parallel lines, contrasting white and black planes, and juxtaposed angles and curves.[80] However, while *Female* and *Dodsworth* were partly set in factories, the Polglase musicals and most other important films in this field had domestic, commercial, or artistic settings, which softened the machine aesthetic of architectural modernism. Newspapers noted that modernist set design in Hollywood involved "less metal chairs of austere, uncompromising lines" and even "a happy blend of modernism and classicism: the streamline motif adapted to period furniture."[81]

Toward the end of the 1930s, a decline in the relative prominence of modernist set design coincided with a renewal of traditional American iconographies. This was evident, for example, in *Mr. Smith Goes to Washington* (Frank Capra, 1939, art dir. Lionel Banks, Columbia), which underlined the meteoric ascent of a small-town Boy Scout leader to senator in Washington, D.C., by strikingly evoking the neoclassical structures of the nation's capital in a montage of sets and rear projection. Throughout the film, the solidity and resonance of the American republic was evident in the brick and stone of the Lincoln Memorial, the U.S. Congress, and a life-size replica of the chamber of the U.S. Senate. Meanwhile, after the bankruptcy and restructuring that affected all the Hollywood majors except MGM during the Depression, signs of economic recovery began to appear. In April 1937, the *Los Angeles Times* found evidence that "art directors are enjoying sumptuous inflation," led by the record $1.125 million sets for *The Adventures of Marco Polo* (Archie Mayo, 1938, art dir. Richard Day, Samuel Goldwyn/United Artists).[82] In that film and others, there was a resurgence in shooting on location too, as filmmakers returned to using the varied Southern California landscapes of Camarillo, Agoura Hills, Chatsworth, Lone Pine, and Big Bear Lake, which lay within 20 to 200 miles of the studios and which appeared on screen, as themselves or in disguise, at a time when the word "location" still appeared in quotation marks in studio publicity and press reports. This trend would become much stronger after World War II, but it was already noted beforehand as "a new and more expansive element in motion picture entertainment" made possible by the "conquest of sound," which had initially been very restrictive.[83]

Having developed in fits and starts since the late 1910s, Technicolor also gained new prominence following the release of the first full-color feature film, *Becky Sharp* (Rouben Mamoulian, 1935, art dir. Ihnen, RKO), which prompted debates about Technicolor's technical, commercial, and aesthetic merits and limits. In fact, sets had always been colored, though not always naturalistically, because variations in color were relied on to create differences in gray tone for audiences and because, as Polglase put it, actors "might easily become depressed by an all gray set."[84] However, Technicolor added yet another consideration to the complex business of designing and choosing materials for sets; it increased the average feature film's budget by 30 percent; it required much more studio lighting than black-and-white film stock to achieve a correct exposure, thereby potentially exposing the details of a set to greater scrutiny; and, at least in Technicolor's early years, it often made sets inhospitable to actors and crews because of the heat generated by the greater number of lights.[85] As Scott Higgins has explained, initial responses to *Becky Sharp* suggested that it was not only dramatically weak but too "radiantly startling" in its color spectrum, leading Technicolor to promote "a restrained mode of design" that could "emulate ideals of artistic monochrome cinematography" and provide "unobtrusive enhancement of story."[86]

This strategy gradually paid off in heightened naturalism and expressive power. The first full-color western, *The Trail of the Lonesome Pine* (Henry Hathaway, 1936, art dir. Alexander Toluboff, Walter Wanger Productions/Paramount Pictures), attracted praise from the *New York Times* for showing "that Technicolor is not restricted to a studio's stages but can record quite handsomely the rich, natural coloring of the outside world."[87] In *A Star Is Born*, Lyle Wheeler's sets avoided striking juxtapositions of color in favor of subdued browns, blue-grays, and beige-golds, especially in the set of the Malibu beach house where alcoholic movie star Norman Maine commits suicide against the backdrop of a glowing sunset.[88] Indeed, notwithstanding the complete reliance of *The Wizard of Oz* (Victor Fleming, 1939, art dir. Cedric Gibbons, MGM) on studio soundstages for the spectacle of the Yellow Brick Road, *A Star Is Born, The Adventures of Tom Sawyer* (Norman Taurog, 1938, art dir. Lyle Wheeler, David O. Selznick/United Artists), *The Adventures of Robin Hood*, and many other Technicolor feature films at this time included significant scenes of nature filmed on location. On the other hand, as art directors, cinematographers, and directors became more *au fait* with the new design, lighting, and filming procedures required, Technicolor features of the early 1940s came to exploit brilliant colors for optical effect in a wide variety of genres and settings, from the Gary Cooper adventure *Northwest Mounted Police* (Cecil B. DeMille, 1940, art dirs. Roland Anderson and Hans Dreier, Paramount) to the war film *Crash Dive* (Archie Mayo, 1943, art dirs. Day and Ihnen, Twentieth Century–Fox) and the period musical *Meet Me in St Louis* (Vincente Minnelli, 1945, art dirs. Cedric Gibbons, Lemuel Ayers, Jack Martin Smith, MGM). Indeed, two Academy Awards for Best Art Direction were awarded from 1940, one each for black and white and for color (a practice continued until the mid-1960s).

Production Design and World War II

The trends of the late 1930s came together in the tour de force art direction of the Civil War melodrama *Gone with the Wind*, for which producer David O. Selznick hired William Cameron Menzies in the elevated new role of "production designer." In order to control the high costs of making a lavish historical epic in Technicolor, Menzies sketched every one of the film's setups in advance, thus producing "a complete script in sketch form" even before the written script had been finished.[89] Hence, in his creation of the film's "storyboard," Menzies accrued some of the functions and credit traditionally reserved to the director and cinematographer while collaborating directly with art director Lyle Wheeler, who managed the rendering of Menzies's sketches in the form of sets—most famously in the scene of the burning of Atlanta, filmed on the back lot of the DeMille/Selznick Studios in Culver City, in which a spectacular part was played by the destruction of a giant wall originally built for the Temple of Jerusalem in DeMille's *The King of Kings* and subsequently reused to restrain the apocalyptic ape in *King Kong* (Merian C. Cooper, Ernest B. Schoedsack, 1933, art dir. Carroll Clark, RKO). Not storyboarded, however, nor requiring a significant budget, were the many strikingly beautiful shots of natural rain cloud formations interspersed throughout *Gone with the Wind*: these were filmed impromptu by special effects cinematographer Clarence Slifer in the evening that followed the now-legendary March 1938 rainstorm that flooded large parts of Los Angeles, causing 115 deaths and $50 million worth of property damage.[90]

I highlight this detail as a rare but revealing example of the place of unmediated, chance-based images in the totalizing aesthetics of art direction at the height of the Hollywood studio era. The three-year production schedule of *Gone with the Wind* meant that World War II had already started in Europe when it was released in Britain in April 1940. Things changed significantly during the war years. A report in the *New York Times* in August 1942 explained that where the film industry "once prided itself on its sublime disregard of costs," now "scarcely a branch of film production remains unaffected by war freezes. . . . Inroads into personnel have been great and will become greater. . . . Metals, lumber, paints, and burlap; fiber-board, wallpaper, muslin, and dress materials; rope, make-up, electric wiring and lamps; even the raw material of the movies—the film itself—are not to be had or are budgeted in their purchase and use."[91] Studios struck every set with great care, salvaging and recycling as much as possible, even the nails, and the average prewar art direction budget of $50,000 seemed enormous in comparison with the new government-imposed limit on sets of $5,000 per picture.

That limit caused anxiety among studio bosses and art directors. Cedric Gibbons estimated that $10,000 was the absolute minimum with which one could make worthwhile sets, although Leo McCarey argued that the new limit might lead to "better pictures" in the long run: "It's going to require better direction, better acting, and better story plots or situations and less depending upon lavish and expensive props to put over a picture. After all, if you've got excellent direction, excellent acting, and an excellent story, you can shoot just as good a picture in front of a two-by-four as you can inside a marble palace."[92] Indeed, by the end of 1942, conditions became even more austere as the studios' prewar stockpiles of materials ran out and nationwide gasoline rationing put a brake on the use of locations. Looking back, in August 1944, *Life* magazine noted that the vast majority of Hollywood films since Pearl Harbor had been shot on indoor soundstages.[93] Indeed, Thomas Schatz has explained that the war years saw the production of fewer historical epics and westerns, and more musicals, melodramas, screwball comedies, and war films, as well as the gradual emergence of film noir.[94]

The most innovative new tendency, film noir was primarily urban and up to the minute in settings. It moved away from a focus on the beauty and efficiency of modernity (which Art Deco and streamlined modern had expressed in the 1930s) and instead presented New York, Los Angeles, and other cities with images of dilapidated downtown streets, dull commercial offices, licentious nightclubs and love nests, and pretty but morally corrupt suburban homes. These were mostly studio renderings, with liberal use of matte shots and rear projection to evoke the outdoors in the cityscape vistas and scenes of driving that were important to the action and existential meaning of the films. This mix underpinned Carroll Clark's art direction for *Murder My Sweet* (Edward Dmytryk, 1944, RKO), which counterpoints the high-rise Art Deco apartment of the villain Amthor on Sunset Boulevard, the palatial Rococo home of the Grayle family in Brentwood, and various bars and back roads that detective Philip Marlowe navigates in his sleuthing. But that production was relatively studio-bound. Other key examples of the genre made during the war, such as *Double Indemnity* (Billy Wilder, 1944, art dir. Dreier, Hal Pereira, Paramount Pictures) and *Mildred Pierce* (Michael Curtiz, 1945, art dir. Grot, Warner Bros.), gave free rein to the expressionistic chiaroscuro in which Dreier, Grot, and other Central European expatriates in Hollywood had been trained, while giving a prominent role to location-shot sequences as well. Indeed, the latter would increasingly displace studio-bound art direction as film noir became more prominent and influential after 1945.

Art direction from the coming of sound to the late 1930s had been shaped by a variety of technological, economic, and ideological factors whose combined effect was to constrain it quite strictly within the limited, but supposedly infinite, and infinitely variable, space of the soundstage. Subsequently, although slightly delayed by World War II, and although the major studios continued to aspire to superlative set design, the most important trend in art direction was its adaptation to the real world outside. The art director—and, increasingly, the production designer—would seek to minimize any tension between the set's contrivance and the immediacy of location shooting, but such a tension would be more and more evident both on the screen and off. Throughout 1945–1947, the thousands of painters, decorators, carpenters, and electricians who made the art director's ideas into reality went on strike against their exploitative working conditions in the longest and most violent labor dispute in Hollywood history.[95] Their strike would have a decisive influence on the restructuring of the industry, which was forced by the anticommunist blacklists, the Paramount decrees, and the rise of independent and runaway film production, and of television, in the late 1940s and 1950s. Hence, the gradual decline of the studio system originated in part in a backlash against the art department's capitalist rigor and make-believe, as a turbulent dispersal of the unsustainable high pressure of fixed-site studio production.

3

POSTWAR HOLLYWOOD, 1947–1967

Merrill Schleier

After World War II, as labor historian Irving Bernstein noted in his in-depth economic analysis of the film industry in 1957, Hollywood was "at a crossroads," plagued by financial, industrial, and social forces, which ultimately transformed the studio system and, in turn, its art production practices.[1] During the classical era, the Big Five studios' art departments were run by powerful men such as Cedric Gibbons at MGM (1924–1956), Hans Dreier at Paramount (1923–1950), Anton Grot at Warner Bros. (1927–1948), Richard Day (1931–1946) and Lyle Wheeler (1947–62) at Twentieth Century–Fox, and Van Nest Polglase at RKO (1933–1957). These men would, in turn, assign films to art directors who each managed a staff of sketchers, draughtsman, storyboard artists, matte painters, and construction crews, among others. According to Academy Award–winning designer Edward Carfagno at MGM, if a producer at the studio sought a particular art director for a film, permission was required from Gibbons.[2] In addition to dispensing assignments, and in accord with many of his counterparts at the Big Five, Gibbons also approved the designs and took credit for them even though he often had little if anything to do with their invention.

With the decline of the studio system after World War II, powerful independent producers such as Sam Fuller, Robert Wise, and the Mirisch brothers and talent agencies such as MCA emerged, selling pictures as package units, thereby transferring the control of art directing from the studio's chief art director to a collaboration between the independent production designer and the director, and often the producer. Although there was an overlap in the tasks performed by art directors and independent production designers, the latter participated much more actively and collaboratively in the formulation of a film's visual appearance, which transcended simply producing the set designs.

The perceived public desire for more authentic settings led to the rise in location shooting, which presented a host of additional challenges. Often sent out with the location staff in post-classical Hollywood, production designers were entrusted with the task of creating a film's sense of place, which included the development of physical settings and their animation by actors. Artful set designs were required in these putative natural environments where there was less control than in the circumscribed back lots or soundstages. An acknowledgment of the requisite creativity was corroborated by the Academy Award for Art Direction given to Richard Day for *On the Waterfront* (Elia Kazan, 1954), a black-and-white film, shot in Hoboken, New Jersey. The search for heightened reality also prompted filmmakers to employ more thrilling effects and often far-flung settings in order to simulate tourist experiences, which further complicated the job of production designers—who were now often responsible for selecting multiple sites and entrusted with the supervision of enormous staffs on split-location films. The creation of expensive and extravagant sets for these places might require the research skill of a historian, an archaeologist, or an industrial designer.[3]

Finally, declining revenues caused, in part, by the competition from television led the studios to produce or finance fewer yet grander and more expensive films as a way to differentiate the cinematic experience from other visual and recreational activities. Extravagant biblical and historical epics such as *Quo Vadis* (Mervyn LeRoy, 1951, art dirs. Edward Carfagno, Cedric Gibbons, and Richard Horning), *Ben-Hur* (William Wyler, 1959, art dirs. Edward Carfagno and William Horning), and *Cleopatra* (Joseph Mankiewicz, 1963, art dir. John DeCuir) were created; while the era began with budgets of $7 million per film, it ended with *Cleopatra*'s production costs skyrocketing to $44 million. Profligate spending was extended to a film's production design, and publicity departments were eager to broadcast the expense and labor involved, hence, the new selling of the sets.

New widescreen technologies such as Cinemascope also heightened the desire for grandiosity or the epic effect, which characterized diverse film genres from westerns to science fiction to musicals.[4] This, in turn, changed the entire mise-en-scène, which now required a more horizontal emphasis in the sets and actors across the entire composition. Size and a new chromatic palette, the latter made possible by the use of Technicolor and other such processes, were geared to heighten viewers' awe and engender a vicarious experience. As early as 1946, British art director David Rawnsley predicted that there would be "great new fields of experiment in the proper use of color," making it possible "to convey varying mental states" through cinematography and production design, anticipating the collaboration of Alfred Hitchcock and designer Robert Boyle.[5]

From these diverse developments that characterized the film industry in post-classical Hollywood, several key factors, which affected the character of production design, warrant further scrutiny. One involves how the studio system's divorcement and the concomitant rise of the independent producer resulted in an expanded function for the art director, who was more frequently dubbed a production designer in the new era. No longer subject to the Big Five's rigid art department hierarchy, the latter sought a professional identity that was consonant with directors rather than second-line staff members whose works were associated with the crafts. However, production designers' more inclusive participation in the filmmaking process was not simply a result of financial exigencies, but also represented their wish to achieve more creative autonomy and an enhanced role as members of the production team. In accord with the independent producers with whom they worked, production designers became free agents, too. An understanding of their educational credentials, varied training in art and architectural practice, and rise up the studio hierarchy helps to explain their preparation and success in the postwar era. During this politically charged time period, their collective relationship to both management and online workers sheds additional light on their quest for professional legitimacy. A second factor involves the emergence of location shooting, leading to exponential changes in their professional scope of practice, which now included multidimensional responsibilities such as the search for and creation of a sense of place.

Boris Leven's work on the film *Giant* (1956) with independent producer and director George Stevens, producer Henry Ginsberg, and author Edna Ferber provides an example of one production designer's more all-encompassing tasks while pointing to the myriad ways in which the entire profession was transformed. A blockbuster, the film reflects many of the efforts of postwar filmmakers to lure lost viewers back to the movies, from its star-studded cast to its expanded historical scope to its runaway location. At the same time, it traversed various film genres—western, historical epic, melodrama—while appealing to the new youth audience with the casting of James Dean, Elizabeth Taylor, and Rock Hudson. *Giant* serves as a microcosm of the manner in which production designers worked on location and within the framework of the independent production system in the new era. Leven made multiple visits to Texas that he chronicled in a journal and performed extensive architectural research that was later incorporated in a series of sketches and small-scale models, which served as springboards for the final sets. He was selected by producer and director George Stevens and acted as a semiautonomous member of the production crew. Indeed, Leven's cinematic architecture functioned as one of the stars of the film, and was promoted as such by the Warner Bros.' publicity department.

The Independents and the New Production Designer

In 1947 stage and screen production designer Mordecai Gorelik wrote a trenchant article entitled "Hollywood's Art Machinery," criticizing studio art departments, which, he believed, compromised creativity in the service of profit. Often stock or recycled sets and backgrounds were recommended for cost efficiency, resulting in what he termed sarcastically "*Prix de Rome* type picturesque architecture," which often had little to do with the plot.[6] However, the importance of Gorelik's postwar assessment is his recognition of the rise of the independent producer and a new paradigm for creative filmmaking. Yet the studio-employed producer still remained an obstacle, largely concerned with pecuniary matters, possessing little concern or knowledge about the art department's methods. Gorelik observed a new generation of directors who sought "dramatically minded artists" working "side by side with them from the script to the cutting room."[7] In order to break the stranglehold that denied the latter both creative control and due credit, he argued that directors and associate producers with more clout were still needed on the movie lots. Perhaps the most exciting development he noted as early as 1947 was the appearance of independent film companies, which were beginning to have a beneficial effect on filmmaking in the United States, making it possible for art directors to work with directors on individual films "beyond the jurisdiction of the art machines."[8]

Yet it would be simplistic to suggest that art departments in the late 1940s and early 1950s were composed solely of disgruntled and wholly disempowered staff deprived of ingenuity.[9] Exceptions to Gorelik's assessment under the old studio system may be found among producers and prestigious directors such as Alfred Hitchcock or Vincente Minnelli, who challenged the status quo, and were authorized to either select their own production designers or work independently from powerful department heads such as Cedric Gibbons. This empowerment is seen especially in the relationship between producer Arthur Freed, who was in charge of MGM's musicals division, director Minnelli, costume designer Irene Sharaff, and production designer Preston Ames. When he first arrived at MGM under Freed, Minnelli encountered immediate resistance from Gibbons, who was unwilling to relinquish creative control at first, announcing to a studio executive that he refused "to work under any conditions with any man designing settings unless he is brought through to me as a member of my department. . . . I do not feel that any of my men should take orders from anyone other than myself in the matter of set design."[10] Minnelli insisted on artistic autonomy that engendered conflict with Gibbons, which persisted for twenty years. Yet he refused to capitulate and, by 1951, set decorator Keogh Gleason claimed that the director could basically make his own aesthetic choices and Gibbons "wouldn't touch him."[11]

Donald Knox's book *The Magic Factory: How MGM Made "An American in Paris"* (1973) provides a useful case study of the way in which a powerful director such as Minnelli supervised the artistry of his films while fostering a collaborative team effort in production design. As we know, Minnelli had previously worked as a window dresser and art director, and was known to have an encyclopedic clipping file of architectural sites and a sophisticated knowledge of the fine arts; hence his definite ideas on the nature of production design.[12] However, Minnelli's expertise has too often led to the obfuscation of the production designer's role in the formulation of the set designs; indeed, most of the scholarship on the director barely mention production designer Preston Ames—who worked with Minnelli on ten films.[13]

Although the film takes place in Paris, all of the sets were fabricated on the MGM studio lot, with a second unit sent to the French capital for establishing shots.[14] Ames was largely responsible for creating the film's streets and garrets from the perspective of a struggling artist. Referring to his designs, he recalled in 1952: "This is the way I remember the Left Bank of Paris when I was a student at the *Beaux Arts*: An attic room with twisted stairway, a street with its shops and cafes, a flower stand hidden behind some old shoring, a cellar converted into a night club."[15] Various views of Montmartre were a synthesis of Ames's designs of the street from below and traveling matte shots by Warren Newcombe, which provided for dramatic scenes of Paris and its iconic monuments "in all its glory" from above.[16]

On the whole, the production design process in *An American in Paris* was interactive, with Minnelli at the helm. For example, Ames suggested a way to realize the Parisian Quai scene, which Minnelli approved. The director authored the scenes in which Lise (Leslie Caron) was placed in frames with diverse colored backgrounds to reflect her various personalities, which were, in turn, augmented by the costume designer Sharaff's matching outfits.[17] Sharaff often suggested chromatic schemes such as the Van Gogh sequence at the Paris Opera, which Ames realized in three dimensions.[18] Hence Minnelli's rebellion from Gibbons's "medieval fiefdom" and his fostering of a cooperative creative environment paved the way for Ames to win the Academy Award for Art Direction for his work on the film, breaking the tradition of Gibbons garnering all the credit.[19]

Many other postwar, award-winning production designers, such as Edward Carfagno, Robert Boyle, Henry Bumstead, Edward Carfagno, and Albert Nozaki, disagreed with Gorelik's categorization of the studios as bastions of mediocrity. Unconcerned with the apportioning of recognition for their efforts, they arrived as budding young architects or aspiring artists, thankful to have jobs during the Great Depression. All five studied in the architecture department at the University of Southern California, the only such program of repute on the West Coast, in which a traditional curriculum was offered in concert with Paris's École des Beaux Arts while keeping students abreast of International Style developments. Paramount's Hans Dreier was so impressed with the program's thoroughness that he recruited art directors from the school, prompting their art department nickname, the Dreier Academy. The German émigré believed that newcomers should begin as apprentices who learned various skills before becoming full-fledged art directors. As Leven reported, "You'd spend so many years as a private—draftsman; then you'd become a corporal—an assistant art director and so on."[20] In later interviews, Boyle and others further idealized Paramount as a perfect laboratory for learning, claiming that they were less class conscious. Waxing poetic about the good old days, they spoke of a time when shared offices afforded them close proximity to all aspects of the art-making process, from the sketch to the finished studio construction.[21] Hence an education in architectural practice and history prepared them well for drafting, completing blueprints, and supervising the building of partial structures, made whole by the camera's artistry, which was augmented by studio camaraderie. This experience was supplemented by extensive historical study from the studio research departments' vast resources to create a believable simulation of a place. At MGM, Gibbons was reportedly a "stickler for research" and amassed a substantial research library, while at Twentieth Century–Fox, art chief Lyle Wheeler lauded his own personal files and vast corpus of materials in the Research Department under its head, Frances Richardson.[22]

After the 1948 Paramount decision, which called for the separation of the tripartite practices of the production, distribution, and exhibition of films by the studios, the so-called assembly line or vertical method of art production design began to unravel. This trend began just after the war, but already by 1945 there were forty independent production companies, and by 1947, the year of Gorelik's article, there were one hundred.[23] Due to a record decline in revenue, which has been explained by numerous factors, including the competition afforded by television, the mid-century move to the suburbs and away from urban theaters, and new patterns of leisure time, the studios rented out their soundstages and back lots, provided full or partial financing, and managed distribution and public relations to independent producers, production companies, or talent agencies who were now in charge of selling the story, managing the budget, and putting together the whole creative team.

The rise of the independent producer in the post-classical period had a direct bearing on the selection of production designers and the manner in which they worked. Rather than art department heads doling out assignments, the independent might simply seek the chief's advice or arrive with his own production designer, often introducing a package unit to the studio. Commenting on the heterogeneous power-sharing arrangement, Alexander Golitzen, the chief art director at Universal (1954–1973), provided insight into how the independent system of production altered the relationship of the production designer to the studio. For example, when the sovereign Hitchcock came to Universal, Golitzen claimed that he recommended, and the former secured, Robert Boyle and Henry Bumstead for *Vertigo* (1958) and *North by Northwest* (1959), respectively.

However, there was a great deal of diversity among the independents' working methods, even among those affiliated with the same studio. While some adhered to the chief art director's counsel, others arrived with their own production teams. Golitzen reported: "Ross Hunter's set-up was entirely different from Walter Wanger's set-up. Earlier, . . . I had a lot to do with both. . . . So eventually Bob Wise did the same thing, and Hitch did the same thing. They were kind of a company within the company within the company type of thing. . . . I think when Bob Wise first came over and formed his own company, he brought Boris Leven and the production man. . . . That was the nucleus of his company."[24] Participating much more actively in the entire filmmaking process, production designers enjoyed more creative autonomy and collaborated actively with the director, screenwriter, and cinematographer.

In response to the path blazed by independent producers, many of the more prominent, well-seasoned production designers also opted for freedom from the studio system beginning in the late 1940s, forging film-by-film contracts. They were inspired, in part, by new tax laws, which enabled them to count their revenue as capital gains rather than income.[25] After World War II, Boyle, who was employed at Paramount from 1933 to 1941 and is perhaps best known for the four films he worked on with Hitchcock, became an independent. His colleague Boris Leven, who was also on staff at Paramount and then Universal in the early years, became a free agent in 1948 and collaborated with independent producers as well as directors George Stevens on *Giant* and Robert Wise on five successive projects. Ken Adam, too, teamed up with producers Cubby Broccoli and Harry Salzman on seven James Bond films, beginning in the early 1960s, and several with Stanley Kubrick. The majority of these successful independent production designers were white men in their fifties or sixties who were trained as architects or visual artists and had enjoyed the comprehensive training afforded by the studios' apprentice system during the previous two decades.[26]

Art directors enjoyed additional autonomy from the labor disputes that roiled Hollywood in the mid- to late 1940s. They were under the jurisdiction of the Society of Motion Picture Art Directors (SMPAD), a nonprofit corporation, which was formed in 1937 to act as a collective bargaining agent and as a professional guild, and which fostered educational, social, recreational, and charitable enterprises. The makeup of SMPAD's board of directors, which included Cedric Gibbons, Van Nest Polglase, and Wiard Ihnen, speaks to the allegiance between art directors and studio system management.[27]

In contrast, their art department confederates, who included model makers, set and costume illustrators, and set decorators, were under the jurisdiction of the radical Confederation of Studio Unions (CSU), headed by the legendary union activist and alleged communist Herb Sorrell. In 1945, Sorrell called a strike, leading to a lockout a year later and the final ouster of the union boss. The historian Gerald Horne claimed that the Hollywood moguls had a stake in ridding themselves of CSU in order to gain almost absolute control of the production process while avoiding the conditions imposed by "union auteurs."[28]

There was a perceived difference between the more elevated practice of the SMPAD art director and that of CSU's so-called art craft members. During the period of maximum labor strife, SMPAD members–studio employees were able to maintain a modicum of independence; they were not required to cross the picket line while still collecting their checks from the studios. Not until 1958 did SMPAD agree to join the International Alliance of Theatrical and Stage Employees (IATSE), the studio-approved union, and two years later a new charter was forged that included television employees; in this they were demonstrating their hybrid loyalties, linked to the old system by temperament if not completely by ideology.

Evidence of the production designer's aim to forge a more visible occupational profile in mid-century Hollywood is seen in the SMPAD publication *Production Design Bulletin of the Society of Motion Picture Art Directors* from 1951 to 1953.[29] Commencing as a few mimeographed pages, by the second issue it was enlarged to a twenty-page magazine devoted to articles on various aspects of the profession. It served as an art gallery for its members' pre-production sketches and production designs; for example, there were two articles in 1951 and 1952 by Preston Ames, accompanied by images from *An American in Paris*.[30] Functioning as a way to explore the complex and multitudinous tasks involved in production design from theory to practice, it featured articles on topics from conducting research to pre-production planning to building models. For example, the head of the Research Department at Warner Bros., Carl Milliken, wished to demonstrate that art directors were not only dependent on the studio's architectural library, but also beholden to its knowledgeable staff who for "ten or more years, has traveled (vicariously) all over the world, and has examined the everyday lives of people in every century."[31] Lastly, *Production Design* brought new, more efficacious and cost-effective methods for set designing to its constituency while serving secondarily as an advertisement for their respective studios. For example, Herman Blumenthal claimed in "Cardboard Counterpart" that Lyle Wheeler's systemized use of small-scale replicas at Twentieth Century–Fox was a crucial element for visualizing sets before construction, and paved the way "for a better understanding between producer, director, cameraman, and art director" of all the "important information as to design, action, and production, and technical problems" involved in filmmaking.[32]

The expansion of the art director's status from a subordinate to an active collaborator after World War II may be traced to William Cameron Menzies's work as "production designer" for *Gone with the Wind* in 1939. In a famous memo, David O. Selznick wrote of Menzies that "his work in the picture, as I see it, will be a lot greater in scope than is normally associated with the word 'art direction,'" reporting that the latter would provide "a complete script in sketch form, showing actual camera set-ups, lighting etc." prior to shooting.[33] The development of the storyboard ensured the production designer's input into the directorial process by animating the sets in time and space. Even if pre-production drawings were not ultimately employed as initially conceived, as they were in Hitchcock's films—the mythology of his visualization of the entire film prior to shooting notwithstanding—the storyboard prompted discussions and, in some cases, a negotiation between the production designer, screenwriter, director, and cinematographer.[34] Following Menzies, many designers sought to follow suit. For example, during Ken Adam's tenure under Menzies on Mike Todd's *Around the World in Eighty Days* (1956), on which Adam designed many of the sets, he observed that Menzies was with Todd "from morning to night influencing everything—I said, 'I think I would like to widen my field.'" Adam decided thus to market himself as a production designer rather than an art director because he wanted "to be involved in the whole production."[35]

Adam's career serves as an example of the possibilities available to the independent production designer in the 1960s. He was an integral part of the James Bond franchise, an international production that was financed by United Artists. Adam studied architecture at the Bartlett School and interned for the Bauhaus-inspired MARS group in London before becoming an art director at Pinewood Studios.[36] *Dr. No* (Terence Young, 1962) established his credentials as an autonomous agent who conferred with a design team, developing his signature style. He is best known for his futuristic torture chambers and gadgets, ultra-modern bunker-like architecture, and exotic fish tanks filled with man-eating predators. His most famous sets are the war room in Stanley Kubrick's *Dr. Strangelove* (1959) and his creation of the interior of Fort Knox in *Goldfinger* (Guy Hamilton, 1964). A testament to his creative autonomy is seen in Adam's claim that while director Terence Young was on location in Jamaica filming *Dr. No*, he was in London's Pinewood Studios, designing and building at least five of the sets without supervision.[37] He is also responsible for selecting memorable exotic settings for the sets he built, including the extinct volcano on Japan's Matsu Island in *You Only Live Twice* (Lewis Gilbert, 1967). After *Dr. No,* Adam's images often preceded the scripts. Adam's part in creating the Bond look corroborates C. S. Tashiro's assertion that films have a visual trajectory that is parallel to or even independent of the story.[38] While the directors in the Bond films changed from film to film, Adam's designs remained the constant, which prompted David Sylvester to refer to him as both a collaborator and an auteur, the latter moniker customarily only applied to a film's director.[39] Additionally, Adam's preparatory sketches not only projected the action to take place in his architectural settings, but they are regarded as works of art in their own right, demonstrating that pre-production designs after World War II have enjoyed an autonomous, extracinematic identity.

Location, Economics, and the Creation of Place

The upsurge in location shooting after the war, which prompted a substantial increase in the production designer's practice, can be explained by several factors. Motivated by economic and aesthetic factors, both the French New Wave directors (and their apologists) and the Italian Neorealists advocated for more authentic experiences in the street and the vagaries of everyday life while decrying the artificiality of the studio-produced set. In the United States by 1945, in films such as *The House on 92nd Street* (Henry Hathaway, 1945, art dirs. Lewis H. Creber and Lyle Wheeler), *The Lost Weekend* (Billy Wilder, 1945, art dirs. Hans Dreier and A. Earl Hedrick), and *The Naked City* (Jules Dassin, 1948, art dir. John DeCuir), real urban landscapes were used.[40] The quest for realism of detail and topography was also a response to the competition posed by television after the war. By shooting in places other than Hollywood (later referred to as runaway productions) in vivid color and employing various widescreen technologies, producers sought to provide a vicarious sense of being there. Further inspired, in part, by the invention of Cinerama in 1951, many films looked much like travelogues while generating new audience pools comprising film enthusiasts and would-be tourists. As Karen Dubinsky has shown, domestic recreational travel to iconic destinations like Niagara Falls increased exponentially after the war due to the middle class's expendable income, and Europe became a destination as well when airplane excursions became more affordable in 1958. After reading the script for *Niagara* (Henry Hathaway, 1953, art dirs. Maurice Ransford and Lyle Wheeler), for example, which was eventually shot on location on the Canadian side of the tourist attraction, Twentieth Century–Fox producer Michael Abel wrote enthusiastically to Darryl F. Zanuck, asserting that the millions who knew of Niagara's wonders would vicariously experience it, and for those who had already visited, the film would provide an opportunity "to relive that experience by seeing the highlights of Niagara Falls once again."[41]

However, the depiction of place in cinema is not simply the selection of a particular geographical location; rather it is fabricated, a synthesis of the real and the artistry offered by production design, which is subsequently animated further by camera angles, lighting, props, and the movement of actors. Often a false dichotomy is set up between the authenticity of location shooting, which is linked to a specific geography, and the artificiality of the soundstage-located set design. But as Simon Schama has shown, even landscapes are not natural but human constructions replete with myth and memory that lie beneath the surface and require excavation, a characteristic that Walter Benjamin referred to as its "embedded" character when referring to architecture.[42] The idea that cinematic settings are nothing more than a "construction" in the service of particular ideologies was recently echoed by Elena Gorfinkel and John David Rhodes: "Place and cinema share an intriguing and morphologically consonant doubleness: both are felt and have been understood to be simultaneously natural and constructed, to be effects of both ontology and the articulation of a code or codes."[43] For example, in *Giant*, an ideologically laden or coded view of Texas is seen in the discrete landscape settings selected, which were interpreted through the subjective filters of the author, director, and production designer.

The decision to shoot films outside of Hollywood was also affected by changing audience patterns in the United States as occasioned by the middle class's exodus to the suburbs, which fostered new leisure pursuits (e.g., television, sports, hobbies) in turn, leading studios to increase their attention to European markets. Plummeting domestic revenues created additional dependence on transatlantic viewers, which made up 45 percent of studio profits in 1956.[44] The tax advantages of shooting abroad coupled with the availability of previously blocked European funds served as additional "pull factors."[45] In order to solidify their worldwide audience, both the studios and independents began to internationalize their productions and opt for a more cosmopolitan viewership, which, according to Vanessa Schwartz, resulted in the international array of stars and locations that characterized the era's runaway productions.[46]

Ironically, shooting on location, especially in international locales, generated an economics of plentitude and profligate budgets for experienced production designers while creating hardship for others. The fewer but more extravagant movies provided ample opportunities for runaway production designers who had risen up the studio hierarchy, especially those who were of European descent or bilingual, such as Ken Adam, Edward Carfagno, and Boris Leven. But these multimillion-dollar projects were accompanied by massive layoffs among the studio's production staffs. Irving Bernstein's study is again useful for gauging the scope of the downsizing: between 1946 and 1956, 53 percent were let go at the same time that real wages fell among Hollywood's craft workers in comparison with analogous jobs in construction.[47] Thus, while experienced American designers enjoyed economic rewards, increased autonomy, and the tax advantages of independent productions, the less prestigious experienced a reversal of fortune, their labors outsourced to foreign workers for lower wages. Herb Krizman, president of the Society of Motion Picture Art Directors, tried to stem the bleeding, arguing in 1957 that runaway productions were an "overall waste and extravagance," claiming that it was well known "that art directors especially felt the sting . . . since it was common knowledge that they were not hired on such projects." In answer to those who sang the praises of authenticity, Krizman claimed that art directors could simulate any setting at a lower cost and with more artistry.[48] Perhaps the most egregious example of the squandering of resources occurred in *Cleopatra* at Rome's Cinecittà Studios, where many postwar runaway productions were filmed. The set designs added to the film's already bloated budget that ultimately skyrocketed to $44 million, which almost ruined Twentieth Century–Fox financially, and heralded the end of the era's historical epic. John DeCuir's sets had escalated to almost unmanageable proportions; the land on which his replica of Alexandria stood had to be dredged for live World War II mines, his fake Roman forum cost $1.5 million and dwarfed the real one, and his extensive use of aluminum tubing led to a countrywide shortage.[49]

A Place of Contrasts: Boris Leven's Set Designs for *Giant*

Giant epitomized many of the important, seemingly optimistic developments in mid-twentieth-century cinema—large in scale (shot at a 1:74 aspect ratio), epic in scope, based on a best-selling novel, created by an independent production company, and filmed on location—yet Texas and its residents are seen as deeply troubled and roiled by class, gender, and racial tensions.[50] The historian J. E. Smyth claims that director George Stevens "was caught up in the Hollywood of the 1950s and its own kind of fascination with size and wealth. The scope of widescreen filmmaking and the lushness of Warnercolor were celebrated and the Texas elites emerged more or less unscathed."[51] I argue that the representation of social and economic conflicts in the film were both underscored and created by Boris Leven's production designs and his formulation of place, which were a combination of physical geography and artistry. The sets emphasize the contrast between privation and excess in Texas, but the sheer display of economic plenitude may also have "signaled the hope of salvation for a film industry suffering" from a decrease in revenue.[52] Leven's designs are not merely subservient to Ferber's narrative or the script by Fred Guiol and Ivan Moffatt, but often generate their own sense of visual meaning, which is contiguous with it.

The importance of Texas as place is underscored in the film's prequel, which announces its epic intentions and serves as an advertisement for the filmmakers' wish to establish the supposed authenticity of the film's locale. Gig Young, the film's star, provides a tutorial on the state, flanked by an enormous map, and a brief history lesson, but he is also keen on zeroing in on the previously unknown city of Marfa, where most of the film was shot. Leven emphasized the state's significance in his formulation of the sets—"It had to be Texas . . . because people travel too much these days to be fooled by California backgrounds for a Texas locale"—while crediting Stevens for his commitment to so-called realism.[53]

In accord with postwar films shot abroad, *Giant*'s Texas is seen as a huge entity unto itself, a view originating with its own history as a fiercely independent republic from 1836 to 1845, which Ferber emphasized in the novel, referring to it as "a different country altogether. A country all by itself that just happens to be in the middle of the United States."[54] Its putative detachment is illustrated in *Giant* by Bick and Leslie's lengthy train journey to the interior.

Boris Leven's imposing Victorian Reata mansion (the Benedict family home) is the most photographed set of the film—a synecdoche for wealth, separation,

FIGURE 18: Publicity photograph of James Dean in front of the Reata mansion.

dysfunctional femininity, repressed family memories, and a time gone by. A publicity image of Reata that echoes various shots in the film features a relaxed yet defiant Jett Rink seated in Bick Benedict's luxurious Duesenberg automobile, feet propped disrespectfully on the dashboard with the imposing mansion in the distance, referencing his class envy and his subsequent domination of all that the house embodies (figure 18). Yet few know that the lone mansion against the vast, empty horizontal expanse of the Texas plains was Leven's invention (figure 19).

FIGURE 19: Reata against the flat Texas plains. Frame enlargement from *Giant* (George Stevens, 1956, prod. des. Boris Leven).

Indeed, this scene is so enduring and iconic that it served as the springboard for a 1981 Levis commercial for women's 501 jeans, in which a cowgirl dressed like Jett Rink addresses a man emerging from an old house, and exclaims, "Travis, you're a year too late," underscoring the dwelling as an indication of a time gone by.

In February 1952, Stevens formed George Stevens Productions, "to produce, sell, and distribute films and television," acquiring the rights to Ferber's property the same year.[55] Stevens and Paramount executive Henry Ginsberg also teamed up with the author in May 1953 to form Giant Productions for the sole intention of producing *Giant* and other properties by her, an agreement that was dissolved on 31 August 1957.[56] Formal shooting began on 15 May 1955, and lasted until mid-October.[57] Warner Bros. financed the independent production where most of the first-unit work took place. Leven's participation on the film commenced at the beginning of 1954 with his use of the studios' research facilities.[58] According to the daily production reports, Leven was present during location shooting in Marfa, which lasted from 6 June to 21 July 1955.[59]

Giant comprised an artful combination of location shooting for exterior scenes and elaborate studio fabrication, uniting Stevens and Leven's quest for a kind of documentary realism with more obvious constructed fictions. Detailed notes in Warner Bros.' files identify Leven's thirteen major location and studio sets and a host of additional minor ones, for a total cost of $489,000, which was the largest budget spent by Warner Bros. up until that point.[60] The exterior views of Maryland (actually Charlottesville, Virginia) and Texas were shot onsite, while the complex interiors were constructed on Warner Bros.' soundstages. Lynnton, Leslie's former home, was the extant Classical Revival Belmont mansion in Maryland, meant to convey old money and tradition, while the Reata exterior was an elaborate, studio-built set that had to be shipped to Marfa.[61]

Leven's research was complex and multidimensional, beginning with a close reading of Ferber's novel, which reveals a consideration of her visual descriptions and themes—from the awe-inspiring view of the mansion to an adaptation of the painting of Frederic Remington for Bick's office.[62] With camera and sketchbook in hand, he supplemented Ferber's text with a trip around the Lone Star State late in 1954, ultimately producing hundreds of photographs and numerous drawings.[63] MGM production designer Edward Carfagno reported on the practice after the war: "You'd go out with a location man. That's the way they used to do it and that made a lot of sense. You go out and you find it, and take pictures and bring them back."[64] However, Leven's charge was much more amplified, and had him serving as a location seeker, a sketch hunter and artist, an architectural researcher, and an ethnographer of sorts. Augmenting his location investigations, Leven made extensive use of Warner Bros.' vast photographic archive. Many of the images he borrowed were not returned to the studio's files, and provide a rare glimpse into the evolution of his visual inquiries and their subsequent deployment in the film's set designs.[65] Myriad requests were also sent to Warner's Research Department for illustrated articles, books, and clippings on a wide array of topics from colonial houses to oil fields, which further affords us the opportunity to gauge the full range of the postwar production designer's varied responsibilities.[66] Warner Bros.' research records and announcements to the trade press also disclose that the same was true for Stevens, who traveled to Texas subsequently with Leven and others to concretize shooting locations, finally selecting Marfa as the main site.[67]

The Moscow-born Leven (1908–1986) came to the United States during the Bolshevik Revolution.[68] He earned a degree in architecture from the University of Southern California in 1932, followed by a year at New York's Beaux Arts Institute of Design.[69] At this time, he also began a career as a watercolorist, assisting Professor Paul Sample in the teaching of his painting course, well on his way to combining his joint interests in architecture and the fine arts, often drawing on his vast corpus of knowledge in both fields in the forging of his set designs.[70] Leven worked for a brief time at MGM in 1938, then moved to Twentieth Century–Fox where his career took off, earning the first of nine Oscar nominations for *Alexander's Ragtime Band* (Henry King, 1938).[71] Following his departure from the studio system in 1948, he worked with such legendary directors as Robert Siodmak on *Criss Cross* (1949, Universal), Fritz Lang on *The House by the River* (1949, Republic Pictures), and with independents such as Otto Preminger on *Anatomy of a Murder* (1959) and Robert Wise on five films, including *West Side Story* (1961), for which he won an Academy Award, *The Sound of Music* (1965), and *The Sand Pebbles* (1966). A testament to his individual prestige and to production design as a marketable commodity is seen in the full-page ad that Twentieth Century–Fox took out in one of the trade journals for *The Sand Pebbles*, which was a full-length enlargement of Leven's head superimposed on the massive San Pablo mast, the ship that he designed for the film (figure 20).[72] At a cost of $250,000, it was the most expensive single prop for a film at that time.[73]

FIGURE 20: Publicity image of Boris Leven for *The Sand Pebbles* (Robert Wise, 1966, prod. des. Boris Leven). Photograph from the Boris Leven Collection, Courtesy of Cinema and Television Library, University of Southern California, Los Angeles.

When Leven became part of the *Giant* team, both he and Stevens were well respected and prominent members of the film industry, each having ascended the studio hierarchy before assuming their roles as independent production designer and independent producer and director, respectively. Visual Arts curator Denise Olsen claims that Stevens and Leven had analogous temperaments, which were beneficial to their work together on *Giant*, free of studio interference.[74] Looking back on his career in 1978, Leven regarded himself as a full-fledged partner in the tradition of Menzies: "The rapport between the director and the production designer is the major factor on which the success of their efforts depends. There must exist between them a complete trust and understanding. The relationship must grow, flourish, give out creative impulses, and above all create a feeling of respect and interdependence."[75] Similar in age and sensibility, both believed in the importance of the visual in a film. Stevens was notorious in Hollywood for his numerous retakes and the time he spent in the editing room, which in the case of *Giant* was over a year. According to art critic John Rosenfield, Stevens believed that "by its own pictorial poetry the picture can tell the essential story," rendering him a production designer's director.[76] Lecturing to the Theater Owners of America in Chicago, the director urged exhibitors "not to be afraid of terms such as 'art' and 'beauty.'"[77] Stevens and Leven's collaboration paid off on *Giant*; both garnered accolades at the twenty-ninth annual Academy Awards ceremony, where the former won as best director and the latter was nominated for art direction.

Stevens requested that Leven complete drawings prior to shooting in order to provide him with directorial ideas. Two "production breakdown" meetings in December of 1954, which were designed to review the script and to concretize the layout of several scenes, attest to Leven's formulation of place and space. The following is typical of Stevens's requests and Leven's creative input: "This page lists scenes at the Swimming Pool of Reata and can either be shot on stage utilizing a tank, or at the exterior tank on the lot. However, this sequence is not going to mean much unless there is a direct tie-up with the Reata house. Mr. Leven was instructed to do some planning on this."[78]

At the time of his death, his longtime friend from Paramount's Dreier Academy, Robert Boyle, recalled Leven's legendary "intolerance of mediocrity and his protectiveness of the integrity of his work." Boyle reported that on the set of *Giant*, when Stevens was blocking out action in front of the Reata set, "a speck appeared on the horizon, followed by a plume of dust. The speck grew larger, becoming a speeding automobile that skidded to a stop at the bottom of the rise." At the sight of Leven, who disembarked from the car, "Stevens wheeled around to his crew and exclaimed in mock terror, 'What did I do now?!'" corroborating that the former was an imaginative force to be reckoned with.[79]

Leven surveyed Texas's vast landscape on a location-seeking journey that commenced at the end of November 1954 with a ten-day, 2,500-mile trip across the state, paralleling the film's epic scope; he had been sent there by Stevens to scout possible filming locations and to conduct research for his architectural set designs.[80] The film's unit manager, Mel Dellar, and location manager, Joe Barry, accompanied him, which was announced to the trade press.[81] Beginning in El Paso in the west, they headed southeast to Deming, New Mexico, and Marfa, Del Rio, and San Antonio; east to Houston, and then north to Dallas and Forth Worth; continuing west toward Vernon; and northwest to their last stop, Amarillo: ultimately eighteen cities in all.[82] Recording his observations in a journal, entitled "Ten Days in Beautiful Texas," Leven included lengthy accounts of the landscape for possible filming locations, the numerous ranches and mansions he visited in search of models for Reata, the plethora of diverse objects he encountered, which would later serve as springboards for the building's interior, and descriptions of typical Texans or "local color" he met on the way.[83]

In spite of the diary's complimentary title, Leven's prose was peppered with negative remarks about the Texas landscape and its startling inequities in wealth, offering insight into some of the characteristics that were infused into his set designs. In San Antonio, he recorded simply "segregation" and "40% Mexican."[84] Surveying wealthy *Alga Diferente* and categorizing it as a nightmare, he noted the ostentatious millionaires' homes all around San Antonio. Perhaps the most derogatory comment, which demonstrates Leven's awareness of the state's class disparities and racial oppression, is in a conversation he recorded with a waitress, about dramatic contrasts that were absorbed into the set designs: "Morning. It is still dark. A loose sash is cracking in the window frame. . . . The breeze swings the old Victorian chandeliers. The roosters yell: 'I hate this place!' *Me too!* Waitresses put in fifteen hours a day. 'They run this place just like a plantation.' 'No unions here.' 'Had niggers . . . wait on tables before—made the change to get more business.'"[85] Leven's record of the discussion also establishes his awareness that the plights of poor whites, Mexicans, and African Americans were similar in Jim Crow Texas. He also expressed to a colleague the desire to capture the abject poverty of Mexican workers' dwellings in the sets: "Enclosed you will find several stills showing the transient camp. Some are photographs of the sketches we made, and some are copies of the actual camps. Even though at first glance each group appears to have character of its own, and occasionally even a sense of the picturesque, they will all have the same predominant note—poverty. This is exactly what we wish to show—the great poverty. To me, poverty means having very little, little of everything—little of canvas, wood, pots and pans, of cardboard or paper. Our camp should look empty and lonely."[86]

Soon after the production designer's "Ten Days in Beautiful Texas," in January of 1955, Stevens made his first trip with Leven to "personally inspect location sites."[87] Subsequently he sent a publicity man and a still photographer on 22 or 23 February 1955, in order to interview types, take photographs of their clothing, and tape record their speech to achieve a greater degree of "authenticity."[88] Stevens was so intent on capturing representative Texans that he commissioned Southern Methodist University fine arts professor Ed Bearden to complete a series of portrait studies and storyboard-like drawings before casting the actors for *Giant*. The drawings were displayed on the set to the makeup and costume crews.[89] Several days later, Stevens traveled to San Antonio again to meet with the two men and to attend a livestock show, collecting information for an appropriate breed of cow for the roundup scene.[90] On 28 February, he met with Leven and members of the construction crew in Texas again to finally "set" twelve of the location sites, including three scenes involving Reata (e.g., gates, barbeque, interior), finally selecting the Worth Evans Ranch in Marfa, twenty-one miles outside the city, Jett's land and shack, and the Mexican settlement, among others.[91] While Leven was largely responsible for developing the sense of physical locale, Stevens focused more on achieving a level of believability for the actors—their dress, speech, and demeanor.

In order to emphasize the contrast between the state's forlorn barrenness and the *nouveau riche* Texans' ostentation, Leven created a massive masonry mansion in the Victorian Gothic style for the Reata ranch. The house served a similar purpose in announcing its sumptuousness to the audience; of the film's thirteen major sets, Reata's $155,000 exterior and the $105,000 interior, which was built on a soundstage, were by far the most expensive and elaborate.[92] Characterized by lofty verticality, the Gothic is here meant to awe; the outside of the tripartite-walled fictional dwelling was seventy-six feet, and the other two sides measured one hundred feet tall each, while its interior preserved the "Victorian scale" with three stories and high ceilings.[93] Yet the style also signified a mysterious and exotic otherness, a haunting of an unresolved past, which referred to the dysfunctional relationship of Bick and his sister Luz Benedict, and the mistreatment of workers in their domain, representing the wholesale oppression of Mexicans in Texas (color plate 5). Under the control of the domineering matriarch Luz, the house's forbidding presence and initially dark and lugubrious interior represented her personality. A Warner Bros. publicist claimed that Reata resembled the decaying Tara in *Gone with the Wind* and the brooding melancholy of the house in *Wuthering Heights* (William Wyler, 1938, art dirs. James Basevi and Alexander Toluboff).[94] Leven's desire to create a feeling of unease is corroborated by his titling of an independent painting of a lonely Reata against the barren landscape, *Ghost of Giant*.[95]

Leven had surely read Ferber's description of Reata, which "rose like a mirage" against the sky, "a vast edifice all towers and domes and balconies and iron fretwork" which "in size and general architecture . . . somewhat resembled the palace known as Alhambra, with a dash of Missouri Pacific Railroad station."[96] Although he and Stevens rejected the Spanish palace's Mediterranean fashion, the stony Gothic of the railroad station with its numerous towers and turrets was partly retained. Leven maintained that a Texas friend of his suggested that he go to Decatur to see the Waggoner mansion, but it is also likely that Ferber's invocation of the great house and other Texas ranches also affected Leven's itinerary, prompting him to visit both the Waggoner Ranch in Vernon and Old

Waggoner House in Decatur.[97] Serving as the model for Reata, the latter is a huge limestone house, built in 1883 and still standing. It was commissioned by cattle baron Daniel Waggoner, who owned over a million acres and on whose land oil was discovered in 1911, much like Bick Benedict in *Giant*.[98] Leven's encounter with El Castille, as the mansion was nicknamed, was accompanied by a "cold wind blowing like mad." Leven described the encounter in his journal: "The Old Waggoner House. An old beauty. Victorian. With a real flair for elegance and scale. 16' 0" high ceilings. Grand porch. Windows. Once it stood alone. It must have been a proud edifice. From its windows and porches one could see the flat horizon many miles away."[99] The solitary house against the Texas prairie also evokes Edward Hopper's painting *House by the Railroad* (1925), which depicts a similar mansard-roofed Victorian dwelling affected by the encroachment of train travel, or modernization, suggesting a time gone by that is consonant with its meaning in *Giant*.[100] When Leven showed Stevens his sketch of the large house placed incongruously on the prairie, the director reportedly put his arm around the designer's shoulder and said, "This is the best damn thing that has happened to this picture."[101]

Leven also produced preliminary sketches of Reata from a variety of vantage points, thereby circumscribing the action that was to take place in its midst, later employed by Stevens in the film, including a view from an approaching car driving across a long roadway, which emphasized the spectacle of the house for the first time from Bick's and especially Leslie's point of view. The couple's passage through its eponymous iron gate was borrowed from the Waggoner mansion, which is defined by an equally imposing entranceway with "El Castillo" emblazoned at the crest.[102] Leven's other sketches of Reata's horizontal, stage-like porch that faces the prairie, which was inspired by the Waggoner Mansion's main stairwell; Bick's office, where much of the drama takes place; and the dining room represent his creation of architectural views for the film's main action.[103]

The dark, wood-paneled interior, an architectural anachronism in 1925 when the *Giant* saga commences, combines with its imposing three stories to create a stultifying sight from Leslie's vantage point, which changes when she becomes the first lady of the house. One of Leven's preliminary drawings reveals his highlighting of the innumerable doorways and balconies, uniting with his use of expressive angles for the ceilings and busy Victorian fretwork to underscore the house's oppressive sumptuousness (figure 21). At the foot of the stairwell, Reata is intimidating for a new bride whose previous Virginia colonial abode is appointed with light-colored, small rooms that are emphasized by numerous close-ups, representing the intimate emotional tenor of her prior family life. Subsequent to the death of Luz, production designer by proxy Leslie redecorates the house in pastel tones, thereby lightening the mood and claiming ownership. Leven remodeled Reata (with the help of set dresser Ralph Hurst) three times during the course of the narrative's twenty-five-year period. For example, when the Benedicts' fortune

FIGURE 21: Boris Leven drawing for the interior of Reata, n.d. Photograph from the Boris Leven Collection, Courtesy of the Cinema and Television Library, University of Southern California, Los Angeles.

increases after the discovery of oil, "the home then takes on a note of sophisticated elegance with Empire and Louis XV furniture, Venetian mirrors, contemporary paintings, crystal chandeliers and Aubusson rugs" and "a pool and tennis court" that are added to emphasize wealth, taste, and modernization.[104]

As a counterpoint to the main house's grandeur, Leven fashioned the abject Mexican town of Vientecito to accentuate the dual tropes of racism and class oppression (color plate 6). The set cost $25,000 to build and was the fourth most expensive, attesting to its importance in the film.[105] Leven created the town as a warren of decaying, simple adobe hovels, which are bordered by ramshackle fences and peeling chicken wire. The interior of one worker's dwelling features a supine Mrs. Obregon (wife of a Reata employee, played by Pilar del Rey) on an old mattress with soiled and bedraggled bedding, trying futilely to attend to her dying infant Angel II, who is lying in an old wooden box, a modern-day nativity scene. Leven was particularly proud of his ability to tell a story by creating textures—or "aging," as it was referred to by production designers—to convey the passage of time, and in this case the effects of poverty and neglect.[106] Cinematographer William Mellor employed low-contrast lighting in several such scenes to emphasize "the feeling of sorrow that prevailed," showing the connection between set design and cinematography.[107]

Perhaps the most telling aspect of the wretched outpost is that it is bordered by a cemetery or a heterotopia; in one shot, the graveyard dominates the frame and speaks to the deaths of countless Mexicans who worked on Reata over the decades, and perhaps those who died during the Mexican American Wars.[108] Later in the film, it serves as the site for the funeral of a now adult Angel Obregon II (Sal Mineo) whose body is returned after World War II, underscoring another classed and raced martyrdom. Leven's fictional creation may be an adaptation of Shafter's Mexican cemetery, which is located south of Marfa. Several studio photographs show various gravesites determined by the deceased's former class, including pedestaled tomb sites crowned by large ceramic crucifixes and wrought iron enclosures, simple wooden crosses, and mounds of rocks for those unable to afford a decent burial.[109] Preserving the general design, Leven replaced the prosperous-looking markers with simple wooden crosses and fences and a scattering of rubble-like graves to establish the abjection of the cinematic place.

A further political commentary may be gleaned from the monumental Frederic Remington–like mural in Bick's office, which acts as a signpost for several of the most troubled scenes, from the death of Luz to the exploitive attempt to deprive Jett of his inheritance to Bick's final capitulation to the realities of oil. Leven's selection of Remington may have been suggested by Ferber, who equated Bick and Leslie to the figures in one of his colorful, romanticized prints.[110] At first glance, the cinematic mural serves as a means to reference both the Benedict family's livelihood while aligning it with the western cinematic genre. It is similar in spirit to the cowboy artist Remington's deceptively realistic images, here showing cowherds aggressively chasing down and subduing steer either for branding or for sport, which was the custom. Indeed, the link between the animals' and humans' fates is shown in one of the film's last scenes, in which Bick's passive, aging body is placed directly below the restrained steer.

One of the most dramatic of Leven's sets is the plethora of oil rigs and derricks that he designed for Jett Rink's newly acquired Little Reata, inherited after Luz Benedict's death. Since Marfa is located in an area of Texas where no oil was discovered, all the equipment had to be fabricated from scratch. Indeed, it is the discovery of oil at the end of the first part of the film just before the intermission that constitutes a major turning point, marking the beginning of Reata's transition from a cattle-breeding ranch to an oil-producing one, and signaling another aspect of Texas's modernization. It also reinforces the class tensions that undergird the film, announcing the ascent of Jett Rink from a poor cowhand to a multimillion-dollar oil baron, and the decline of Benedict family hegemony. Everyone on *Giant*'s production team understood the import of oil in the story; studio research notes show that the portions of Ferber's novel dealing with the discovery of oil were blocked out for special consideration. Leven and others requested an additional investigation of the King Ranch, which served as a partial model for the Benedict family's transition to oil, followed by articles on refineries in popular magazines. To achieve further accuracy, in December of 1954, Leven ordered two clippings about Independent Petroleum in California and ten clippings of their oil fields.[111] Some of the long shots of oil rigs were even photographed on location in Bakersfield, California.[112] The production company was so proud of the realism of the sets that the publicity department trumpeted the gushing of the *faux* oil for a group of tourists: "Art director Boris Leven and

FIGURE 22: Publicity photograph of Boris Leven and James Dean in front of a miniature oil derrick and Reata, n.d. Courtesy of Margaret Herrick Library, Academy of Motion Picture Arts and Sciences, Beverly Hills.

set designer Ralph Hurst constructed an oil well and derrick with a cable tool percussion-drilling rig. Special effects man Ralph Webb whipped up ersatz oil. In the authentic Texas setting the special liquid looked like the real thing."[113] For the end of the film, Leven fashioned a miniature oil derrick seen on a pedestal adjacent to the Remington-like mural and adjacent to the slumped body of Bick. The publicity department made further use of the miniature sculpture; a publicity photograph that was distributed to the press shows Leven explaining its workings to an interested Dean, which served as a ploy to introduce the production designer to the public and increase his star power (figure 22).

The oil rigs and derricks are rendered in contrast to the nuanced, detailed depictions of architecture, illustrating various aspects of Leven's multifaceted style. His ability to create layered surfaces is also seen in the other films on which he worked, such as *Two for the Seesaw* (Robert Wise, 1958) and *Anatomy of a Murder* (1959). However, the artist also created bold, stylized shapes that convey a modernist, functional logic for the industrial structures, producing geometric silhouettes against the sky; and when seen in multiples in a long shot they communicate their wholesale domination of the landscape and Texas's economy. Leven employed a similar grid-like efficiency for the steely fire escapes, grillwork, and bar-like enclosures and gates in *West Side Story*, a combination of meticulous realism and pared-down abstraction. The two poles of Leven's sensibility serve as an encapsulation of cinematic production design—the creation of a believable setting by recourse to mimesis, combined with poetic license and abbreviation for the fabricated cinematic place.

Part of the publicity strategy for *Giant* focused on the unprecedented magnitude of its production design; hence Leven's efforts became part of the marketing of the film. Vivian Sobchack has noted that the language of surplus was employed in the historical epic films of the 1950s and 1960s as a way to legitimize them, not through specific events so much as creating a "general historical eventfulness," that is, generating drama and hype prior to the actual drama. "This was achieved often through *empirically verifiable* and *material* excess—entailing scale, quantification, and consumption in relation to money and human labor" as a way of exceeding its excessive screen boundaries and creating its own history.[114]

After boasting about moving more than a million dollars of equipment and over two hundred personnel to the small city of Marfa, population 3,500, publicity copy focused particular attention on exceeding the boundaries of traditional location shooting through production design. Instead of just equipment, this time Hollywood "decided to take its own mansion along." In an unprecedented way, both Reata and the designer were singled out for special credit: "The house, a magnificent three-story Victorian structure designed by art director Boris Leven, was built in the Warner Bros.' prop department and then shipped to the Worth Evans Ranch . . . on five railroad flat cars."[115] Other promotional material bragged that it was "the biggest shop-made prop ever built in Hollywood" and that it required twenty-five men to assemble it.[116]

Indeed, the house became both a star and a tourist attraction in its own right during the filming of *Giant* and thereafter. It could be seen for miles, drawing the public like a magnet. A testament to architectural production design's continued extracinematic identity continues to this day in the tourist pilgrimages to Marfa to see the Paisano Hotel, the meeting place of the cast and crew, and the extant skeleton of Leven's Reata mansion, the remnants of which stand like a lone ghost on the flat prairie.

I have highlighted Leven's particular contribution to the visualization of *Giant* not as an auteurist paean, but rather to illustrate how the job of the production designer changed in post-classical Hollywood from being subservient to the director, chief studio art director, and producer to a valued part of a more collaborative creative team. Now free agents, production designers such as Leven were in high demand and in a better bargaining position to negotiate both their economic and creative requirements. Ironically, it was the very studio system that many sought independence from that provided the new production designer with a host of heterogeneous skills that would later foster such autonomy and inventive input. In addition, the rise of location shooting in the postwar era necessitated a new expertise that was necessary to formulate a sense of place, which was dependent upon onsite study of the setting, thorough research of the landscape, architecture, and its history, and often the experience of an engineer. These abilities were required in order to construct a convincing visual story that was both parallel to and independent of the narrative, done in active collaboration with the director. Leven was at the forefront of a group of such designers as Ken Adam and, later, director and designer Ridley Scott (along with industrial designer Syd Mead and production designer Lawrence Paull) of *Blade Runner* (1982) fame, who believed that scenography was at least as important as the actors and script in cinema. Scott referred to his method as "pictorial referencing," whereby he studied a wide array of visual images from the fine arts, popular culture, and architecture to create "total environments," a strategy that was foreshadowed by the work of Leven in collaboration with George Stevens, Robert Wise, and others.[117]

4

THE AUTEUR RENAISSANCE, 1968–1980

Charles Tashiro

As with any cultural phenomenon, the shift in American filmmaking in the late 1960s and 1970s toward more personal, often critical expression is best understood as the product of multiple factors. In examining the contributions of art directors and production designers to this phenomenon, we should consider both the critical and ideological assumptions underpinning the development and production practice within the film industry. This dual perspective is necessary to understand what happens when the ideology of auteurism confronts the reality of material practice. To make this argument is not to deny that such a thing as an "auteur" exists, nor to claim that the work of individual filmmakers cannot be differentiated. Recognizing the role of technicians in creating visual style does, however, make attributions and descriptions more precise.

There is also the further problem of imprecise periodization. The question is muddied further by competing labels for roughly the same period, such as "The New Hollywood" or "The Hollywood Renaissance." For the sake of this discussion, I assume that "The Auteur Renaissance" coincides roughly with "The New Hollywood," that is, it can be said to begin with the popular and critical success of *Bonnie and Clyde* in 1967 (Arthur Penn, art dir. Dean Tavoularis). Its end date is more problematic, since the notion of auteurism as an ideology has hardly ceased. Directors' names are still used to promote films. And yet clearly we are no longer in a period of directorial dominance. For the sake of simplicity, I consider the "The Auteur Renaissance" to have ended with the financial failure of Michael Cimino's *Heaven's Gate* (1980, prod. des. Tambi Larsen), mainly because, rightly or wrongly, the director's profligate arrogance was blamed for the film's failure. Alarms sounded across Hollywood about the need to "manage" directors in ways that would have been unthinkable even five years earlier.

Auteurism

Why was auteurism able to have such an impact on production and popular conceptions of the medium? And why was that impact so strong in the United States in the 1970s? To understand the relationship between designers, directors, and cinematographers in that decade, or, indeed, to understand why such a relationship is important in discussing the period at all, we should briefly revisit the theory.

There are arguably not one but three "auteurisms." The first, formulated by François Truffaut and his associates at *Cahiers du cinéma* in the 1950s, extolled Hollywood production for the ability it gave directors to use purely cinematic (i.e., visual) devices to tell stories.[1] Truffaut contrasted this approach with the literary prejudices of the French so-called "tradition of quality." And yet, ironically, by referring to the journal's writers' favorite directors as "auteurs," Truffaut introduced a contradiction within auteurism that has never fully been reconciled between the literary connotation of the label and the anti-literary bias of the initial theory. If you wish to discuss visual style, for example, why not posit a "*Politique des Peintures*"?

The *Cahiers* formulation of auteurism was the starting point for an American critic, Andrew Sarris, to domesticate the argument into the so-called "auteur theory."[2] Sarris, like Truffaut, was interested in raising the stature and reputation of Hollywood directors based largely on their technical skill. At the same time, however, Sarris reintroduced literary consideration by stressing that consistent visual style was not enough to make a director an "auteur" by itself, that his or her films (though almost always his) must exhibit repeated thematic interests for him to be included in Sarris's infamous "Pantheon."

In short, with Sarris's help, literary expression returned through the back door. As Pauline Kael pointed out in her rebuttal of the theory, however, Sarris's formulation made it virtually impossible for a writer-director to attain auteur status because there was no "tension" between the imagery and the script.[3] While that observation was trenchant, Kael herself eventually evolved into an auteurist in all but name and, like most auteurists, skirted the question of the relationship between literary content and visual style. That failure to address this central concern is important, given the disproportionate influence Kael and Sarris exercised in film criticism at the time.

It is arguably this reductionist definition of auteurism that influenced the third form of the theory, which underpinned the film school educations of many American directors who rose to prominence in the 1970s.[4] This third form of auteurism assumed that because the director is the most important person in a film production, his or her vision would shape the final result much more than the script. If the director has a strong enough personality, a distinctive style would eventually emerge. Questions concerning the origins of content are secondary, as the "tension" between visual and literary expression was once again elided and ignored to concentrate on personality. What remains as a legacy of the various formulations of auteurism was the idea that the director's first form of expression would be visual, even if he or she also wrote the script. This emphasis was as true for directors without a film school education, but perhaps was more pronounced and important for those with degrees in production, such as Francis Ford Coppola or Martin Scorsese. As a result of this prejudice in favor of visual expression, technicians like the cinematographer and designer increased in production importance, but rarely in critical recognition or discussion.

The Look of a Film

One of the first consequences of the incorporation of auteurist theory into popular criticism was the attribution of visual style to the director. If you accept the idea that the director is the most important person in the creation of a film's form, it is logical to assume that the director is as responsible for the look as he or she is for the actors' performances. When discussing the work of directors whose work demonstrates a consistent visual style, regardless of their collaborators, such an assumption makes sense. The work of an Alfred Hitchcock or a Max Ophuls has much more in common visually with other films by those directors than it does with work done by their cinematographers or designers or others, for example.

The problem arises in assuming such control over visual style for all directors. It is as if the rise of directors obscured any awareness of those who help achieve the visual style accredited to them. David Thomson's article "The Art of the Art Director: Designing the Film" appeared in *American Film* in February 1977 and was one of the rare efforts to credit the art director's role in the creation of mise-en-scène. Thomson confronted the myth of the director's sole responsibility head on, opening his discussion of art direction with reference to a film directed by one of the most revered of classical era auteurs, Howard Hawks, *The Big Sleep* (1946, art dirs. Carl Jules Weyl, Max Parker). The passage could well have been written by an enthusiast praising Hawks's visual style, but Thomson goes on to say:

> This account of the first ten minutes of *The Big Sleep* could fit a celebration of Howard Hawks. As director of the movie, he stands to receive

> credit for its structure, its effect overall and in detail, and every facet of its appearance. I have been describing the film Hawks made, or organized, but I have concentrated on what is called "art direction" or more inclusively, "production design." Although we are accustomed to identifying the contributions of photographers and composers, it is unusual to see intelligent praise or blame leveled at the art director.[5]

With auteurism's increased emphasis on the image, we would expect the contributions of visual technicians like cinematographers and designers to rise to prominence, but recognition such as Thomson's was rare.[6] Some prominent cinematographers, such as Vittorio Storaro, John Alcott, Nestor Almendros, Gordon Willis, Vilmos Zsigmond, and others did become almost as famous as the directors (Bernardo Bertolucci, Stanley Kubrick, Terrence Malick, Francis Ford Coppola, and Robert Altman, respectively) with whom they worked. And yet their equivalents in the design profession, people like Richard Sylbert, Dean Tavoularis, Ferdinando Scarfiotti, Leon Ericksen, or Polly Platt, rarely received as much attention, despite the fact that they often contributed as much to the looks of the projects on which they worked as the cinematographers. Even when offering an overview of the decade in 1975, Axel Madsen could refer to the "key people in the crew," including the sound recordist and property master, but *not* the art director/production designer.[7] This omission is all the more glaring when one considers that Madsen was writing after the success of such design-intensive films as *The Godfather, A Clockwork Orange, Cabaret*, and *Barry Lyndon*, not to mention European contributions such as *Red Desert, Blow-up, Juliet of the Spirits, Doctor Zhivago, The Conformist*, and countless others.

Indeed, in the same issue of *American Film* in which Thomson's article appeared, veteran art director Harry Horner described his collaboration with classical era directors, and made a peculiar plea:

> Early in my designing life I was confronted with a problem: Directors or producers expected me to be a background illustrator. . . . But the designer should not be confined to a previously conceived idea. Sometimes an idea is so firm in the mind of the director that he will say, 'I must have it this way because otherwise it just doesn't work with my concept.'
>
> These things should come out of exchanges. Directors should have the strength of self-protection, but they cannot, unfortunately, work alone on a movie. . . . He might as well take advantage of the possibilities offered by a person who thinks in visual terms.[8]

Horner's comments suggest that the designer is often unnecessarily subjugated by directors. But not just directors. When critical recognition of subsidiary contributors does occur, often the praise given to cinematographers should really

1: The set design in *Hugo* (Martin Scorsese, 2011, prod. des. Dante Ferretti, art dir. David Warren, set dec. Francesca Lo Schiavo) depended greatly on computer-generated imagery (CGI).

2: The visual look of the biopic *Klimt* (Raoul Ruiz, 2006, prod. des. Rudolph Czettel, Katharina Wöpperman, set dec. Georg Resetschnig), with its use of abstract superimposition and gilt makeup, mimics the painter's style

3: Bagdad, as seen from the palace in *The Thief of Bagdad*, realized in a “Maxfield Parrish blue.” (Raoul Walsh, 1924, art. dir. William Cameron Menzies)

4: The Phantom in *Phantom of the Opera* (Rupert Julian, 1925, prod. des. Ben Carré, art dir. Charles D. Hall, Elmer Sheeley, set dec. Russell A. Gausman) ominously poised atop a statue on the roof of the Paris Opera.

5: Interior of Reata with Luz confronting Leslie. Frame enlargement from *Giant.* (George Stevens, 1956, prod. des. Boris Leven)

6: Mexican town of Vientecito. Frame enlargement from *Giant.*

7: *Barry Lyndon*'s (Stanley Kubrick, 1975, prod. des. Ken Adam, art dir. Roy Walker) painterly past.

8: The messy pastiche of film noir conventions in *Farewell, My Lovely* (Dick Richards, 1975,

9: In *Dick Tracy*, Universal's generic back lot is saturated with funny pages red, yellow, green, and blue (Warren Beatty, 1990, prod. des. Richard Sylbert, Touchstone).

MAYOR

10: Black-and-white diner deco clashes with riotously colorful cubism in *Pleasantville* (Gary Ross, 1998, prod. des. Jeannine Oppewall, New Line).

11: A steel mill was digitally "ruined" by CGI for this shot from *Atonement* (Joe Wright, 2007,

be credited to the designer. This situation results from a basic misunderstanding of the role of both technicians. While the responsibilities can overlap and vary considerably from one project to another, the distinction between the two professions can be grossly defined as the difference between the look of *what* is photographed (the designer's role) and *how* it is photographed (the cinematographer's responsibility). Just as the qualities of a still photograph or a painting result from the interaction between subject and artist, the look of a film's physical world arises from the collaboration among director, cinematographer, and designer.

This confusion between the roles of director, director of photography, and designer can be attributed at least in part to the realistic image, its central role in cinematic expression, and the medium's power to persuade viewers temporarily that the events unfolding in front of them are "really" occurring. Put another way, a confusion between cinematography and design occurs because of the reality of the physical world that both manipulate in the service of narrative illusion. In that manipulation, the cinematographer has a greater opportunity for abstract expression because the designer must first and foremost convince viewers that the world photographed exists physically, whereas the cinematographer is largely dealing with the ineffable qualities of light.[9]

To step outside the auteurist period for a moment, consider the example of film noir, and the recognized importance of lighting to that genre. It is a cliché of noir that lighting setups should be dark, that much of the set will be in shadow, and that a considerable part of the impact of the scene will result from blatant, exaggerated lighting schemes. When characters stand in the horizontal stripes cast by lights through Venetian blinds, it is correct to attribute the effect to the director of photography. What is taken for granted is the presence of the blinds that provide the excuse for the opulent lighting setups. In other words, it is the designer's responsibility to provide something from the physical world that, when photographed, must convince for itself (the blinds must look like real blinds) and for the expressive purpose to which they are put by the director of photography (with both answering to a director visually sophisticated enough to say, "I want Venetian blinds in this scene in order to cast horizontal stripes").

In short, the designer must always present an object world that at least seems physically possible and plausible in its context. It is then up to the cinematographer to bring out the qualities of that physical world that will enhance its appearance. To make this observation is not to suggest that design can only be capital R "Realistic." In fact, to the extent that viewers are aware of film design at all, it is likelier to be in relation to more stylized genres such as fantasy, musicals, and science fiction than in more realistic ones such as melodrama or the crime film. The point is that even in the most stylized environments, the designer must deal with basic physical laws that cannot be ignored completely without running the risk of arousing the viewer's skepticism or amusement. In order to succeed, the cinematic illusion must occur in a physically consistent universe. In most cases, that means a material world superficially similar to the one we occupy; which means further that the design profession must always deal with the vexed issue of realism (which often makes their labor "invisible").

The Look of the Seventies

If a concern with physical reality and plausibility is central to cinematic expression and the designer's role generally, it was especially true in the cinema of the late 1960s and 1970s when emphasis on the director reached its peak. In *Hollywood's Last Golden Age: Politics, Society, and the Seventies Film in America*, Jonathan Kirshner asks rhetorically, "What, then, was the seventies film?"[10] After citing how many films of the period were morally ambiguous, character driven, and often politically motivated, he goes on to note:

> The seventies film, in its search for a more 'realistic' cinema, often had a characteristic visual style, one with a new emphasis on source lighting, location work, and in many ways 'worse' picture quality—less pristine and more often shaky, darker, filtered, or grainy—as well as a willingness to depart from 'invisible' editing that seamlessly matched images and adhered to standardized notions of continuity. In sum, with the stories chosen, their content and purpose, the way they were told, and their technical presentation, the seventies film was at odds with the political and technical conventions of the classical Hollywood studio system.[11]

Further, by emphasizing the interest in and influence of the French New Wave for many filmmakers of the era, Kirshner implies that a value was placed on individual, even idiosyncratic expression, on the presence of a recognizable directorial signature or voice. What, then, were the consequences of these assumptions for designers?

The first, most obvious observation is that an emphasis on realism makes it even less likely than usual that there will be much scenic stylization. If directors are going out of their way to provide the illusion that their stories are taking place in the "real world," and if they are reinforced in that goal by cinematographers using techniques selected for their roughness and lack of polish, in a specious equation of documentary surface with veracity, designers will not be encouraged to develop self-consciously formal or stylized settings. Quite the opposite, they will be likelier to err on the side of a forced realism, overemphasizing physical details that might otherwise be taken for granted, or perhaps not included at all. Even an outer-space-set science fiction film like John Carpenter's *Dark Star* (1974, prod. des. Dan O'Bannon), for example, wallows in a kind of fake naturalism, with the messes surrounding the astronauts reminding the viewer that even in space, human beings produce a lot of waste. It is as if the more dirt there is, the truer the vision of space, and thus the more authentic the representation. Similarly, the heavy literalism of the special effects in *The Exorcist* (William Friedkin, 1973, prod. des. Bill Malley), one of the most commercially successful films of the 1970s, seems calculated to prove to an audience that they are in the presence of the Devil because he has the ability to move heavy objects at will and otherwise distort the physical environment constructed at great effort and expense.

Kirshner links this realism to the political and cultural upheavals of the seventies, including an increase in crime and violence in America's cities. The heightened angst and paranoia made commercial success possible for those films that explored or exploited the world of urban decay. Films such as *The French Connection* (William Friedkin, 1971, art dir. Ben Kasazkow) or *Death Wish* (Michael Winner, 1974, prod. des. Robert Gundlach) or *Taxi Driver* (Martin Scorsese, 1976, art dir. Charles Rosen) unfold in down-at-the-heels environments that convince by immersing the viewer in a calculatedly unpleasant physical environment. While *Taxi Driver* may be the most relevant in an auteurist context because of the film school educations of both director Martin Scorsese and scenarist Paul Schrader, it offers only limited insight into this issue because of its virtually exclusively underclass settings. Art director Charles Rosen had to do little but select appropriate spaces and allow the decayed settings to speak for themselves. To have done otherwise would have worked against the film's nightmarish hysteria, since the rotting, hellish environment is at least partially responsible for Travis Bickle's (Robert De Niro) alienation.

A truly realist aesthetic has to move beyond naturalism's tendency to seek life's seedier details in order to explore the everyday with an eye that can recognize both the beautiful and the ugly. The results may prove just as unpleasant, but a realist does not choose the negative to make a point. He or she leaves the conclusions to the viewer. In this sense, the environments created by designer Robert Gundlach for the Charles Bronson vehicle *Death Wish* may be more exemplary, precisely because of the matter-of-fact lack of visual appeal. The film's infamous rape scene, which sets the plot of retributive vengeance in motion, takes place in an unassuming, middle-class New York apartment. The white-walled decor is, in a word, ugly, with the cinematographer's high-key lighting and wide-angle lens photography doing nothing to make it even remotely attractive. Unlike *Taxi Driver's* decrepit, crumbling interiors, the furniture in the apartment is arranged neatly, surfaces are clean, but the cumulative impression is of an overwhelming cheapness, vulgarity, and lack of style. (The protagonist, Paul Kersey, is a successful architect, so the generally shabby air cannot be attributed to his lack of education or financial means.) In short, in the effort to evoke the lived world of mid-1970s Manhattan, the design reveals ugliness and lack of distinction even among those whose ways of life would suggest the means for more appealing externals.

Death Wish provides a broadly realistic environment, thus fulfilling the classical Hollywood function of invisible design. The approach differs significantly from classical practice only in the use of location photography instead of studio sets. The tendency of American films to use unassertive physical environments was noted early on by Léon Barsacq. Discussing the decline of directors in Hollywood in the 1930s, Barsacq observed: "As directors became dethroned, the era of producers and businessmen began. Because the industrial methods introduced by the big Hollywood studios were incompatible with aesthetic experiment, American . . . film decor began to evolve mainly in the direction of a rather impersonal technical perfection."[12]

While Barsacq did not link that impersonality to the general American film emphasis on narrative, it is plausible to assume that once the more character-centered realism of the seventies became the norm, there would be a shift in design emphasis within realist parameters. In the classical realist model, physical environment does not call attention to itself. It is realistic to the extent that it reinforces the general milieu of the story, but impersonal in relation to individual characters. A character-oriented realism, on the other hand, while remaining plausible overall, is likelier to use elements of design that provide details about individuals that exceed narrative requirements. Thus, while unvarnished visions of mainstream contemporary American life can permeate action films from the auteurist era like *Death Wish*, they also shape environments more richly expressive of individual characters' lives.

The combination of realist characterization and contemporary decor is probably most evident in films directed by Robert Altman. The consistency of the realistic environments in his films is all the more striking given that the only designer with whom he worked repeatedly was Leon Ericksen, and with him almost exclusively on his most stylized films of the period (including *McCabe and Mrs. Miller* [1971], *Images* [1972], and *Quintet* [1979]). Many of Altman's contemporaneous films, including *Nashville* (1975), do not even credit a designer or art director. The absence of a designer, however, does not mean an absence of design, even if the filmmaker is consciously seeking a quasi-documentary look. That very choice guarantees a verism that at least convinces us that we are looking at events as they occur, as most spaces may take on a presence of their own almost in spite of the filmmaker's intentions.

Nashville makes a particularly striking example of the realist design illusion, both in the sense of convincing the viewer she is witnessing events as they occur, and in the metaphorical sense of a structuring myth. Shot largely on location in real bars, restaurants, clubs, homes, churches, and hotel rooms, the film also employs fluid cinematographic techniques, like zooms and frequent pans, that record the physical environment with the glancing objectivity of documentary filmmaking. The design of the space preexists, and seems largely to be a matter of selection with only a few details (such as posters for the "Replacement Party" candidate Hal Philip Walker) added to serve the story's requirements. Explicit stylization is largely a matter of costuming: the sequined, Elvis Presley–style leisure suit worn by Haven Hamilton (Henry Gibson) to signify his investment in glitz as a form of entertainment; the Bicycle Man's outlandish, oversized glasses and wide-brimmed straw hat to give Jeff Goldblum a visual presence that allows him to stand out without saying a word; the tight one-piece suit worn by Gwen Welles to emphasize that her character (Sueleen Gay) has only her body to offer; and so on. This reduction of the design principle to costuming can be seen as a logical end game for character-based narrative, for when character is all, what they wear is their most directly visual expression.

Nonetheless, even within these preexisting spaces, details are used expressively, less to advance the story than to add to a sense of texture and to externalize character specifics. For example, the hotel room occupied by Bill (Allan Nicholls) and Mary (Cristina Raines), a musical couple about to separate, is modern, functional, with blank white walls and furniture obviously purchased for economy. The room is the definition of impersonal. Indeed, precisely because it is a space whose occupants will constantly be changing, a hotel room cannot have a specific character presence, except when it begins to reflect the lives of the people renting it. So the filmmakers do not just show the impersonal room. Instead, Bill lies on his bed wearing nothing but a bathrobe; Mary, in the other bed, her back to Bill, wears only an oversized T-shirt. As Bill tries to get Mary to talk, a room service tray with dirty dishes sits prominently at the foot of his bed. Irritated, Mary gets out of her own bed and crosses over his (rather than walking on the floor), nearly pushing the tray off his bed in so doing (figure 23). The tray and the mess serve no narrative purpose. We see neither character eating. The details do, however, economically convey the characters' use of and familiarity with an otherwise impersonal space, grounding their actions in a bit of textural detail that is immediately convincing. In doing so, it vivifies the space, lending an otherwise dull,

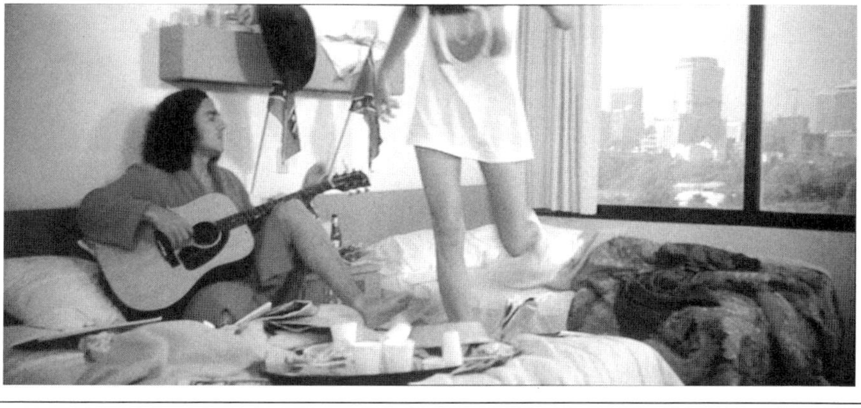

FIGURE 23: The impersonal/personal hotel room in *Nashville* (Robert Altman, 1975, art dept. and set dec. Robert M. Anderson) serves the realistic function of an impersonal hotel room while filled with details that silently demonstrate how the occupants use it.

routine room a lived presence. It also opens up the narrative imaginatively, since the refuse implies a meal before what we witness. The effect is to ground the moment in a resonant environment in which the narrative is just one thread in an ongoing, lived world.

A more explicit link between a character's life and her surroundings is provided by Sueleen's cluttered bedroom. Sueleen, a talentless waitress who aspires to musical stardom, lives amid a disorganized mess of personal details. Movie star photos hang on her walls (as does a crucifix, a not incidental detail given the sexual humiliation to which she is eventually subjected). The top of her dresser doesn't have a square inch of free space, piled with makeup, hair dryers, a goldfish bowl (!), religious kitsch, and a lava lamp. It is a mess, in other words, accentuated further by the fact that her closet is left open (again, without any narrative reason) so that several of her dresses and a nightgown hang out limply (figure 24). The cumulative effect is a pathetic image of a woman living in a fantasy world, incapable of recognizing her own lack of ability and yet also too sweet to be an object of fun. But it is a fantasy world built entirely on cheap quotidian detail that serves simultaneously as silent commentary *and* expression.

It is the accumulation of such details that adds up to the "design" of a film like *Nashville.* Real locations, barely dressed for the occasion, but selected for their resonance, slowly, quietly build an indictment of the depicted world, which, paradoxically, leads to the "myth" of realism. For as convincing as the milieu may have been in 1975, when *Nashville* was released, the passage of time renders these details as quaint and antique. It is not that people no longer live in cheap surroundings or no longer create messes in hotel rooms. But the very assertiveness of the details, after time, reads less as "real world" than "so seventies." In other words, time has the effect of rendering visible the very details and behaviors that initially were incorporated for their invisible tendency to reinforce the sense

FIGURE 24: The cluttered mess of Sueleen's bedroom in *Nashville* provides a wealth of information and insight into the woman's character.

of reality. In rising to prominence, these details begin to distance rather than involve the viewer by inviting recognition of the objects and the image as themselves, rather than as simple background. By so thoroughly evoking the time and place, the environment is eventually condemned to being patronized.

This is the paradox of datedness, and never more a problem than in those works that most successfully, if temporarily, convince the viewer that he is witnessing events. It is therefore interesting that when Altman embarked on period re-creation in *McCabe and Mrs. Miller*, he felt the need to work with a designer, Leon Ericksen. It is as if the director recognized that to achieve the realist effects of his contemporary films in a period setting, he would paradoxically have to resort to a form of stylization.

Like *Nashville, McCabe and Mrs. Miller* also uses the open frame form of composition, with the camera frequently panning and zooming to follow characters or emphasize details. And as with most of Altman's most famous work, the actors often improvise dialogue, thereby providing a strong sense of momentary presence. Even within these similarities, however, there are significant differences. Vilmos Zsigmond's cinematography, for example, is far more blatantly stylized, relying on heavy diffusion filters and reduced lighting to add to the moody texture. And because the era of the film (the late nineteenth century) and its setting (the Northwest frontier) are considerably less materially abundant than the present, there are fewer objects, with a more limited range of connotation, to express character. (For example, there are no automobiles to provide short cuts to tastes in expensive commodities, while the roughness of the frontier setting provides few opportunities even for wealthy characters to display their acquisitions.)

At the same time, Ericksen, in a far more consistent, even radical fashion, relies on "mess" as a trope of presence. The town of Presbyterian Church in which the story unfolds is constantly under construction. Very few buildings are complete (even the church that gives the town its name is only half done) and one of the few that is, Sheehan's bar and hotel, is a fetid, unpleasant hole in the wall. There is no pavement; people have to walk in the mud and slush, and plumbing is the nearest tree. As if to emphasize just how repellent the surroundings are, the film has an otherwise gratuitous scene in which the newly arrived McCabe is shown the hotel's sleeping quarters, a filthy congerie of rough wood, dirty sheets, and unwashed occupants in which you can practically smell the atmosphere. And while McCabe turns up his nose in disgust at the possibility of staying in Sheehan's hotel, it is only Mrs. Miller's greater attention to comfort and hygiene that eventually makes both of them successful business partners. Nonetheless, even at the peak of their success, the sets are shot in asymmetrical compositions, in half-completed rooms, frequently with out-of-focus details obscuring part of the frame, to emphasize the transitory, unkempt nature of the spaces. In short, the environment is foregrounded in an unusual fashion, becoming not so much a character as an active issue.

This combination of an abundance of period details with fluid camerawork, structured by an awareness that the era dramatized in *McCabe* was rougher than the present, works to create an immersive, momentarily convincing illusion of the past. Of course, filmmakers in the seventies did not invent historical verisimilitude, nor were they the first to recognize the importance of research in building convincing physical re-creations of past eras. What sets period design from the auteurist era apart from its predecessors was the recognition not so much of the superficial difference of period fashion as the difference in practical, everyday activity, of the way spaces in the past were used and lived. And one of the most obvious of these differences is dirt.

McCabe and Mrs. Miller is just one of many period films from the seventies to use dirt, sweat, blood, urine, excrement, sputum, and the daily activities surrounding them as active elements of design. The work of Sam Peckinpah, for example, would obviously be entirely different if he did not dwell obsessively on blood in his action sequences. The swashbuckling antiheroics of Richard Lester's *Musketeers* films (1973 and 1974, prod. des. Brian Eatwell) or *Royal Flash* (1975, prod. des. Terence Marsh) or *Robin and Marian* (1976, prod. des. Michael Stringer) revel in moments of physical pain and pleasure, actively supported by props and details in the images. Ridley Scott's first feature, *The Duellists* (1977, prod. des. Peter J. Hampton), drenches the characters in a wet, smoky physical environment, producing a profound sense of physical presence that exhausts the viewer as much as its dueling characters. Even as fastidious a period re-creation as *Barry Lyndon* (Stanley Kubrick, 1975, prod. des. Ken Adam) includes narratively inconsequential scenes of shaving or vomiting or drunken excess. In short, in period films of the seventies, the human body becomes as much an object as a subject in the design, exploited by directors and designers alike to create a purely visceral identification in the viewer.

Barry Lyndon makes a useful counterexample to *McCabe and Mrs. Miller* because, aside from a similarly heavy reliance on zoom lens shots and diffusion, their photography and mise-en-scène are markedly different. While Altman, Ericksen, and Zsigmond work deliberately to create a messy environment to aid in producing the period illusion, Stanley Kubrick, cinematographer John Alcott, and production designer Ken Adam go to the opposite extreme, with each camera setup as deliberately composed as a painting. Certainly the details in *Lyndon* are as historically accurate as those in *McCabe*, perhaps more so, and as such are well within the realist goal of providing a plausible physical environment. The difference lies in the emphasis. In *McCabe*, the period details are a jumble, with very few registering individually. In *Lyndon*, the historical accuracy and assembly of details are featured, as emblems of the care going into the re-creation. The environment in *McCabe* is lived; that in *Lyndon* is displayed (color plate 7).

Altman and Ericksen create the past as a present. Kubrick and Adam evoke the pastness of the past. Rather than trying to place the viewer in the space, events are distanced. The effort to evoke eighteenth-century paintings by its very nature is an intellectual as much as a visual exercise. Realistic settings remain essential parts of the re-creation, but only in the sense of being archaeologically correct. The approach is closer to the classical model, except that by shooting in real spaces and period locations, the historical nature of the image can never be entirely avoided. The impersonality of classical period re-creation is replaced by the personal obsession of the director for the re-creation of a past moment, expressed either in settings extant from the period (such as Schloss Ludwigsburg in Germany or Castle Howard in England) or in evocations of art works associated with it.[13] One way to view this difference is to think of a Hollywood classical film set in the eighteenth century, say the MGM production of *Marie Antoinette* (W. S. Van Dyke, 1938). The art director Cedric Gibbons and the MGM art department went to great effort to get period details correct, but the fruits of their labors were invested in sets and costumes assembled on a soundstage in Southern California. For Kubrick, the accurate details achieve full resonance only when shot on location in images that reinforce the period setting through content and composition.

Taken to one extreme, this archaeological approach can result in a fetishism of antiques, and, as such, the beginning of the end of expressive realism in favor of cultural exploitation. One of the most blatant examples of this degeneration of the realist impulse is Jack Clayton's version of *The Great Gatsby* (1974, prod. des. John Box), which was promoted at least as much on the basis of its period fashions (designed by noted fashion designer Ralph Lauren), Gilded Age locations in Newport, Rhode Island, and excessive, expensive props and backgrounds as for any intrinsic merits.[14] At another extreme, cinematic re-creations of the past become pastiche. *Barry Lyndon* cannot imitate the filmmaking of an era when the technology did not exist, but the evocation of period paintings points in the direction of imitating surfaces to achieve period feel. Post-cinematic eras offer the seductive opportunity to use the medium effectively to imitate itself.

A film like *Chinatown* (Roman Polanski, 1974, prod. des. Richard Sylbert) offers a pivotal case at many levels. In design terms, it is squarely within the realist approach. Sylbert's environment is almost a textbook example of intelligent, unassertive art direction. Cars, clothes, and architecture are carefully designed or selected to evoke a recent past. They also are firmly linked to character. The literally chintzy stucco bungalow apartment of Ida Sessions (the faux Evelyn Mulwray), for example, is light years from the rich, manicured home of the real woman (Faye Dunaway). Jake Gittes's (Jack Nicholson) own one-bedroom apartment, seen only briefly, is almost bereft of personal detail, as if any kind of home life were alien to his character. The office of Water and Power Company executive Yelburton is the image of solid respectability. Unlike in *The Great Gatsby* this accumulation of details is not emphasized. They work in quiet support.

And yet, as Peter Lev has observed about the film, *Chinatown*'s social critique and realist impulse have a dual edge, one in which events expose the evils of contemporary society, but where surfaces seduce. Describing the nihilistic despair at the end of the film, he notes: "Nothing can be done. . . . But this brings us back to the surface of *Chinatown*, to the pleasures of sight and sound and taste and sex. If action is futile, we are left with self-indulgent passivity of a stylish yet empty Los Angeles."[15] In short, even if Polanski and Sylbert did not intend to create an artifact of nostalgia, they did so unwittingly. The carefully constructed images of Art Deco–era Los Angeles have an innate appeal beyond the narrative content. The design may have been created as invisible support for a period film, but it acquires a presence in spite of itself because of its very success in re-creating the aura of a past *cinematic* age.

For the appeal of *Chinatown* rests in no small part on its evocation of classic detective fiction, as noted by Jonathan Kirshner. This is the key difference from other realist milieus, because *Chinatown*'s resonance depends on its antecedents, particularly the work of Dashiell Hammett and films (such as John Huston's *The Maltese Falcon*, 1941, art dir. Robert M. Haas) based on that literature. The filmmakers are no longer making a direct response to existing conditions, or even trying just to re-create those conditions. Thus the design cannot be truly invisible. Like everything else in the film, the design is layered, not innocent. It now serves three functions: minimal plausibility for the story, a collection of period-specific sets and artifacts that produce the illusion of period, *and* a meta-narrative of "thirties detective fiction" based on previous films.

This kind of meta-cinema reaches its most exaggerated form in *Farewell, My Lovely* (Dick Richards, 1975, prod. des. Dean Tavoularis), an adaption of a Raymond Chandler novel, previously filmed as *Murder, My Sweet* (Edward Dmytryk, 1944, art dirs. Carroll Clark and Albert S. D'Agostino) with Dick Powell. In design terms, *Farewell* takes the principle of realist period evocation to its furthest conclusion, by not just providing period-specific details, but by consciously evoking the look and feel of forties film noir at every level. Viewers are never allowed to forget they are watching something set in the 1940s, and not just because of the inevitable period costuming and cars. The voiceover narration interweaves the story with the baseball career of Joe DiMaggio. Advertisements for period products are plastered wherever they seem plausible. Soldiers and sailors are frequently visible in the background. And of course, every interior is dimly lit, with as many Venetian blinds as possible (color plate 8).

With this pastiche of noir conventions, the tendency of seventies design to objectify the characters as much as their environments achieves an unprecedented exaggeration by the casting of Robert Mitchum, himself a veteran of noir films, in the lead opposite Charlotte Rampling, whose resemblance to the young Lauren Bacall is exploited to the fullest. As a result, in *Farewell, My Lovely*, design permeates *everything*. The gentle balance of character-based realism tilts so that the people are no longer shaping the environments. The sets are defining the characters. This is particularly true of the overstuffed, filthy home of Jessie

Florian (Sylvia Miles), an alcoholic ex-actress who gives Marlowe some important information. Her home is so cluttered with trash that Marlowe can barely walk amid it without tripping. While it is too much to blame designers for a shift in tendency toward material overload, it is fair to suggest that as audiences' expectations began to shift, the heightened importance of the design profession was a sign of changing times.

Dean Tavoularis

The career of the designer of *Farewell, My Lovely*, Dean Tavoularis, is, in many ways, a yardstick of the evolution of his profession during the seventies. As Beverly Heisner has noted in her study of contemporary production design, Tavoularis is among the most successful and respected production designers in Hollywood.[16] He was a central participant in the New Hollywood, earning his first art director/designer credit for the seminal *Bonnie and Clyde*. In addition to working with Arthur Penn, he has collaborated with other leading directors, including Michelangelo Antonioni (on *Zabriskie Point*, 1970) and Wim Wenders (on *Hammett*, 1982). He is probably most famous, however, for his work with Francis Ford Coppola, including the three *Godfather* films (1972, 1974, and 1990), *The Conversation* (1974), and *Apocalypse Now* (1979). As Jonathan Kirshner has noted, "More than any other picture, Arthur Penn's *Bonnie and Clyde* (1967) heralded the arrival in America of a 'New Cinema.' . . . It was a big hit. *Bonnie and Clyde* not only made lots of money; it also resonated with the culture, even influencing fashion trends. Set in the past, the movie was nevertheless obviously aimed squarely at the big issues of the present; it reflected new sensibilities and sparked controversy for those reasons."[17]

As art director for *Bonnie and Clyde*, Tavoularis was responsible for the film's uncharacteristically gritty look. Working on a limited budget of $55,000,[18] he used locations for their evocative power, more or less creating a realistic environment as much out of necessity as from plan. There is nothing glamorous about any of the settings. Interiors are uniformly drab, the furniture cheap, decoration minimal. Given the fact that the Barrow gang is constantly on the move, there is little opportunity for them to affect spaces in a way that would express their character. The very emptiness of the settings becomes a form of character expression, for these are people with no lives beyond their bank robberies.

One of the few exceptions to this *lumpenproletariat* norm is the porch scene between undertaker Eugene Grizzard (Gene Wilder) and his date Velma Davis (Evans Evans). Every other home seen in the film is decrepit, poorly maintained, often with peeling gray or brown paint, broken windows, and torn screens. This house is freshly painted white, with a neatly tended yard, and, at the moment Grizzard realizes that someone is stealing his car, there is a brief flash of bright color as the camera catches a trellis laden with blooming red flowers. It is the kind of detail that is easy to overlook, but which subliminally sends a message of "middle class," or at least sufficient personal wealth to add a little color to their lives. This higher social standing is reinforced by the fact that the suit Grizzard wears fits him more closely than the clothes worn by Clyde and his brother, while the loose, more diaphanous dress worn by Davis is an entire class away from Bonnie's long skirts and beret.

At the same time, as Kirshner noted, the success of *Bonnie and Clyde* inspired fashion trends, and there is no denying that the lower-class clothing worn by Beatty and Dunaway has a rakish verve that contradicts the lower-depths realism of the rest of the design. It is not that their costuming is unbelievable as anything the real Bonnie and Clyde could have worn, only that when stars wear it, under carefully controlled conditions, what may have started as plausible detail acquires a life of its own. This tension between verism and stylishness is not unique to Tavoularis's work, as we have noted already, but it does seem to be a recurring pattern in much of his design, regardless of the director for whom he is working. (It should be noted in passing that costume designers often work independently of the production designer. In this case, the clothing was designed by Theodora Van Runkle.)

This tension is all the more apparent in Tavoularis's collaboration with Antonioni in *Zabriskie Point*. In at least its first forty-five minutes or so, *Zabriskie* has a rough, edgy, nearly documentary surface. In the first scene, for example, a political meeting of campus radicals, the camera pans, zooms, and cuts with all the spontaneity of documentary shooting. Later, when Mark (Mark Frechette) visits a campus in turmoil with the intention of shooting a cop, the camerawork follows the action with the confused, messy flux of an eyewitness record. And when Mark visits the industrial areas of Los Angeles, the hand-held camerawork, zooms, and abrupt cuts again produce a sense of documentary veracity, even as the sound track becomes more stylized.

FIGURE 25: The High Modern office in *Zabriskie Point* (Michelangelo Antonioni, 1970, prod. des. Dean Tavoularis, set dec. George R. Nelson) surrounds businessman Lee Allen (Rod Taylor) with the trappings of cold, hard-edged power.

Intercut with these documentary-like sequences, however, are obviously staged scenes in which Tavoularis's contributions as set designer are more apparent. Daria (Daria Halpern) is a temporary office worker who attracts the attention of the head of a real estate development company, Lee Allen (Rod Taylor). His offices are located in a Los Angeles skyscraper, designed in High Modern style, with cold granite surfaces, ample glass, and shiny metal structural details (figure 25). The calculated order of the settings and the way they are treated could not be further removed from the willful chaos of the scenes with Mark, but in both cases the characters are at the mercy of, if not controlled by, equally inhuman spaces.

When the action moves to the California desert, however, the visual style necessarily shifts and there are few opportunities for sets. The "design" in these sequences is largely a matter of selecting locations and deciding on how those spaces are shot and cut, although a few details suggest the designer's input. When a family touring the desert pulls up to an observation point overlooking Zabriskie Point, for example, the absurdity of their hitching a boat to their trailer as they drive in the desert is underlined by a camera move showing decals of where the family has toured. Or when a highway patrol car pulls up in a vaguely threatening manner to Daria, the single outhouse behind which Mark hides with a gun has no reason for being there except to be used in the scene. The details, in other words, while firmly grounded in realistic possibility, have a presence beyond their function—which is not entirely clear in any event.

In the film's famous concluding sequences, Tavoularis's contributions are critical. For not only must the showcase house in the desert fulfill its realistic function of being a believable model home in a high-end real estate development. It must also contribute to the expressive significance necessary for the final explosion of the house, shattered into a thousand details of consumer artifacts, to be more than a pretty pictorial conceit. In short, the set must *disgust* in a way that makes its destruction understandable, if not desirable.

Tavoularis achieves this revulsion through incongruity. In purely logical terms, nothing about the house should be there. In the middle of a desert, it has a swimming pool overflowing its edges with water from an underground spring. Cut into the side of a mountain, with no trees anywhere in sight, the interior decoration has an abundance of wooden fixtures and details. Defiantly Modern in architecture and conveniences, the decor is nonetheless in an egregiously false antique style, with a strangely nautical slant. (One of the most incongruous details is a ship's wheel used as a finial on a staircase.) The house cannot be defended even at the level of a necessary domicile, however elaborate, since it has been built on speculation. In purely rational terms, in other words, the house exists only as a grotesque monument to waste, technological arrogance, and the pursuit of wealth and needless development for their own sake.

Tavoularis's collaboration with Antonioni gave the designer the rare opportunity to work with a director for whom setting and architecture are central concerns. In the designer's most famous work, his collaboration with Francis Ford Coppola on the *Godfather* trilogy, he was working in the more familiar territory of narrative support and period re-creation. Which is not to suggest, however, that Tavoularis's contributions are any less important to the results. Quite the contrary, the look of the *Godfather* films is central to their impact, combining a simple but effective visual scheme with an understated period sensibility that strikes a perfect balance between realism and stylization. The overall design of the films was neatly captured by Pauline Kael in her review of the first installment in 1972: "The visual scheme is based on the most obvious life-and-death contrasts; the men meet and conduct their business in deep-toned, shuttered rooms, lighted by lamps even in the daytime, and the story moves back and forth between this hidden, nocturnal world and the sunshine that they share with the women and children" (figure 26).[19]

The simplicity of this contrast also provides a good example of a collaboration between director, designer, and cinematographer (Gordon Willis). The design concept may have been Tavoularis's or Coppola's or both, but in any event that visual concept (dark vs. light) becomes the structuring mechanism for future decisions. For the designer, this concept requires choices of materials (wood, heavy furniture) and colors (browns, blacks, and deep reds) for the interiors that will appear "dark" on screen. For the cinematographer, elements of the design (such as the shuttered windows) put restrictions on what kind of light can be used, how bright it should be relative to exteriors, whether it needs to be shaped in particular fashion, and so on. And in the case of any question, it is the director who makes the final determination. Tavoularis described this crucial relationship as an open, creative one: "He [Coppola] gives you a general direction. He

FIGURE 26: The contrast between light and dark in *The Godfather* (Francis Ford Coppola, 1972, prod. des. Dean Tavoularis, art dir. Warren Clymer, set dec. Philip Smith) expresses a simple but powerful contrast between the characters' good and bad activities.

describes how the idea is born. Then I move, comfortably, around the axis. Coppola gives you the freedom and opportunity to explore your potential."[20]

The *Godfather* films also provided Tavoularis with the further challenges of period design. As with his work on *Bonnie and Clyde*, some of the interiors are legacies from the period in which the story is set. Unlike *Bonnie and Clyde*, however, the characters in the *Godfather* films have the time and means to live in and affect the spaces they occupy, so that individual sets may provide a wealth of information about the people who control them, but without calling attention to themselves. As Kael further noted:

> The period details are there—a satin pillow, a modernistic apartment-house lobby, a child's pasted-together greeting to Grandpa—but Coppola doesn't turn the viewer into a guided tourist, told what to see. . . . Like Renoir, Coppola lets the spectator roam around in the images, lets a movie breathe, and this is extremely difficult in a period film, in which every detail must be carefully planted. But the details never look planted: you're a few minutes into the movie before you're fully conscious that it's set in the past.[21]

Leaving aside the problematic attribution of this achievement to the director rather than to the designer, Kael's comments ably convey how the first two *Godfather* films strike a balance between period re-creation and stylization. (The third, produced outside the timeframe of this discussion, is in any event considerably less successful in this regard.) That this need not be the case, even with as skilled a designer as Tavoularis, is ably attested by his work in *Farewell, My Lovely*, discussed above. Our awareness of design in that film demonstrates that a wealth of period detail is both too much and not enough. There must be a governing concept that guides the filmmakers in deciding which, if any, details should be emphasized. Or as Tavoularis himself expressed this issue in discussing *The Godfather*, "In a period film, detail is important. You can't just put a can of soup on the shelf—it has to be the right can of soup."[22]

While Tavoularis has gone on to design many films since the seventies, including more with Coppola, it is multiply appropriate to conclude this brief overview of his career with *Apocalypse Now*. It is not only the last film he designed during the period under discussion. It is also, because of its late entry, an example of where production design as a profession and big-budget filmmaking generally were to head in the coming years. The film also provides an excellent opportunity to deal with issues of realism and design's ambivalent relationship to that style.

For on the one hand, *Apocalypse Now* superficially offers an ultra-realistic depiction of the Vietnam War. Blood, explosions, and death are in ample abundance. The dialogue is over-ripe with expletives. The characters are (in what is also a generic convention of war films) a cross-section of American society, particularly American youth. The film was shot on location, in the Philippines, if not Vietnam, and great effort and expense were employed to give the viewer a sense of "being there" in the jungle while watching events.

At the same time, however, *Apocalypse Now* is anything but realistic. Instead of an objective examination of the situation, it provides a moral parable that unfolds in a series of incidents calculated to provide ever-deepening mystification and horror. While the lives of the soldiers in the film are presented in vivid detail, the story moves from the (exaggerated) reality of a modern, technological war to the bare conflict of "natives" fighting with spears. From a design perspective, this requires Tavoularis to work from the simple realism of a hotel room, a general's field headquarters, and the deck of a patrol boat, to the stylization of the ruins of an unnamed ancient civilization that provides no starting point for the "re-creation" of an architecture and era that never existed. In a word, the final set is a fantasy.

The challenges created by this situation are ably demonstrated by the sequences in the ruined temple. For, despite the huge set, we in fact see very little, and often what we do see is barely discernible in the rich shadows of Vittorio Storaro's cinematography. The first meeting between Willard (Martin Sheen) and Colonel Kurtz (Marlon Brando) is particularly murky, with Brando's head going in and out of shadows so deep that there is virtually no way to gauge his relationship to the space. Even the daytime exteriors are limited largely to Willard imprisoned in a bamboo cage, where we see little more of the surroundings than he does.

That Tavoularis is able to make what we do see of the ruins believable testifies to his ability to create plausible environments. They nonetheless have no grounding in anything other than a vague Southeast Asian exoticism. In other words, in the effort to continue a realistic physical environment, one that seems plausible in the narrative context, Tavoularis evokes a sense of the art and architecture of the Indochina region. Since the story is deliberately obscure about where, exactly, the action occurs (other than "Vietnam" in the broadest sense), however, the design cannot have the specificity of successful realist design. Moreover, since the film becomes increasingly stylized as it progresses, the final designs transcend realism to achieve a poetic, if not archaeologically correct, truth unique to the film. They have to provide the kind of resonance that the accumulation of details throughout *Zabriskie Point* gave to the house at the end.

To put the matter simply, the design of *Apocalypse Now*, lush, extravagant, and brilliant as it may be, does not know quite where it wants to go.[23] While that uncertainty can plausibly be attributed to a production that was notoriously out of control, it also is part of a turning point in Hollywood cinema. At the tail end of the Auteur Renaissance, design was beginning to take on a life of its own, as visual style evolved from being the sign of an artist with a distinctive worldview to being an end in itself.

Looking Forward—or Backward?

As a sub-discipline of an expensive industrial commodity, production design must please, or at least not get in the way of expectation. As such, designers must adhere to a set of standards that may differ in style, but not in the goal of providing physical environments that can be accepted as "real." During the late 1960s and 1970s, audience expectations included a more comprehensive realism beyond mere surface. As social attitudes began to change, however, the ambiguous, critical nature of realism became less commercially viable, as more escapist product began to dominate. This shift in consciousness did not affect production design's materialist foundation. In some ways, the designer's role became even more important as ever less realistic stories and characters relied on the physical realism of the settings to construct the narrative illusion. The most outlandish situation could be made acceptable if dressed sufficiently well. Furthermore, the stylish undercurrent that runs beneath all glossy, designed images has an innate appeal regardless of purpose. For this reason, as audiences sought greater escape and as films retreated from their previously serious explorations of character and action, physical surroundings rose to prominence. In the process, production design moved from service to an auteur to serving the commodity fetish.

5

THE NEW HOLLYWOOD, 1981–1999

J. D. Connor

By 1979, it seemed eminently possible that Hollywood could produce grittiness without grit—that the image and its profilmic origin could be clean yet still deeply marked by class differences. Patrizia von Brandenstein explained that when she made the "big jump" to designing *Breaking Away* (Peter Yates, 1979, Twentieth Century–Fox), she chose particularly monochrome interiors for budgetary and narrative reasons: "Close-valued colors are not as expensive to produce. Everything was washed and bleached. It kept the values close; it made the family less prosperous." Yet as she would discover, once the clean image was given any scale, it tended toward the monumental and the classical. For the famous quarry swimming scenes, she decided to have the walls sandblasted to remove the moss and layers of graffiti that generations of locals had left behind. The results were stunning (figure 27). "The image of a Roman bath, that pristine quality, was something we brought to it by sandblasting the whole quarry, which was quite an undertaking. We used pontoon boats and we sandblasted the walls of the quarry. We heaped up tremendous boulders, stacked them up, and cleaned everything so it was as clear as possible. The sand acted like a filter: as it settled to the bottom of the quarry, it cleaned the water so it had that sparkling blue quality."[1]

Breaking Away is deeply embedded in the landscape and institutions of Bloomington, Indiana. In this university town, a group of aimless townies have

FIGURE 27: The "Roman bath" of the sandblasted quarry in *Breaking Away* (Peter Yates, 1979, art dir. Patrizia von Brandenstein, Twentieth Century–Fox).

been left behind by American deindustrialization, debarred from the usual routes of class advancement—higher education—by cultural and economic forces as ironic as they are irrefutable. As Dave's dad Ray (Paul Dooley) explains to him on a night walk through the university campus, "I cut the stone for this building. . . . I was damn proud of my work. And the buildings went up. When they were finished, the damnedest thing happened. It was like the buildings was too good for us. Nobody told us that, just—just felt uncomfortable, that's all. Even now I'd like to be able to stroll through the campus and look at the limestone, but I just feel out of place." He asks whether Dave and his friends still swim in the quarries, and muses, "So the only thing you got to show for my twenty years of work is the holes we left behind." With the quarry walls cleaned up, the "hole" now matches the pristine walls of the campus buildings, and the kids' furtive attempts at self-assertion through graffiti give way to a classical purity. For former star quarterback Mike (Dennis Quaid), the blankness of the quarry walls allows him to wallow in a particularly athletic nostalgia. The quarry is a Roman bath, a ruin generations in the making.

The contrasts between Mike's professional failure and von Brandenstein's success capture and condense a much longer transformation in American labor. The film suggests that football—here, the midcentury industrial sport—gives way to cycling—a more individualist team sport, one coded as European, less masculine, and corporate-sponsored—just as industrial labor has given way to the sort of cultural facility possessed by Dave Stoller (Dennis Christopher) and von Brandenstein. At the same time, the film also makes clear just how much labor is still involved in these new, neoliberal forms. Dave pushes himself to the limit training and he encounters resistance at home (his father), while von Brandenstein struggled for years against the union gatekeepers who prevented her from making the transition to art director.[2] Once she had made her "big jump," she was nominated for an Academy Award as part of the *Ragtime* (Milos Forman, 1981, Dino De Laurentiis/Paramount) team two years later and won for *Amadeus* (Milos Forman, 1984, Saul Zaentz/Orion). That her work was so immediately recognizable as among the best in the industry, and was so immediately recognized, demonstrates the profession's structuring imbalance as the eighties began. The residual barriers to entry for new talents created the possibility for dramatic breakthroughs. Gone were the stable art departments and regular ladders to success they seemed to offer. In their place were new paths for individual achievement and new pressures and contingencies along those routes.

The new contours of the profession were shaped by the overarching economic and political forces of the moment. The art department might be organized according to older industrial models, but the processes, technologies, and contexts had changed decisively. Designers, individually and as a group, took note of these pressures and discussed them widely in trade publications and other sites of professional discourse. But if everyone in the biz knew that things had changed, did those changes show up on screen? Measuring the effects of the world of work in the designs themselves poses real difficulties. A host of other factors impinges on any transmission of economics to design. Crucially, there is the project's overall budget, which would seem to be so overwhelmingly the proximate cause of a film's look as to occlude any representation of some industry-wide trend. There are also genre demands (the rise of the action movie), culture-wide aesthetic swings (the preppy resurgence), technological demands (the rise of video and the need to "shoot for the box"), and individual hallmarks belonging to directors or other creative personnel.

How would one even begin to judge design? Here, the work of Charles and Mirella Jona Affron is essential. In *Sets in Motion*, the Affrons propose a hierarchy of design intensities that cuts across period and style. This hierarchy includes sets that perform the most basic function—denoting a space—as well as designs that amount to a form of narration in themselves—those sets that dominate the story world of a film. Their typology possesses a singular advantage for our purposes. On their account, the function of a given design depends on its intensity, which in turn depends on a proleptic reading of the script. From the beginning, the art director searches for what they call the film's "narrative imperatives." Assuming that "the reading of the décor is intended to be inseparable from the reading of the narrative," then those readings of the narrative that are "conventional" will require a conventional degree of design intensity; "unconventional" readings require higher intensity designs, and so on. This is almost a linear relationship. "The weight of the art direction in that reading [of the script] will vary . . . primarily in accord with the degree of design intensity applied to the décor."[3] We can judge designs based on the obtrusiveness they bring to the film's "narrative imperatives."

One difficulty with this model is that it presumes a rather overweening primacy of narrative, or at least the script. In practice such a privilege might be less problematic since it accords with typical Hollywood processes, where production designers read scripts as part of an initial budget breakdown and suggest location shifts and other cost-containment strategies. Yet if the Affrons' "set theory" assumes that design functions are narratively determined, narrative demands might not be the only pressures designers face. Hence the Affrons' turn in the final chapter of *Sets in Motion* to "Judgment and Prize." There they continue to press the narrative argument by contending that judgments by reviewers and critics are "most persuasive . . . when they integrate narrative and decorative functions"; and that the judgments of industry peers embodied in the Academy Awards celebrate "the nexus of art direction and narrative."[4] Yet the integrative reading the Affrons prize, following the collapse of the classical studios and during the period of studio reascension, is under sustained assault. There is no doubt that production designers in the eighties and nineties were valued for their ability to support film narratives through designs of the properly calibrated intensity, but they were also required to support what we might call the "career narratives" of their creative workers and the "franchise narratives" that might extend beyond a particular filmic incarnation. Budgetary efficiency, narrative sufficiency, and artistry were values that existed alongside recognizability and extendibility. Every set—like every script, performance, cut, or close-up—bears a potentially split address. It finds its role within the production it serves, the career it constitutes, and intellectual property it extends.

By reconfiguring design intensity as the product of a reading, the Affrons suggest that every set might be seen as a choice, but such readings need not be limited to the script. Each production, each set, might emerge as "legible" in ways beyond those privileged by the Affrons, and each set might be the result of a multivalent negotiation over the value of a set's obtrusiveness. In what follows, I want to isolate several contexts for the emergence of alternate legibilities. My assumption is that the sum of those eruptions of design will constitute both an outline of the situation of design in general and a map for further attempts to isolate its importance to the revivified Hollywood of the era.[5]

The Way It Is Now: Location Shopping and Self-Advertisement

On *Reds* (Warren Beatty, 1981, Paramount), Richard Sylbert retained much of the executive authority that had made him a plausible studio head in the mid-1970s. He was notoriously prickly to his crew, as Sylvia Townsend documents. Most notoriously, Sylbert sought and received sole credit for the design of the production's 144 sets. He did not submit art director Simon Holland's name for the Academy Award. Holland was incredulous. "I said, 'Dick, do you really have to do this?' and he said, 'It's the way it is now, kid.'"[6] Holland may have been slighted, but others who did not anticipate credit beyond their job title found a way to cater to Sylbert's need for control. Set decorator Michael Seirton (who *was* nominated) noted that if he showed excitement over a particular item, Sylbert "would discount it. But if Seirton ignored or played down the treasure, Sylbert, crediting himself for the great find, would appreciate it."[7] The flipside of this complex managerial dance was Sylbert's mastery of his relation with Beatty. The two of them joined forces in a campaign against what they regarded as excessive craft insistence. Beatty told Sylvia Townsend that he and Sylbert "coined the phrase, 'I'm here, too-ism'" to describe "a director or a production designer or a costume designer who wanted to be present on the screen and would do something either with a camera angle or use of a particular hat, or something that would distract from the theme or the story to this element."[8]

The anecdotes about Sylbert suggest that the upwelling of professional pressures ("the way it is now, kid") had reached a point where the management of those pressures on screen ("I'm here, too-ism") had become a principal task of key creative personnel. Aesthetically, only a sustained insistence on story values could hope to contain the overwhelming need for occupational validation on the part of the independent contractors assembled for the show.

As Max Horkheimer and Theodor Adorno had contended in 1944, "Today every close-up of a star is an advertisement for her name, and every hit song a plug for its tune. Advertising and the culture industry merge technically as well as economically."[9] By the 1980s, the danger was that every knick-knack would be an advertisement for the set decorator. Sylbert's on-set unpleasantness and his ability to ingratiate himself with directors such as Beatty, John Frankenheimer (*The Manchurian Candidate,* 1962, United Artists), and Brian De Palma (*The Bonfire of the Vanities,* 1990, Warner Bros.) should be seen less as a personal quirk and more as the embodiment of a particular strategy for aesthetic management.

Those baked-in conflicts were more likely because the department Sylbert was running was composed of British locals. When department heads are parachuted in to run productions outside Hollywood, there is invariably friction through culture clash, personality clash, or both. But in the cases of *Reds, Yentl* (Streisand, 1983, prod. des. Roy Walker, United Artists), and *Amadeus* we encounter a particularly consistent New Hollywood form: these historical dramas are shot in well-preserved locations well outside the usual industrial settings. The industry could then recognize them not only for their designs as such but also for their frisson of historical authenticity and organizational difficulty. Location scouting in search of lands time forgot had been essential to the Auteur Renaissance's Great Depression fascination in films such as *Bonnie and Clyde* (Arthur Penn, 1967, art dir. Dean Tavoularis, Warner Bros.), *Paper Moon* (Peter Bogdanovich, 1973, prod. des. Polly Platt, Paramount), and *Boxcar Bertha* (Martin Scorsese, 1972, art dir. David Nichols, AIP). As Michael Atkinson explained in *Sight and*

Sound, "The idyllic vision of the Depression captured in the 1970s had everything to do with economics. . . . In the Nixon years there were huge portions of the southern and midwestern US that hadn't changed appreciably in 40 years, having been left out of the post-war development loop by virtue of sheer poverty and neglect. Conveniently, if not coincidentally, these were the same states and regions that many of the gangster-era crooks used to prowl, giving film-makers ready-made locations that were both authentic and inexpensive."[10]

But where directors in that previous era were eager to put distance between themselves and studio oversight, in the eighties, the search for historically preserved locations gathered momentum with the gradual opening of Soviet bloc countries to outside filmmakers. The first efforts were fitful. For *Reds,* Beatty, Sylbert, and cinematographer Vittorio Storaro hoped to shoot in the USSR, but the Soviet authorities would not grant permission without script approval. For a figure who chafed under studio authority, political preclearance was intolerable, so the production shot exteriors in Finland (for St. Petersburg exteriors) and in Spain (the agitprop train), used interiors at Lancaster House (for the Winter Palace), and did studio work at Twickenham, in England. *Yentl* was shot in Prague and New York, *Amadeus* entirely in Czechoslovakia.

Late Soviet-era and emerging post-communist nations possessed an ideal combination of below-the-line talent (hung over from the state film industries), "fresh" locations, and a crying need for foreign exchange. As Forman put it, "Prague was absolutely ideal because thanks to Communist inefficiency, you know, the 18th century was untouched."[11] As liberalized markets took hold across Eastern Europe, legacy cultural institutions of all sorts became potential streams of income for states in various stages of traumatic privatization.[12]

For New Hollywood filmmakers, the prospect of authentic and inexpensive locations once again proved impossible to resist. At the same time, though, the novelty of these locations—of designing into "new" places—could become part of the film's marketing, to popular audiences and industrial colleagues alike. Finally, the prospect of making "something different" appealed to production designers who needed to create a recognizable career. So von Brandenstein was "honored" to work on *Amadeus* after the contemporary, working-class drama of *Silkwood* (Mike Nichols, 1983, Twentieth Century–Fox) because "I wanted to do something violently different." And she followed *Amadeus* with *Beat Street* (Stan Lathan, 1984, Orion), another contemporary film set in the hip-hop-and-graffiti-art world of New York, because "I wanted something to get me out of [*Amadeus*] so I wouldn't be stuck in the eighteenth century for the rest of my life."[13]

Von Brandenstein's trilogy of artist movies—*Amadeus, Beat Street,* and *A Chorus Line* (Richard Attenborough, 1985, Embassy/Polygram/Columbia)—are hardly the titles that come to mind when one thinks of the decade's "high concept" mainstream. But they do exemplify the porous relationship between narrative and style that, to the film scholar Justin Wyatt, seemed paradigmatic.

"In some cases the style of the productions seems to seep through onto the narrative; issues of style or image become crucial to the functioning of the characters and the development of the narrative. Consider, for example, the importance of style in performance to *Flashdance* [Adrian Lyne, 1983, prod. des. Charles Rosen, Paramount], style in aviation to *Top Gun* [Tony Scott, 1986, prod. des. John F. DeCuir Jr., Paramount], or personal style to *American Gigolo* [Paul Schrader, 1980, art dir. Ed Richardson, Paramount]. . . . Furthermore, the reliance on bold images in the films reinforces the extraction of these images from the film for the film's marketing and merchandising."[14] One might add to this list the marketing and merchandising of film's design professionals. In this, high concept and the heritage film share a commitment to intensity.

Wyatt's sense that these high-concept narratives are "more" about marketing and design than narrative has been criticized by David Bordwell, who contends that such films are still governed by classical canons of linear, causal storytelling. Here, our revised understanding of the Affrons' intensity scale is useful again. For if there is a cycle of films that, as Bordwell admits, "display bold music and slick visuals" and possess a "fashion-layout gloss," then we ought to recognize them as a trans-generic layer of design. And if the box office results of those films are not guaranteed—Bordwell highlights the relative success of "stylistically unprepossessing" films such as *9 to 5* (Colin Higgins, 1980, prod. des. Dean Mitzner, Twentieth Century–Fox) and *Terms of Endearment* (James L. Brooks, 1983, prod. des. Polly Platt, Paramount)—then we ought to be looking for other dimensions of success beyond box office. Wyatt, following critic Howard Kissel, sees the new emphasis on smooth surfaces and backlighting as a triumph of visual control: "Tony Scott's *The Hunger* [1983, MGM] is supposed to be about such themes as death, immortality, violence and love, but it's really about art direction."[15] Neither Kissel nor Wyatt credits production designer Brian Morris or art director Clinton Cavers, but that is likely because they assumed that Scott, like his brother Ridley or fellow Brit Adrian Lyne, was the prime mover behind his films' look. This was the first generation of advertising-trained, MTV-ified directors, and their art departments received less critical attention even when they were being recognized for their prepossessing "I'm here, too-ism."

A look at the Academy Awards for Art Direction/Set Decoration over the decade suggests an explanation. Between 1980, when Pierre Guffroy and Jack Stephens won for *Tess* (Roman Polanski, Columbia), and 1988, when Stuart Craig and Gerard James won for *Driving Miss Daisy* (Bruce Beresford, Warner Bros.), every winner was a historical costume drama. Thirty-six of the decade's fifty nominees were period films (or featured extensive period sequences), with the remainder divided between science fiction films and a handful of contemporary dramas (including Polly Platt's characteristically precise work on the "unprepossessing" *Terms of Endearment*). The run was broken only by Anton Furst's victory for *Batman* (Tim Burton, 1989, Warner Bros.). For the decade, then, industrial

FIGURE 28: Judd Nelson's Alec Newbary is the loneliest yuppie in the world, lost between his new Nikes and his giant Nike billboard in *St. Elmo's Fire* (Joel Schumacher, 1985, art dir. William Sandell, Columbia).

recognition all but required narratively justified, high-intensity design work in the context of a prestige picture. The only genre work that found any recognition at all was of similar intensity, yet the broad membership of the Academy apparently found it difficult to take seriously.

The exemplary case might be William Sandell, who designed or art-directed such crucial films as *St. Elmo's Fire* (Joel Schumacher, 1985, Columbia), *Robocop* (Paul Verhoeven, 1987, Orion), and *Total Recall* (Verhoeven, 1990, Carolco), but had to wait until 2003 to be nominated for an Academy Award, for *Master and Commander: The Far Side of the World* (Peter Weir, Twentieth Century–Fox). What the Brat Pack film shares with the two sci-fi movies is its commitment to intense branding. Take the giant Nike billboard that fills Judd Nelson and Ally Sheedy's loft (figure 28). At one level, the branded backdrop seems to be of a piece with the overarching use of larger-than-life images—a similarly scaled Billy Idol image in Demi Moore's apartment; a Coca-Cola machine that seems bigger than its customers. At another level, though, the population of the ad and the population of the film seem interchangeable. Producer Lauren Schuler described the assembly of the Brat Pack as a matter of design: "When we were casting the film, we looked for people that would 'go together,' so it looked as though they were friends."[16] So these Nike runners "go with" these yuppies. Their class origins might be stipulated in the script, but like the quarries of *Breaking Away,* they have been visually sandblasted. The results, though, are a peculiar sort of theatricality, in which a viewer is able to shift his attention from the character to the set without missing a beat—at least, director Joel Schumacher was:

> But it is always amazing that we get angriest at the people that we're supposed to be in love with. And I'm not wise enough to figure that one out. That's a great Nike billboard in the background. That was a great photograph of runners having come from a marathon in the rain. It was

> a particularly arresting image. And you know, photography is art. It's certainly not a hard sell for the product. I like the idea of a young couple not being able to afford art maybe getting a billboard from a junk heap or even tearing one down in the middle of the night, and using it as art in their loft.[17]

It would be difficult to find a more encapsulating registration of high concept's effects: the image is ready to be valued as art, or turned into narration, or used to sell something outside the film. Similarly outsized ads appear in Sandell's other films, usually with a cheekier affect attached to them, but nonetheless just as "legible" as the future worlds they populate.

Sandell was forced to wait for decades, but the trend toward "excessive" or intense contemporary settings was rewarded just a few years later. The stark distinctions between characters and set that were encouraged by backlighting and industrial settings and that encouraged extracinematic consumption were finally able to break through residual standards of design decorum when that constellation could be narratively and generically motivated by comic book source material. The grit-free, "immaculate" imagery of high concept inspired a new graphism, a tendency that only became more pronounced as the dramatic changes brought on by digital revolutions in production and post-production gathered force. *Batman,* which won the Oscar in 1989, is set in a contemporary Gotham, but it is a city that remains enveloped by Art Deco skyscrapers and clothes while it is crisscrossed by the Joker's boxy mid-sixties cars and toggle-switch gadgetry.[18] The resulting asynchronies add up to a world where major characters carry private temporalities with them. In contrast, Richard Sylbert's *Dick Tracy* (Warren Beatty, Touchstone), which won in 1990, gives us a version of cartoon deco that has swallowed up every character and spit them out in the limited color-palette of the Sunday funnies.

Sylbert had inherited the palette when he took over the role from Dean Tavoularis; he fought for his usual khaki backdrops; and he uncharacteristically asked his designer brother Paul for help. When the dust settled, though, Sylbert was able to take credit for the look he had resisted. And while Townsend paints Sylbert's success as ironic, a look at the film shows that irony was essential to that success.[19] The colors were severely restricted and announced their artificiality at every turn, yet Sylbert and Rick Simpson managed to populate the world with seemingly authentic objects—radios, crockery, furniture, cars—that did *not* seem arbitrary, that seemed to have been drawn from the world's largest warehouses of candy-colored commodities. At the same time, those commodities were rigorously de-branded. "A café was called 'Café' and a newspaper was the 'Daily Paper.'" Even the car grilles were redesigned: "The worst thing for a scene in *Dick Tracy* is for somebody to say, 'God, isn't that a beautiful Ford.'"[20] That mix of willful limitation and almost magical availability found its exterior equivalent in the exteriors on the Universal lot. Townsend notes that Sylbert considered the lot "the McDonald's of the motion picture business" and that the buildings on its New York and brownstone streets appealed to him because they were "totally generic. . . . Those buildings are not buildings; they're icons of certain kinds of architecture" (color plate 9).[21] They came, in other words, pre-interpreted: for Sylbert to use them was to acquiesce to very particular, willful limits, and yet however degenerate the buildings might be, they were available, almost magically. They carried a kind of ironic prolepsis with them, the mark of ready exploitability. That irony extended to *Dick Tracy*'s tie-ins as well. Like other Disney blockbusters of the era, the film was cross-promoted at McDonald's that summer. The red-and-yellow "*Dick Tracy*" logo fit all too well with McDonald's house colors. What the film managed to do was combine the raw appeal to the mass market—Disney, McDonald's, Madonna—with enough arty credibility to put it over with Academy voters—Sylbert, Storaro, and composer Stephen Sondheim.

For such pop-slumming to be effective, though, creative workers had to maintain their reputations across several motion pictures. So it is particularly striking but not surprising that the designers most identified with the cartoon deco at the end of the eighties paired their work on those nostalgia fests with films of a similarly intense, contemporary, financialized urban realism. (Furst, who died in 1991, is an exception.) Sylbert paired *Dick Tracy* with *Bonfire of the Vanities;* von Brandenstein swerved from *The Untouchables* (De Palma, 1987, Paramount) to *Working Girl* (Mike Nichols, 1988, Twentieth Century–Fox). Both *Bonfire* and *Working Girl* showed their designers bridging New York's class gulfs, following their protagonists down, or up, the economic ladder. Both of them relished the high-style domestic spaces that accompanied *Wall Street* (Oliver Stone, 1987, prod. des. Stephen Hendrickson, Twentieth Century–Fox) and the era's deal making. In the protagonist's apartment in *Bonfire,* for example, Sylbert's work aimed to "ignite the flames of greed and covetousness under people all over New York," as author Tom Wolfe put it. Julie Salamon, in her account of the making of the film, detailed the $350,000 spent furnishing this single set: "Richard Sylbert was amused by the studio's constant nattering about money. In his mind, the entire point was excess. . . . The walls were lacquered (four layers thick to achieve the right glow), the vases were Chinese, the chairs were Chippendale, the floors were parquet, and the couches were covered with flowery Mark Hampton prints. Sylbert had loaded chintz upon chintz, detail on detail . . . 'Anglophilia,' he said. 'It's a recipe, like a cookbook.'"[22] To pull it off, Sylbert had to be the authentic stylist, the one who knew Mark Hampton, Colefax & Fowler, and Aubusson carpets. When the elites mingled with hoi polloi, the display of marked class differences was not, in any of these cases, a *Breaking Away*–style exploration of the actualities of lives lived below the 1 percent. Instead, the realism (or fantasy) of the working-class spaces served to legitimize the protagonists' desire for escape. Yet however motivated these contemporary films might have been and however rigorously these designers managed their careers, they went industrially unrewarded: *Untouchables* was nominated, not *Working Girl; Dick Tracy,* not *Bonfire.* Stephen Hendrickson, who designed *Wall Street,* had to wait, like Sandell, until he was nominated by the Art Directors Guild and the Television Academy for his work on the Depression-set *Annie* miniseries (Rob Marshall, 1999, Disney).

Paratexts: The Making of Production Design

As unanchored individuals, designers were required to manage their careers along those axes that could be recognized industrially. But as members of creative collaborations in the new conglomerate era, they were also subject to forces that offered an opportunity for the reassembly of the social context of production. The Hollywood mode of production had shifted to what we might call collective "I'm here, too-ism." The manic, deal-driven, package-unit system of assembly threatened to undermine the overall coherence of every project. Each craft might take aim against those centrifugal forces, attempting to reassert Hollywood's more traditional values of coherence and causality.

Yet it would fall to design to offer a theory that might integrate story and style within the film, and that might bind a particular project to its downstream or synergistic incarnations. We can register that grand effort in two genres of design paratext: the making-of monograph (or DVD extra) and the theme park attraction. Both of these reach a peak in Rick Carter's work on *Jurassic Park* (Spielberg, 1993, Universal).

Mid-century roadshow audiences were often given elaborate pressbook-style souvenirs that touted the films' "surge and splendor," to use Vivian Sobchack's phrase.[23] These served as models for later, more complete "art-of-the-film" monographs, and they routinely made space for discussions of the elaborate settings and historical accuracy of the epics. By the late seventies, book-length treatments became increasingly common—in addition to *The Art of Star Wars* and *Superman,* there were books on *Heavy Metal, The Dark Crystal,* and *Tron.*[24] Such paratexts offered ample space for concept art, storyboards, and construction photos, introducing readers to the workings of the art department, and allowing them to see how a film made the transition from script to screen. As popular literature, such books nearly always gave the impression that the pathway was smooth, and that the below-the-line workers were laboring in service to the auteur's vision. However sanitized the vision of collaboration they offered, though, such books also publicized the work of increasingly independent production designers, art directors, and set decorators to the industry.

In *Production Culture,* John Thornton Caldwell had detailed the relentlessness with which contemporary craft workers self-market.[25] The forms that marketing takes are the products of the particular convergence of the overall industrial configuration and technologies of display. Today's designer websites with their digital sizzle reels are the evolved versions of eighties videotapes. The technologies of professional self-marketing, their extension and intensification, run in parallel with transformations in the modes of motion picture distribution. When videotapes were priced inexpensively for consumers in the mid-eighties, home video libraries became possible.[26] At the same time, the major studios acquired publishing companies and the U.S. bookselling industry saw the dramatic expansion of Barnes & Noble/B. Dalton and Borders/Waldenbooks.[27] The overall effect was an explosion of book titles to serve an audience more expert than ever.[28] Every superstore featured a row of oversized *art of* books along the top shelf of its Film & Media Studies section.

Despite the changes in media, however, the core of the production designer's self-presentation for both professional and popular audiences has remained what we might call the triptych of incarnation: first, there is the presentation of a particular draft version of an image—an elevation, a piece of concept art; then there is a scene of construction; finally, there is an image from the completed film—ideally a particularly striking moment—that demonstrates the deep interplay of setting and story, proving to the reader/audience/potential employer that the work of the designer has been essential to what seemed merely to be "the movie." On the page, the triptych usually spans the gutter; on a DVD extra, the editor makes liberal use of the fade. Both discourage the consideration of the design artifact as an independent expression (figure 29).

In the case of *Jurassic Park,* perhaps the most confidently self-conscious of its generation of blockbusters, the *Making of* book appears in the film itself, on

FIGURE 29: The development of the *Jurassic Park* visitors' center in Don Shay and Jody Duncan's book *The Making of Jurassic Park* (1993).

a shelf in the visitor's center dino-store. Surrounded by T-shirts and inflatables, the book seems to be a behind-the-scenes account of the making of the park, but its authors, Don Shay and Jody Duncan, are the real authors of the making of the film. Hollywood had long been able to acknowledge its own backstory on screen—consider Cary Grant's joke in *His Girl Friday* (Howard Hawks, 1940, art dir. Lionel Banks, Columbia) about Ralph Bellamy looking like "What's his name? Ralph Bellamy." The difference here is that the *Making of* book is part of a projective scenario of desire: it is buyable in a way that makes the audience want to buy it. This new mode of consumption forecasting eroded the paramountcy of the script as the anchor for a film's future and supplemented it with the transmedial timeline of a franchise.

The movie announces itself as a ride just as proleptically. Carter would work with Universal on the Jurassic Park ride even before the film was released; Spielberg had a legendary deal that gave him 2 percent of the park's gross.[29] It was a cliché that action movies had become rides. The cliché had several aspects: It referred to visceral mechanics of the plots, the regularity of the narrative arc, the attenuation of character, the lack of an anchor in contemporary reality, and so on. But at the peak of the neoclassical Hollywood era, the interchangeability of the film with its ride was an opportunity for further exploitation, not a sign of structural weakness. Rides must maintain the design integrity of the underlying property, but they usually do so without the resources of the cinematographer and editor, and in the context of a radically reduced narrative.

The revelation of design work in behind-the-scenes accounts and the extension of that work into rides show how paratexts form a professional surround to the core work of the production designer. But such instances required more sustained theorization than the winking self-acknowledgments in *Jurassic Park* could provide. To work through the new configuration, one might bear down more insistently on the nature of virtuality within the film. Many of *Jurassic Park*'s defining images do just that: the "Objects in mirror are closer than they appear" shot of the T. Rex, the projection of the letters in a DNA sequence onto the (virtual) head of a velociraptor, and the reflections of the velociraptors in the polished steel of the industrial kitchen. All of these images foreground the film's behind-the-scenes obsession with the perceptual reality of the new CGI characters.

Jurassic Park might put its reflections on franchise extension and the new digital modes of production at the center of its narrative and design, but only when the movies in general but not movies in particular became the center of the mediascape would there be a stable way of dealing with the era's pluralization of modes of attention. If making-of books, coverage on infotainment television programs, and extra features on videodiscs and DVDs provided new ways of focusing on design, the new media conglomerates required design extensions into other realms. In the classical era, art directors might move between theater, film, and television, but very few worked directly in consumer venues and products (the Disney team was the significant exception).[30] In the newly ramified entertainment industry of the nineties, design became a paradigm of synergy.

That self-reflection took two forms. In the first, new studio-based theme parks could convey the durability of movie properties as rides within a framework that made "the movies" the star. Disney opened Disney–MGM Studios in 1989; TimeWarner bought half its licensee Six Flags in 1990; Universal launched Universal Studios Orlando that same year; and Paramount bought a chain of parks in 1993 and rebranded them. The second major expression of the new blockbuster-centered entertainment universe was the restaurant chain Planet Hollywood. Writing in *Esquire,* Tad Friend captured the way "I'm here, too-ism" became marketing: "It sounds like one amazing project: you've got Arnold *Terminator* Schwarzenegger and Bruce *Die Hard* Willis, plus director John *Home Alone* Hughes, producer Keith *Sophie's Choice* Barish, designer Anton *Batman* Furst, and publicist Bobby *Dances with Wolves* Zarem. . . . If it walks like a movie, and quacks like a movie, it's usually a movie . . . but in this case it's a bunch of cool movie guys opening a restaurant where you can eat turkeyburgers and feel like cool movie guys."[31] The aim was, according to Furst, "a fun place for the jeans brigade, not upmarket or smart," but nevertheless an atmosphere where they could experience what Friend called "instant artifacts."[32] For such synthetic nostalgia to work, customers needed to do more than "remember where you were when you first saw *City Slickers.*"[33] They needed to know that the creation of *City Slickers* (Ron Underwood, 1991, prod. des. Lawrence G. Paull, Castle Rock/Columbia) required the deployment of just the sorts of artifacts that now adorned the walls. It was their ability to attend to and extract elements of the profilmic world that would anchor their desire to consume in the atmosphere of Furst's art direction. With Planet Hollywood, the odd theatricality that made movies product placements for themselves reached its peak.

"I Settled for Reality": Digital Drop-ins

Friend's sniping about Planet Hollywood assumes that the public's desire for faux authenticity is a bubble. The implied contrast, naturally enough, is the classical Hollywood star: "Like tulipomania and the South Sea Company, Planet Hollywood's success rides on a bubble of promotion. Bobby Zarem, the . . . publicist, is sitting surrounded by old Veronica Lake movie posters in his magpie's nest of an office." But here Friend is underestimating the New Hollywood's ability to rewrite the terms of its audiences' desires. For in the nineties, the office of the classical star was the production of desire that she could only fulfill through surrogates. Most of the way through *L.A. Confidential* (Curtis Hanson, 1997, art dir. Jeannine Oppewall, Warner Bros.), Detective Ed Exley (Guy Pearce) is still trying to figure out his partner, Bud White (Russell Crowe). He is particularly

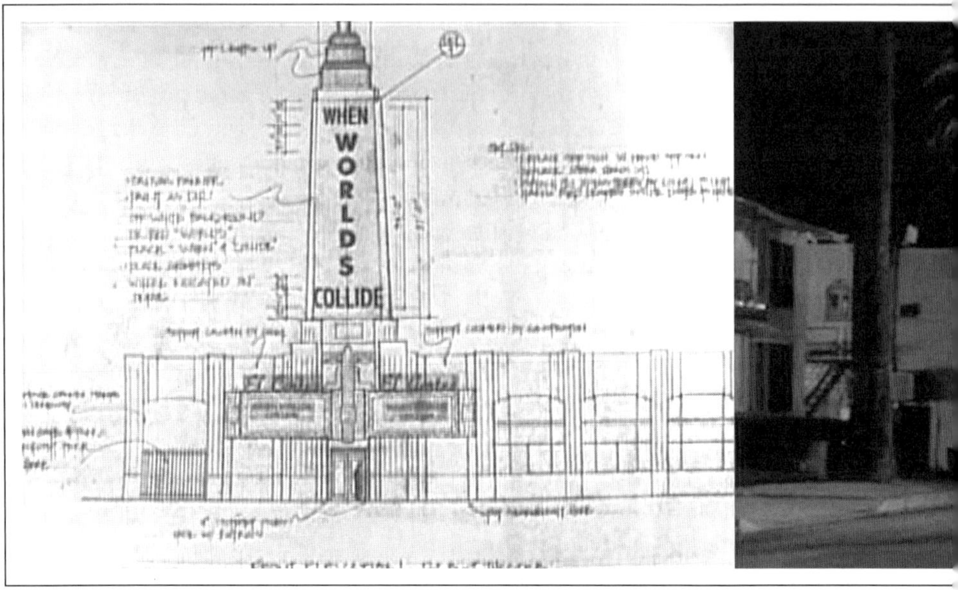

FIGURE 30: Sets in *L.A. Confidential* (Curtis Hanson, 1998, prod. des. Jeannine Oppewall, Warner Bros.) are part of the film's semiotic whirl. A DVD feature shows how the elevation for a movie theater set will form the set-like backdrop to the characters' discussion of blocking and photography.

confused by Bud's relationship with Lynn Bracken (Kim Basinger). Like a host of other women in the film, Lynn is a prostitute who has been made over to resemble a movie star—in her case, Veronica Lake—and boost her value in the sex trade. The others have been "cut" to order in a grimly embodied version of Hollywood's essential fakery, but Lynn has escaped the worst of it and come to terms with her status as ersatz star. As she puts it in the screenplay, "I came out here with a dream. That's gone, but I settled for reality." And the reality is that while she looks like Veronica Lake, she makes her living selling the false promise of sex with Veronica Lake. "Some reality," says Exley.

Given that whoever was to be cast in the film could not be surgically altered to more closely resemble Lake, the Lake effect would have to be carried by other aspects of the movie—by a film playing in the background, a glamor shot on the wall, and a production design in perfect sync with this laconic swirl of semiosis (figure 30). Sets in the movie look like sets, because they often are, because they are being used as part of complicated double-crosses. The Victory Motel is a too-perfectly noirish motor lodge. The TV-show-within-the-film, *Badge of Honor,* is less realistic than *Dragnet,* but between the faux-show and the prowling surveillance of *Hush-Hush* magazine, every location in Los Angeles is on the verge of becoming a set. Even the most functional location in the film, the Police Department offices, is not immune to this flat-ersatz affect, since the department is forever giving birth to new stars.

In keeping with the elevated position of design in the new industrial synergy, Hanson pitched the film to Warner Bros. by touting its look. He didn't play

up its film noir heritage, the sordid romanticism of James Ellroy's novel, or the complicated plotting. Instead, he flipped through a deck of period postcards and images, selling the studio on the desirability of *L.A. Confidential*'s look. In the Affrons' account, productions are designed to provide a backstop for narratives that precede them. But for *L.A. Confidential,* the narrative is a narrative of design and imposture that is unthinkable outside the design of its realization. And it would be the studio's desire to possess that look that would encourage them to settle for the reality of *L.A. Confidential.*

Lynn Bracken looks like Veronica Lake—that's her new reality—but that perceptual duplication makes her one of a host of mid-nineties "drop-in" characters. She joins the title character in *Forrest Gump* (Robert Zemeckis, 1994, prod. des. Rick Carter, Paramount), Buddy Holly (*Pulp Fiction* [Quentin Tarantino, 1994, prod. des. David Wasco, Miramax]), the kids in *Pleasantville* (Gary Ross, 1998, prod. des. Jeannine Oppewall, New Line), and, perhaps, *Jurassic Park*'s T. Rex. The convergence of professional, industrial, and cultural factors resulted in the design of sets that could serve as backing for these drop-in characters. The extractability of filmic elements and the heightened attention to design provided the formal principles that would underlie the profession as it came to terms with the technological changes of the early CGI era. Only in an era where the tenuousness of the real had become a real problem again could "settling for reality" carry the utopian romanticism it possesses in *L.A. Confidential.*

Here Carter's career is illustrative. He had been a mainstream, blockbuster production designer in the eighties. His involvement with computer-generated design begins with work on *Amazing Stories* (Spielberg, 1985–86, Amblin/

Universal) and carries over to *Jurassic Park,* a film where CGI characters came to the fore. That pathway continues through *Forrest Gump,* in which historical settings and historical footage were combined through digital compositing; to *The Polar Express* (Zemeckis, 2004, Castle Rock/Warner Bros.), in which motion capture allowed for the inversion of the usual temporal relationship between set design and performance; and eventually to *Avatar* (James Cameron, 2009, Twentieth Century–Fox) and *Sucker Punch* (Zack Snyder, 2011, Warner Bros.).

What Carter's career illustrates is precisely the importance of career in the industry's management of technological change. When a new technology is being brought to bear for the first time, the combination of industrial risk aversion, open contracting, and actor-networks reduces the scope of the novelty, and that, in turn, allows the particular film to constitute a display of technological novelty and not a wholesale renovation in the mode of production. This may seem to be merely a fancy way of saying, "When there are millions of dollars at stake, hire people you know you can trust," but the point of my formulation is to foreground the changes that were necessary to make such conventional wisdom conventional. Production designers are hired both because they are known to directors who exercise a degree of creative control and because they are known to be good at "this sort" of film, where "this sort" can mean a genre, or a scale, or the level of realism or insistence that the project entails. The greater reliance on digital technologies in both production and post-production threatened to undermine many of the accepted hierarchies and timelines of design. At each step along that way, production designers were evaluated according to the new calculus, and were chosen based on their ability to "fit" the new arrangements.

But Carter's career path is not simply guided by his own comfort with shifting technological and labor arrangements and his reliability as the manager of very large budgets. There is, even within this set of professional constraints, ample room for, and unrelenting demand for, a personal style. As a disciple of Richard Sylbert, Carter designs sets that are replete, if generally less ironically so. Yet where Sylbert's individuals—Bennett Marco, John Reed, Dick Tracy—exist in spaces that seem to have been projected by the characters, Carter's heroes exist in spaces those characters have bought, inherited, or somehow put together, largely off the rack. The grand visitors hall in Jurassic Park is a "temple for dinosaurs" that looks like the Dome of the Rock, but it also, and crucially, looks like a visitors hall.[34] The great doors to the *Jurassic Park* ride in the film look like the doors to Kong Island—Jeff Goldblum's character will ask, "What have they got in there, King Kong?"—but they also look like the-doors-to-a-theme-park-that-wants-to-look-like-Kong-Island. Part of why this easy referentiality matters is that it tracks a particular aesthetic commitment, or a difference of belief. When Marco reads a book, that is Marco's book—he just happened to have to buy it. But in Carter's world, that commodity status never rubs off. His privileged position designing for

Spielberg and Bob Zemeckis meant that Carter was not required to do product placement work, but the essentially commoditized spaces of these films exist in a world where design has been intensified so that the buyability of the object has come to the fore. Drop-in products and drop-in characters are equally at home.

Still, in the nineties, the mastery of design in the context of new technologies was not enough to persuade Academy voters—Jeannine Oppewall and Jay Hart were nominated for *Pleasantville* but lost to *Shakespeare in Love;* Dennis Gassner and Richard L. Johnson were not even nominated for *The Truman Show* (Peter Weir, 1998, Paramount). Like Sylbert before him, Dennis Gassner would win an Academy Award for his work with Warren Beatty, in this case on *Bugsy* (Beatty, 1991, TriStar). And like Sylbert, he paired his historical work (*Barton Fink* [Joel Coen, 1991, Working Title/Twentieth Century–Fox], *Road to Perdition* [Sam Mendes, 2002, DreamWorks/Twentieth Century–Fox]) with contemporary designs for films such as *The Grifters* (Stephen Frears, 1990, Miramax) and *Hero* (Frears, 1992, Columbia). Still, his most intensive designs in this period were for *The Truman Show.*

In *The Truman Show,* the digital revolution that began with characters and effects began to spill over into the design process. On *Dick Tracy,* Sylbert and Harold Michelson sketched fifty-seven mattes to be painted on glass, a technique not much altered from Michelson's work with Hitchcock in the 1960s.[35] But on *Truman,* Gassner designed several buildings using CAD (figure 31). As Craig Barron of Matte World explained, Gassner could then "decide what should be built as a set, so then he would give plans to the construction people to build, say, the first story of the buildings and then we [computer animators] had those

FIGURE 31: The "tradigital" world of downtown Seahaven Island in *The Truman Show* combined practical construction with CGI upper floors. Both relied on the same set of architectural plans developed in CAD (Peter Weir, 1998, prod. des. Dennis Gassner, Paramount).

same plans and we would bring into our computer and start to texture and add more detail to the computer graphics solution."[36] There were still large-scale paintings, such as the sky-and-cloud cyclorama that Truman's boat punctures at the film's conclusion. But single-story office buildings were extended via digital mattes, and the gargantuan dome that encased Sea Haven was an entirely digital creation. Because the initial plans were digital, they became the logically prior design document, and, as a consequence, the authority of the production designer could be maintained.

In the 1980s, depictions of class ascendancy and high finance were the logical career complement to historical work. A decade later, a cycle of quasi-contemporary films insisted upon their artificiality. Instead of a concern with class—however theatricalized—these new films were drawn to questions of their own ontological status. Such explicit interrogations were cued by both the sets themselves—like *Dick Tracy, Pleasantville* shot important exteriors on a lot; *The Truman Show* repurposed a planned community as a mammoth practical set—and by characters' *recognition* of the artificiality of the sets within the narrative (color plate 10). At those moments, the stranger-in-a-strange-land became a figure for the audience coming face-to-face with a newly legible design. The drop-in character allowed a film to explore the digital turn through narrative, whether that was the narrative of an older form, like the network sitcom in *Pleasantville,* or an emergent, and implicitly digital form, like the 24/7 reality television of *The Truman Show.* Whatever form the film world took, the drop-in character had to stand out from it, and that extraction required a world of sufficient design intensity that it could be reacted to. The professionally precarious production designer required the same.

Coda: We're Here, Too-ism: The Art Directors Guild

The Affrons established the usefulness of awards as a metric for industrial recognition, and I have attempted to carry that analysis forward into the New Hollywood era. As they demonstrate, in the studio era, there was a marked concentration of awards in particular genres—historical dramas—and a paucity of awards in some of the "lower" genres such as horror or the gangster film. And while MGM and Twentieth Century–Fox received a disproportionate share of nominations, so did prestige independents such as United Artists and Samuel Goldwyn. In the 1980s and 1990s, that genre concentration was, if anything, more pronounced: only one contemporary film won, and that was *Batman* in 1989. The Academy overwhelmingly nominated and awarded period films of one form or another. Only 21 of the 105 nominees might be classified as contemporary films and, of those, most centered on worlds of extreme stylization (*William Shakespeare's Romeo + Juliet, How the Grinch Stole Christmas,*

Addams Family Values, Batman, The Birdcage, Babe, Hook, Men in Black, What Dreams May Come, Toys) or were substantially set in the past (*Interview with the Vampire, Terms of Endearment, Titanic, Forrest Gump*).[37] The studio/indie balance was also comparable: twelve winners were distributed by major studios, nine by indies. Similarly, the consistencies across nominations and the concentration of winners are comparable to those the Affrons found: 45 of the 105 Art Direction nominees were nominated for Best Cinematography; 43 were nominated for Best Picture; 36 were nominated for Best Director. Two-thirds or more of the winners in each category were nominated in Art Direction. Half the time the Art Direction winner won one of the other three; a third of the time it swept them all.[38]

Individual production designers might be able to balance their work in an effort to maintain their status as valued below-the-line employees, but, as I have shown, no level of aesthetic achievement could bust through the impregnable wall of industry judgment. In response, the Society of Motion Picture and Television Art Directors (IATSE Local 876) launched its own awards in 1996. The new awards coincided with a thoroughgoing change in guild leadership and an intensification of self-promotion. As Jack Da Govia reported in the inaugural issue of guild publication *Trace:* "Shock and strong feelings greeted the results of the recent officers election of Local 876: an indication of its importance. The membership sent a powerful message to the leadership, as real and undeniable as a cow in church."[39] Alongside the awards, the guild launched a website and a lively journal, planned a film series and gallery exhibits, considered purchasing a building, and debated the relative merits of simplifying their unwieldy name. The drive for "prestige and respect" was on.[40] Scott Roth, hired as executive director in 1997, pursued a twofold strategy. On the one hand, he vigorously defended the art director's power. Mired in a budgeting fracas with Local 44, he was adamant: "Jurisdiction is the lifeblood of any labor union. Surrender even one part of it, and the whole of the union may be lost. Eternal vigilance in such matters is essential." On the other hand, he wanted to model the art directors' campaign for respect on the success of the American Society of Cinematographers. "There are seminars, conferences, and conventions at which the cinematographers and other creative guilds have a presence: we should always be there too. . . . We need something like *Visions of Light,* the documentary the cinematographers made, and a journal of production design like the *American Cinematographer.*"[41] Eventually, the rechristened Art Directors Guild would have all these things.

Yet despite these efforts, the field of recognized films did not markedly expand.[42] Given that the Academy nominees originate with the design branch members, it is not surprising that seventeen of the twenty-five ADG nominees were also nominated by the Academy or that three of the five ADG winners won Oscars (all period films). The exceptions were *What Dreams May Come,* the

Guild's one contemporary/fantasy winner, and *Gladiator,* which lost to another historical epic, *Crouching Tiger, Hidden Dragon.* The only contemporary movie nominated by the Guild and overlooked by the Academy was *American Beauty,* a film that won five other Oscars. Finally, of the Guild nominees, no winners and only four nominees were women. The Academy, in contrast, nominated eighteen women over the same stretch, five of whom served as production designer, the other thirteen as set decorators. (For organizational reasons the ADG did not recognize set decorators until 2008.)

The campaign to diversify the films that might come to the Academy's attention had not succeeded. From the beginning there had been important voices in the Guild advocating multiple award categories. Tom T. Taylor wrote, "It seems counter-productive to have an elaborate and expensive awards process which recognizes only one example of excellence in Film and one in Television. Not only does that greatly limit our effort to win greater recognition and visibility in our industry, but I believe it is unfair to be so narrow." Instead, Taylor argued for splitting the award three ways in each medium. "Let's create an attitude of abundance rather than of lack."[43] In 2001, the ADG split its award in two, with "period or fantasy" on one side and "contemporary" on the other. According to Michael Baugh, the second award chair for the Guild and the editor of *Perspective,* the successor to *Trace* and the Guild's answer to *American Cinematographer,* "Contemporary films were separated out from Period/Fantasy based on the realization that a contemporary film would never, ever have a chance to win."[44] Baugh credits Guild publicist Murray Weissman for being "eager to involve more and more films and studios in the process," a process that continued when the Guild split "Period or Fantasy" into separate categories in 2006, arriving at Taylor's tripartite solution a decade after. The end of the New Hollywood era saw greater craft consciousness on the part of the Art Directors Guild, culminating in its move into new headquarters on Ventura Boulevard, a building they would later buy. The Guild's continuing efforts on behalf of its membership are an attempt to expand the visibility of the creative labor of design; whether such an expansion will benefit more than a select group of individuals remains an open question.

6

HOLLYWOOD'S DIGITAL BACKLOT, 2000–PRESENT

Stephen Prince

For the director Ben Affleck, the set designs in *Argo* (2012) had to be carefully articulated in ways that encouraged audiences to become immersed into the period of the Iranian hostage crisis in 1979. The film, which depicts the seizure of hostages from the U.S. embassy by Iran's Revolutionary Guards, has three main settings—Iran, Hollywood, and Washington, D.C. Each of these is rendered in persuasive period detail. Brief glimpses in the film of Iranians in the revolutionary Khomeini period munching Kentucky Fried Chicken at one of that chain's fast food outlets, for example, or the historical artifact of pneumatic tubing present in the offices of the State Department and CIA, were based significantly in period research and documentation.

Affleck regarded production design as a subliminal factor, affecting viewers' reception of a film in ways that are significant but go beyond what an audience consciously notices.

> I believe that audiences care about set decorating . . . they just don't know it. That's how you sink an audience into the reality of something, you know. That's why I photograph it really closely. That's why I incorporate

> it into the scene, because that's taking it from a movie to a real place. Because how we identify reality in our own minds is by the things that are very close to us, the things that are literally the set decoration of our lives. And the set decoration in movies has got to mirror that accuracy in order for the audience to get invested.[1]

The actor Ed Harris has appeared in numerous films since the 1970s and has directed two films, *Pollock* (2000), a biopic of Jackson Pollock, and a western, *Appaloosa* (2008). As someone who has worked in front of and behind the camera, he understands the depth and the nuances that the right set decorations bring to a film. "The more specific, the more detailed, the more authentic. . . . Everything makes a difference. You have to work less as an actor, the more specific things are around you."[2]

As Harris suggests, production design is an art of the specific, defining setting, character, and story through the articulation of sets, props, and costumes. Although digital filmmaking is now firmly ensconced as the norm in Hollywood, production design continues to operate within many of its familiar contexts and parameters. If one looks at the Academy Award winners for Production Design or Art Direction since 2000, one finds that, as in past decades, they are heavily weighted toward period films—films set in real historical periods, as in *Lincoln* (2012), or in fantasy realms, as in *The Lord of the Rings: The Return of the King* (2003). Moreover, as the remarks by Affleck and Harris demonstrate, sets remain of crucial importance to directors and actors, and the digital era has not altered this fact. Director David Fincher notes that digital filmmaking retains the importance of production design. "I do see a day where if you have to go back and do a re-shoot of a scene, you will have made high-resolution photographs of that set and you will be able to just go to a blue-screen stage and call it up. But you still will have had to have built it the first time."[3] Fincher's *Zodiac* (2007), *The Curious Case of Benjamin Button* (2008), and *The Social Network* (2010) are digitally intensive films, and yet, he insists, "sets are really important . . . almost more important for directors than actors."

Production requires sets or locations, and a production designer delegates tasks to an art director and to subsidiary staff. This hierarchy of labor has remained consistent in the digital era. As art director Sarah Horton (*The Bourne Supremacy* [2004], *V for Vendetta* [2005], *The International* [2009]) points out, the production designer helps to establish a film's visual identity and delegates the task of realizing this identity to the art director. "The Production Designer establishes a kind of visual scaffolding, defined by color, light, texture, and contrast in which I [as the art director] am free to operate. In discussions with the Production Designer, the Art Director is responsible for the construction of the sets and they can take many forms. It can be a set in the studio . . . it can be a location where shooting takes place" or a mixture of both.[4]

Sets and Props in Digital Moviemaking

Physical sets and props have maintained their place in production as the industry has transitioned to digital moviemaking. In large part, this has to do with the sense of reality that physical things convey. As Oscar-winning production designer Sarah Greenwood (*Pride and Prejudice* [2005], *Atonement* [2007], *Sherlock Holmes* [2009]) remarks, "I like tangible things. I like lighting, texture and atmosphere that the digital world doesn't have."[5] Doing the research and finding the right sets, props, and furnishings to characterize a film's story world and its characters remain as important today as they were in cinema's analog era.

The Help (2011) portrays the relationship between black maids and the white housewives they work for during the civil rights era of the early 1960s. To aid in visualizing this world, the production design team studied magazines, family photos, books, and home movies collected by people living in the Mississippi locations where the film was shot. Set decorator Rena DeAngelo noted, "The beauty of shooting this movie in Mississippi was that it was all there. I really thought I was going to be driving all over creation looking for all the dressing. But aside from the four trips we made to Memphis, we sourced much of it in the fantastic antique malls of Mississippi. Every one of them was a treasure trove of some aspect of Southern life." DeAngelo obtained access to a department store in Greenwood, Mississippi, that had been closed for thirty years. "It had all the display cases, shelving, mannequins, lighting fixtures, bolts of fabric, signs, hundreds of unopened boxes of blinds from 40 years ago, Christmas decorations and window displays. . . . That store was a gold mine."[6]

Even when a film's story takes place in a fantasy realm, the physicality of real props may be a prized asset for the production. J. J. Abrams, director of *Star Trek Into Darkness* (2013), points out, "Obviously, you can't do a movie called 'STAR TREK' and not have green screen elements, but one of the things we've

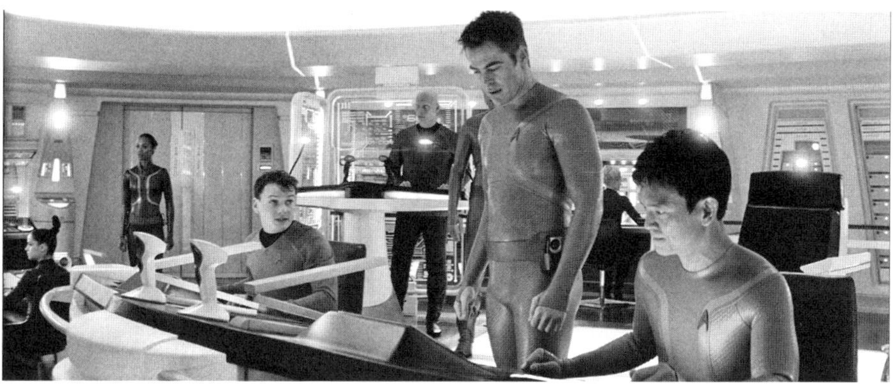

FIGURE 32: Although much in *Star Trek Into Darkness* (J. J. Abrams, 2013, art dir. Ramsey Avery, prod. des. Scott Chambliss, set dec. Karen Manthey) is achieved via digital compositing, the deck of the starship *Enterprise* was built as an extended, connected set in order to facilitate the actors' performances.

continued from the first movie is the idea of finding locations or building sets whenever we could to create a world that isn't synthetic or sterile, but feels very, very real."[7] The starship *Enterprise*, for example, was designed as a large, connected space in ways that would facilitate the actors' performances (figure 32). "We had the opportunity this time to build a set that was contiguous so that we were able to go from the Bridge down a hallway, into the Turbo Plaza area and go around a corner into the Med Bay," Abrams notes. "It gives the ship a sense not only of scale, which is a fun by-product, but a real sense of being interconnected." Set decorator Karen Manthey added: "I understand and believe in the importance of the set during the shoot as a world for the actors to inhabit. When we present a set to the director, the job of that set is to lead to an enhanced performance from the cast and crew, and with that, a better final product. That understanding has become a motivator for me in regard to working at the highest performance level possible."[8]

One of the extraordinary shots and scenes in contemporary cinema is the Dunkirk beach sequence in Joe Wright's *Atonement*, filmed as a single, extended five-and-a-half minute Steadicam shot. Dunkirk was a beach resort in France where the English army in World War II massed for an evacuation, and the filmmakers aimed to capture the surreal quality of wounded and dying soldiers huddled amid a seaside resort. Filming at the town of Redcar on the eastern coast of England, the filmmakers recruited 1,000 extras from town to populate the beach, costumed as English soldiers preparing for the evacuation. The camera prowls throughout an extensive location dressed with often-large sets that include a Ferris wheel, a gazebo bandstand, a tin barge beached on the sand, tents, jeeps, motorcycles, and buildings fronting the sea. In his review of the movie, Roger Ebert remarked that he could not tell if the sequence was CGI, and this ambiguity—is it real or not?—is a new factor at work in the reception of contemporary film, where much that may not be physically real nevertheless can seem to be so. Indeed, audiences might tend to think that the Dunkirk beach scene was created digitally because scenic design on this scale today often is a digital matter. Rather than being built on a large scale, they can be digitally augmented or extended (color plate 11). But in the case of *Atonement*, the beach settings were found and built but not digitally engineered. The sets were dressed and filmed in a traditional fashion, and Greenwood, who won an Oscar for the film, feels that the sequence is special because it was physically designed and staged as the viewer sees it. "If we were making it now, it probably would be CG and it stops being so incredible and amazing."[9] Had the background been a digital creation, it would have been shot differently, she maintains. Although the scene originally was planned to be a montage of discrete shots, the physicality of the sets, the light at golden hour, the ocean tide itself convinced Wright to film it as a single, extended shot (figure 33). It was the weight and the materiality of the location that influenced his shooting decision.

> If you knew that you were going to do it digitally, you'd have done something massive and bigger. Instead of having a thousand people on the beach, you'd have a hundred thousand. But having a hundred thousand CGI people on the beach doesn't make it better at all, actually. What made that shot work was the human drama, and the pain, and every little moment of that sequence told a story. And that was the combination of everything being there on that day, on that moment of the day, of Joe designing to shoot that way, the light and everything just happened to fall into place well. It could've been torrential rain and zero visibility, but if you'd not even attempted it and said that you'd do it in CGI, you would've ended up with a very different moment in the film.[10]

Greenwood speaks from a traditional perspective that values the physicality of real sets and props, and she may be correct in her observation that a digital lure for filmmakers often is toward ever more grandiose expressions. The software Massive enables crowd replications that, as its name suggests, easily facilitates what the film scholar Kristen Whissel has called "the digital multitude," the gigantic hordes seen in films like *The Lord of the Rings* trilogy.[11] And yet, while art director Sarah Horton finds that digital set extensions and augmentations are becoming more prevalent in cinema today, she points out that digital work often is tied to what a production design and set designer have accomplished with real objects and materials. "My own experience is that visual effects are often sourced from the built sets using and extending from the physical surfaces and lighting. It's much more difficult, time-consuming and expensive to start from nothing in the computer."[12] Thus, in an era of digital filmmaking, the physicality of real sets

FIGURE 33: The Dunkirk beach evacuation from *Atonement* is shot in a single, extended take, with the camera exploring a massive location dressed with three-dimensional sets in a traditional fashion (Joe Wright, 2007, art. dir. Ian Bailie, prod. des. Sarah Greenwood, set. dec. Katie Spencer).

and props retains a significant place in Hollywood production. But, though it is significant, the built set or found location is not a prerequisite for production. Digital production design enables films to move far away from the physicality of settings. And that movement is where the striking developments in production design after the year 2000 frequently are found.

Digital Imaging

The most significant trend in Hollywood production design in the new millennium is tied directly to the diffusion of digital imaging tools. This trend is a return to the tradition of back-lot filmmaking, which had been the standard industry practice during the classical studio period. As its name suggests, back-lot filming enabled the studios to make movies using studio properties rather than going on location for production. Errol Flynn, for example, fought the Japanese in World War II in Raoul Walsh's *Objective, Burma!* (1945) not in Southeast Asia, where the story is set, but on Warner Bros. soundstages. Another Flynn epic, *The Sea Hawk* (1940), was a dry-dock picture. Nothing was shot at sea for its story about sixteenth-century naval warfare between England and Spain. All of its seafaring scenes were filmed in a state-of-the-art studio tank so big that it could accommodate full-scale models of period warships and with a painted muslin cyclorama to represent the sky.

In these earlier decades, movie characters interacted in front of rear-projected backgrounds that represented beaches, foreign locales, or the traveling landscape visible outside an automobile window. While there were some exceptions—John Ford shot many of his westerns on location in Monument Valley—the dominant studio practice was to synthesize a location using partial sets, miniature models, matte paintings, rear projection, and composites achieved on the optical printer. During the 1950s, as the classical production system entered a period of crisis, filmmakers began moving outside of the studios to shoot on actual physical locations. *On the Waterfront* (1954) provides a powerful example of what can be achieved by the skillful integration of authentic locales into the aesthetic design of a film. As the studios declined during the 1950s and into the 1960s, location filming increasingly became a normative practice for filmmakers who wanted to eschew the conventions of studio filmmaking. The shift seemed so widespread and permanent that many studios shut down their matte painting departments. The movies that today are known as the American New Wave exemplified the virtues of location work. When Dennis Hopper took a 16mm camera and loaded it with a fast, grainy stock to film Mardi Gras for a sequence in *Easy Rider* (1969), it amounted to an artistic manifesto rejecting the studio tradition of simulated landscapes and highly polished image-making. The documentary-like patina of realism in *The French Connection* (1971) is due in significant part to its canny use of Manhattan streets and the ways that cinematographer Owen Roizman captured them using the available ambient lighting conditions.

As location work succeeded the simulated landscapes of the classical studio period, it came to be seen as a method of achieving greater realism or authenticity in a film. At a minimum, the changeover ushered in a kind of rivalry between what Charles Affron and Mirella Jona Affron called "the advocates of constructed sets and the partisans of real streets and buildings."[13] While each option remains available to filmmakers today, the digital revolution has revived and reinvigorated the back-lot tradition of simulated screen environments. This is because digital imaging has provided filmmakers with a more extensive and effective set of tools for envisioning locations and for making them seem credible within the terms of a given film's story world. While *Star Wars* (1977) was not a digital film, its tremendous success pointed to the future. George Lucas loved matte paintings and the entire tradition of artificial locations that they enabled, and his enthusiastic embrace of visual effects and built environments, coupled with the popular response to the movie, helped to make this tradition real and vital once again. And then Lucas helped lead the industry into its digital future.

These developments were synergistic, one reinforcing the other, because production design in the studio era had always been about more than placing live actors on sets and filming the scripted scenes. Key to understanding production design in the back-lot tradition is recognizing that the sets and the depicted environments to which they pointed tended to be radically incomplete. They were completed when conjoined in a final composite with other image elements that were created separately. When Anthony Keane (Gregory Peck) walked into Hindley Hall in *The Paradine Case* (1948), the actor was filmed on a minimalist set consisting of a floor, a doorway, and a wall, and matte paintings were composited with the live-action footage to extend the set and create the visual impression of a sumptuous mansion. Matte paintings often worked in this fashion to extend and complete partial sets, as did miniature models, especially hanging foreground miniatures that were positioned between the camera and the live-action elements. When Scarlett O'Hara returns to Tara in *Gone with the Wind* (1939) to find it empty and desolate, she enters the mansion house and its staircase and upper floors are a foreground miniature.

Narrative cinema has been an art of the fragment. Shots provide viewers with partial views of the action, and production designers in the back-lot tradition build only what will be seen by the camera, and even that is frequently incomplete at the point of live-action filming. Composite shots blend live action with hanging miniatures, matte paintings, and process photography, making production design about more than sets. The built environment for a feature film consists of the physical sets and props as well as various kinds of composited imagery that extend, elaborate, and fill in what has not been built directly for live action. If all of this is done well, viewers will experience screen spaces that seem holistic and contiguous rather than as the disconnected fragments that they truly are.

Digital imaging has not changed this tradition but, in fact, has intensified it because digital composites can be more seamless and subliminal than photochemical composites achieved on an optical printer and because digital imaging has transformed some of the traditional tools of production design, making them more malleable and articulate than they could be in the analog tradition.

Consider matte paintings, for example. During the era of analog cinema, these were 2D paintings used to extend backgrounds or other portions of a screen environment, and they were composited with live action in post-production. In general, cameras were locked down when filming shots that would have matte paintings added to them because the resulting motion parallax created by camera movement would reveal the painting to be a 2D element and one that was not as far from the camera as its depicted landscape was meant to be in the story world. Introduced in the 1950s, motion control camerawork enabled panning shots to be synchronized on a production camera and a process camera so that a pan executed live on set with actors could be replicated on the matte painting that would later be composited into the shot. But, in general, throughout the era of analog cinema, matte paintings were static, two-dimensional elements that constrained what a filmmaker might do with the camera in shots where they appeared.

The famous pull-back in *Gone with the Wind* is designed to appear as a crane shot. It shows Scarlett O'Hara (Vivien Leigh) and her father (Thomas Mitchell) as silhouettes standing beside a tree, with the mansion of Tara in the distance. The shot composites live action (stand-ins for Leigh and Mitchell playing the characters), a miniature model (the tree), a matte painting of a stormy sky, and a matte painting of Tara. Registration among these elements is less than perfect; they jiggle noticeably when the pull-back begins. The simulated camera move is produced on the optical printer as a zoom-out effect, and the 2D nature of the matte paintings is apparent because there is no motion perspective accompanying what is meant to appear as a camera move.

Digital Environmental Design

In the digital era, matte paintings are dynamic, three-dimensional components of a composited environment. When the actor Mark Ruffalo, playing a police detective, walks down a digitally augmented San Francisco street in *Zodiac*, the urban environment glimpsed at the end of the street is a matte painting, and as the moving camera follows Ruffalo, the matte painting is animated with the motion perspective produced by the hand-held camera (the process is called matchmoving). It undergoes the same kinds of transformations as near-ground objects. The motion control camerawork creates an organic bond between painting and real environment, providing the coordinates that enable the matchmover and the compositor to blend the two as an imperceptible illusion. As this example demonstrates, digital matte paintings exhibit depth, dimensionality, and the perspective changes produced by a moving camera. To the extent that it is interactive with other scenic elements or characters in the frame, a digital matte painting is not a discrete and separable component in the composited scene, as it was in the old analog days. As Craig Barron, the co-founder of Matte World Digital and the co-author of *The Invisible Art*, the authoritative history of matte painting, states, "It is difficult to categorize what a matte painting shot is today. . . . Most filmmakers still call what we do matte shots, and we like that because we see our work as an extension of the original craft. But, it's more accurate to say we are involved in environment creation."[14]

As Barron suggests, matte paintings today are subsets of digital environment creation, and I would suggest that production design itself increasingly is understood as a form of digital environment creation since even pictures shot on real locations will undergo digital image processing in their final stages of production. Accordingly an art director and a virtual art director will collaborate on a production, one handling built sets and the other handling their virtual counterparts.

A digital matte painter works with electronic brush and paints using programs such as Autodesk Maya and Adobe Photoshop. These programs transformed the nature of matte painting. Photoshop, marketed by Adobe in 1990, enabled filmmakers to paint over visible matte lines, blending and blurring image elements, changing pixel information to create perfect matches between different image types. Photoshop integrates well with Maya as part of an image production pipeline, enabling efficient creation and animation of matte paintings. The digital environments that are part of contemporary production design frequently begin life as a concept sketch that can be directly imported into Maya, where an artist can construct the scene geometry onto which a matte painting will be projected. This geometry is a set of primitive cubes and cylinders, constructed of polygons (the building blocks of digital geometry), that will underlie the buildings, streets, signage, cliffs, bluffs, mountains, or whatever other scenic elements may be involved. Maya provides a toolset that facilitates the warping and extrusion of polygons so that they can be extended across the location as sketched. In doing so, the artist constructs the scene's three-dimensional information. The geometry is constructed according to a camera projection that has been preset. This projection establishes the camera's view of the scene in terms of lens focal length, depth of field, camera position, aspect ratio, and camera movement. Maya also permits the creation of lighting and color effects, so that painting can be done during the scene building stage. Directional lights can be established to create shadows and highlights and various compositing passes can be executed. These can include an occlusion pass (to calculate which objects are obscured by other objects according to the camera projection), a specular pass (calculating highlights according to viewing angle and light sources), Z-depth pass (calculating object distances from the camera, essential information for animating scenes with lots of activity), and alpha channel-passes (establishing degrees of translucency and opacity in scenic elements). (Digital compositing is a multi-pass process. Each pass renders discrete types of information, and rendering is the process of converting the 3D computer information into a 2D image suitable for cinema viewing.)

If there is to be a camera move on the painting without a live-action plate, this can be key-framed in Maya as an animated move across scene geometry. If the painting will be composited with a live-action plate that was filmed with a camera move, then the move can be motion-tracked with a matchmoving program and imported into Maya or a compositing program like Shake or Fusion for final render. Maya can save all this information as a PSD file, which is a proprietary Photoshop format, for use in that program. The matte painting will be created in Photoshop, and the artist can import the render information from Maya, which will convey an abundance of lighting and color information. The painter can lift textures from photographs or from miniature models and can clone or tile this information in order to build the matte painting.

In *Cowboys and Aliens* (2011), for example, the alien spaceship appears as a huge tower looming above the desert floor. In many shots the tower was a miniature model. In others, it was a matte painting, and the painting was textured with photographic information derived from the model. *The Lord of the Rings* trilogy featured numerous matte paintings establishing distant vistas, and these were textured with photographic information derived from New Zealand's skies and mountains. The opening shot of *Changeling* (2009) is a crane from the skyline of Los Angeles, circa 1928 (the period setting of the story), to the wooded neighborhood street where Christine (Angelina Jolie), the principal character, lives. The skyline is a camera-projected matte painting animated with a panning shot that is matchmoved to a live-action camera craning down to a suburban street on a San Dimas location. The transition from the matte painting to live action is finessed with some digitally animated trees composited into the shot to hide the join between the painting and the location. As these examples suggest, matte paintings today incorporate numerous image types as well as animation and live-action perspectives. In this sense, they are more than "paintings" and, arguably, they are more important than ever to cinema now that it has entered its digital era.

Roland Emmerich's *Anonymous* (2011) exemplifies the capabilities and artistry of digital environmental design. The setting is the Elizabethan era, and the story recounts an alternative version of accepted history in which Shakespeare is a witless lout fronting for the true author. Most of the film's numerous exterior shots were filmed with actors before greenscreen. (Greenscreen or, alternatively, bluescreen enables the efficient extraction of live-action elements from the colored background so that they may be composited with digital sets, landscapes, or characters.) Many of the exterior locations appearing in the film were digital

FIGURE 34: Many of the exterior locations in *Anonymous* (Roland Emmerich, 2013, art dir. Stephan Gessler, prod. des. Sebastian Krawinkel, set dec. Simon Boucherie) were digital creations into which the actors were composited after being filmed on greenscreen.

creations, and the actors were inserted into these with very convincing results. Only a few shots betray their origins as digital composites (figure 34).

The exteriors were created by drawing on several sources of documentation. One of the film's producers traveled throughout England shooting photographs of surviving sixteenth- and seventeenth-century buildings. Using a Canon 5D camera, a high-end DSLR capable of shooting images at 4K resolution, he compiled a visual record of period architecture consisting of some 50,000 photographs. These were used in several ways. They provided information about the structural characteristics of buildings in that period that the effects artists used in constructing the digital buildings that appear in the film. The photographs revealed that the building materials were often warped and asymmetrical. Visual effects supervisor Marc Weigert said, "I'd always assumed that old buildings like that had started out straight, and had then become crooked through the years. But they were actually built that way, with weirdly crooked timber beams and so on. So we built the houses accurately, with squared lines; and then we went through and warped them and otherwise modified them to make them crooked. It was important that they not look symmetrical . . . and that was a daily fight in dealing with computer models."[15] Indeed, the polygons that underlie digital 3D geometry are plane surfaces enclosed by straight lines. Computer modeling thus has a built-in bias toward symmetry and hard, clean edges, and the artistry of digital modeling in cinema often consists of finding ways of overcoming the computer's preference for symmetrical perfection. Things often need to be roughened up and made dirtier. A "dirt pass" in rendering, for example, consists of adding environmental grime appropriate for the objects in a scene. The irregularities found in many natural forms need to be carefully emulated and added to the characters and humanly made objects in a digitally created scene in order to make it appear natural.

The *Anonymous* designers also used the photographs for photogrammetry (a method of mapping the camera's lines of sight across several images in order to recover the underlying dimensional structure of the pictured objects and their physical layouts). Photogrammetry enabled the film's effects artists to model the photographed buildings in three-dimensional computer space and to use these models for generating hundreds of buildings needed for wide views of London that the film would show. Ground floors, roofs, second stories—these were modeled in a modular and recombinant fashion in order to generate a city's worth of period buildings.

Photogrammetry is widely used in contemporary cinema when artists need to construct digital environments that are modeled on real locations or objects. One of the most audacious shots in David Fincher's *Zodiac* is an aerial flyover of the Port Authority Terminal in San Francisco. Since *Zodiac* is a period film dealing with the Zodiac killings in the late 1960s, the filmmakers could not go on location and simply film the Port Authority—too much had changed in the intervening years. The area no longer looked as it did in the period. The harbor as it appears in the flyover is an all-digital environment built from photogrammetric analysis of city blueprints of the area as well as photographs taken in the period by a U-2 spy plane. Lighting information was recovered as well from the period photographs, enabling the artists to animate shadows and highlights on buildings that were consistent with what would have been found in the late 1960s. The dimensional structure of a real scene can be recovered from even a small number of photographs, and textures from those photographs can be projected onto the digital environments according to the view established in the scene's camera projection. I described this as an audacious shot because the digital artistry is both flaunted and subliminal. The action in the shot takes place in bright daylight, and it's an establishing shot so it is held onscreen for some time. These conditions can be brutal for a digital artist because they can reveal the underlying architecture of the image, but in the case of *Zodiac* the digital environment has been modeled perfectly.

One of the scenic highlights of *Iron Man 4* (2013) is a helicopter attack on Tony Stark's (Robert Downey Jr.) mansion, built on the cliffs of Point Dume in Malibu. Zoning and property restrictions prevented the filmmakers from doing any filming in that area, so all of the exterior action is digitally constructed. (Interiors that show the mansion cracking and leaning from the rocket attack were filmed on sets mounted atop a gimbal, much as Chaplin had done to simulate a rocking ship nearly 100 years earlier in *The Immigrant* [1917], a parallel that demonstrates some of the essential continuities of filmic practice across analog and digital eras.) Unable to film on location, the visual effects house handling the sequence shot photographs at Point Dume and of surrounding buildings "to determine how much texture detail we would see at that time of day, how much the windows would reflect, what the sun did to the buildings over time, what the shadows looked like."[16] This information was incorporated into the sequence's digitally designed environment. The photographs also supplied the photogrammetric information that effects artists used to build a 3D computer model of Point Dume. The visual effects supervisor for the sequence pointed out, "There was no surveying required at all. It was all based off of photographic imagery."

Returning our discussion to *Anonymous*, location photography also provided the filmmakers with the materials needed for a camera move. In the film a dramatic camera move descends into Westminster Abbey during a funeral. Salisbury Cathedral doubled for the location. Several three-dimensional environments were constructed based on a high-angle digital photograph looking down into the cathedral, each environment corresponding to a portion of the image. The photograph was then projected onto the 3D environments and a virtual camera move connected the environments with appropriate parallax effects. The result onscreen was an impressive virtual camera move from the upper story of the cathedral down toward the funeral below. The method employed to construct this shot was elegant and simple and one that numerous other films have used. An aerial flyover of a Cuban location in *Bad Boys II* (2003), for example, was constructed by projecting photographic textures of houses onto a wireframe environment and arranging a series of matte paintings on 2D planes at various removes from the virtual camera. Animating this material brought the virtual environment to life as well as the camera move. A similar effect introduces the Macau location in *Skyfall* (2012), where James Bond has traveled searching for an assassin's employer. An aerial shot introduces an elaborate gambling casino surrounded by water and floating lanterns, with the city in the distance. The casino and its entranceway are a façade built on the Pinewood studio tank; the rest of what one sees are digital environment extensions and a matte painting. The flyover effect that simulates an aerial shot results from the animation of set, CG extensions, and matte painting. The shot combines 2D and 3D effects. The chief villain in *Skyfall*, Raoul Silva (Javier Bardem), lives on a remote island whose deserted metropolis is rendered as a series of 2D and 3D matte paintings (figure 35).

FIGURE 35: The deserted island metropolis of the villain (Javier Bardem) in *Skyfall* (Sam Mendes, 2012, art dir. Chris Lowe, prod. des. Dennis Gassner, set dec. Anna Pinnock) is brought to life as a series of 2D and full 3D matte paintings.

The digital environments in *Anonymous* were created with realism as the aesthetic goal. They were not meant to look like a fantasy locale or like digital creations. The film's wide views of London were built and animated using period maps of the city, and the filmmakers aimed to place famous locations, such as the Tower of London, the Thames, and London Bridge in relation to the city as these were laid out. The film's Elizabethan locations no longer exist, but they can be built using the documentation supplied by maps and photographs, and the digital back lot enabled the film's actors to inhabit Shakespearean London in a convincing fashion.

Nevertheless, the film's extensive use of virtual environments to represent exterior locations is a little unusual in live-action feature filmmaking in 2013. More typically, digital environments supplement live-action sets as extensions and augmentations. Tom Hooper's production of *Les Misérables* (2012) provides some good examples.[17] The story setting is nineteenth-century France, and live action was filmed on sets constructed at Pinewood Studios and on locations in England and France. This live-action material subsequently became a series of "plates" (the industry term for live-action material that has been scanned for use in a digital composite). As Sarah Horton noted, plates often furnish the references used by digital artists for creating color, textures, and lighting in matte paintings or other composite materials. In the case of *Les Misérables*, live-action plates were extended with period details that had been pulled from nineteenth-century daguerreotype panoramas of Paris. This enabled compositors to insert actors and settings filmed on the Pinewood stages into period backgrounds and the surroundings of streets in Paris. The compositing was complex because many shots featured groups of performers moving in complicated ways and camera movement that had to be matchmoved in the digital environments (figure 36).

FIGURE 36: Live-action plates—in this case, the children running toward the camera—have been seamlessly composited with digital environments and elements of real locations to portray the nineteenth-century world of Victor Hugo's novel in the film *Les Misérables* (Tom Hooper, 2012, art dir. Grant Armstrong, prod. des. Eve Stewart, set dec. Anna Lynch-Robinson).

Digital Composites

When live-action plates are used in digital composites, the results are generally seamless. In this respect, composited environments, which have always been a part of production design, can be created today with more precision and a more convincing blend of elements. In the analog era of film, composited environments were created photochemically using optical printers—an interlocked process camera and process projector. The process camera photographed frame by frame each of the optical elements in a composite and used mattes to block portions of the frames on the dupe negative to prevent double exposures. The registration of matted areas often was imperfect, and visible matte lines tended to afflict the composite work. Moreover, a composite shot necessitated the rephotographing of footage to assemble the finished shot, so generational losses of image quality affected the results.

Digital composites do not rely on this kind of photochemical printing. A compositor works by transforming pixels according to numerical operations, and these transformations need leave no visible trace in the final results. Moreover, the alpha channel enables very efficient and clean matte extraction. The alpha channel is one of four channels in which digital images store picture information (the others being red, green, and blue). The alpha channel is grayscale and designates the relative opacity of a pixel (black is fully transparent, white is fully opaque). Using the alpha channel to set black and white values for selected areas of an image enables the creation of the male and female mattes used for extracting characters or other objects from a shot and their insertion into another background or setting. Tools like Z-depth mapping enable precise calculation of dimensional information within the frame, and compositors can use this to control depth of field information and the camera's projection of a 3D computer environment onto the 2D plane of cinema.

The alpha channel and Z-depth mapping facilitate the compositing of live-action plates with digital environment extensions as found in *Les Misérables*. The results are dynamic and spatially immersive. Perspective changes produced by camera movement are replicated uniformly across the live-action and digital elements, creating a perceptually persuasive bond between the elements of a composite. Actors can move into and out of the depths of the digitally augmented environments, so that the domains of live action and optical effects do not appear visibly separate as they did during the era of optical printing.

One of the big set pieces in *Les Misérables* is the funeral for General Lamarque, a hero of the revolution, which the filmmakers staged near the Bastille. The sequence was shot in Greenwich, England, and its wharf, the Admiralty Museum, the Thames River, and the city itself—unmistakable British signatures—were all visible in the shots. The filmmakers had planned to use greenscreens to block those areas in preparation for digital set extensions, but director Hooper was shooting with multiple cameras, and their differing lines of sight were not compatible with greenscreening. Instead, these areas were rotoscoped, that is, their edges were articulated frame by frame as a matte so that they could be extracted from the shots and replaced with digital imagery of nineteenth-century Paris. Historical maps and paintings suggested how the Bastille was positioned relative to surrounding streets and buildings, and these environments were constructed and composited with the live-action plates.

The building that remains a centerpiece in the scene is part of Greenwich's Old Royal Naval College, which also appears at the film's conclusion as cheering throngs mass along a barricade in defiance of the government. The barricade was a practical set created by the art department as a small part of a much larger structure that appears in the film as a digital composite. The full digital extension was created from HDRI (high dynamic range images) of the practical set, used to establish texture references to be incorporated into the digital imagery. HDRI is a widely used application in contemporary film for the construction of digital environments when these are modeled on live-action filming. A high dynamic range image captures all of the visible light values in an environment, and in this respect it differs greatly from what a conventional photograph supplies.

Photography captures only a small spectrum of the visible light in a location. This fact seems to have been overlooked and neglected by theorists who construct accounts of cinema and realism based on the model of photography. A photographer intentionally must exclude from capture significant ranges of detail in the scene being photographed. By setting shutter speed and f-stop, the photographer determines what range of shadow and highlight detail will be preserved. A photograph cannot capture all of the information that the eye can see, but a high dynamic range image can do so. If a series of photographs are taken of a location, using exposure settings that produce a range of images, from under- to over-exposed, this range can be digitally combined to yield a composite photograph that preserves all of the exposure details captured in the individual photographs. The HDRI image provides a full reference of environmental light values, needed by a compositor in order to match the lighting and color in live-action plates with digital materials. In the case of *Les Miserables*' barricade, or the photographs of Elizabethan-era buildings in *Anonymous*, HDRI provides an important tool set for constructing the textures and ambient lighting values needed in digital set extensions.

Movie Magic Is Illusion, Not Fakery

In the analog era, production design followed a sequential process. The designer's plans were sketched, followed by the construction of sets and costumes, and then live-action filming proceeded based on these. Environment extensions were achieved in post-production with matte paintings and other composited effects, produced on the optical printer. The diffusion of digital tools has made compositing and virtual art direction into activities ongoing with production. One of the major innovations of *Avatar* (2009) was the on-set compositing of live action with digital characters and environments. James Cameron filmed his actors in motion-capture gear while viewing their characters as digital avatars in the digital environments where they would appear. Using Maya, the film's virtual art department had constructed low-resolution environments of planet Pandora's flora and fauna that Cameron could composite on set with his actors. Using a camera rig dubbed "Simulcam," Cameron was able to create virtual camera moves as live action in the digital environment. These innovations shifted motion capture from post-production to production and enabled the director to step into the digital world on the live-action stage.

Russell Crowe's major song sequence in *Les Misérables*, when his character, Javert, sings about devotion to the law, is staged with his character atop the roof of police headquarters. The rooftop is a partial set, augmented with a digital panorama of Paris. The film's 3D effects supervisor built the scene in Maya and showed the rendition to director Hooper on set. It showed two camera projections, as the scene would appear if shot using an 18mm and a 24mm lens, to demonstrate the amount of city visible in each perspective beyond actor Crowe. The digital visualization assisted Hooper in his shot choice. Narrative cinema is an art of the fragment. The viewer's experience of wholeness and contiguity is an illusion constructed by filmmakers, and production design very often is about building and compositing environments that viewers are meant to understand as being co-extensive with a film's story world. In fact, however, the spaces of story world and production design are fabricated and engineered to sustain the narrative illusions of contiguity and wholeness. In *Argo*, for example, as an Iranian mob storms the U.S. embassy, several employees escape from the building using a back staircase. Filming and editing this action sustained an elegant illusion. The Veterans Administration Building in Los Angeles was used as a location for filming the interior scenes in the embassy, and Iranian street scenes showing angry crowds were shot in Istanbul. In the finished film, the employees go down the stairs and out the door into the streets of Tehran. In production, the actors were filmed walking toward a Veterans Administration doorway in a corner of the building. On location in Istanbul, production designer Sharon Seymour built a set on a raised platform above an Istanbul street that matched the VA doorway. The set contained a staircase running down to street level and a second door that opened onto the street. In Istanbul, the actors were filmed entering the set's doorway, going down the stairs, opening the second door and stepping out into the street. As edited, the action was seamless and created perfect continuity, but it was an elaborate construction. As the film's cinematographer Rodrigo Prieto remarked, "The shot connects the locations in L.A. and Istanbul as if it had all taken place in Tehran."[18]

Production designer Paul Sylbert's long and distinguished credits include such classics as *One Flew Over the Cuckoo's Nest* (1975). He said, "The campfire scene at night in [the western] *Bad Company* [1972] was done on a sloped floor in a gym in Kansas. We do this all the time in movies. Movie magic is illusion, not fakery."[19] Debra Granik's *Winter's Bone* (2010) was shot digitally using Red One cameras, on locations in the Ozark Mountains that matched those called for in the story. Granik and crew scouted locations for two years before filming began because realism and authenticity were important attributes of the film's style. But filmic style, even a realist one, necessitates construction. A climatic scene shows Ree Dolly (Jennifer Lawrence) taken by night to a pond by two sinister women who are meth dealers. There, Dolly finds the body of her murdered father. Dialogue shots among the women in the boat were filmed on a mock set on dry land, using a low camera angle to hide this fact. Other shots in the scene showing Ree reaching into the water were filmed on the pond. The style is realist, and yet the spaces on screen are not what they appear to be; as Sylbert noted, much is illusion but not fakery.

Filmmakers have always done this kind of thing and always will. Little about the nature of narrative cinema has changed in the digital era, although filmmakers now have tools that are more expressive, powerful, and nuanced than their forbears did in earlier generations.[20] But tools in themselves are not what counts. What counts is a filmmaker's intelligence and taste. Stanley Kubrick pointed out that Chaplin's films will probably last longer than anyone else's because of what Chaplin brought to the screen, not because of his filming methods. "If something is really happening on the screen, it isn't crucial how it's shot. Chaplin had such a simple cinematic style, but you were always hypnotized by what was going on, unaware of the essentially non-cinematic style. He frequently used cheap sets, routine lighting and so forth, but he made great films."[21] Great films will continue to be made in a digital medium, but idea rather than method is what will make them so.

ACADEMY AWARDS FOR BEST ART DIRECTION

Note: The Art Directors Guild only lists awards starting in 1936. The earlier years are culled from other sources.

1927/28	William Cameron Menzies	*The Dove, Tempest*
1928/29	Cedric Gibbons	*The Bridge of San Luis Rey*
1929/30	Herman Rosse	*King of Jazz*
1930/31	Max Rée	*Cimarron*
1931/32	Gordon Wiles	*Transatlantic*
1932/33	William S. Darling	*Cavalcade*
1934	Cedric Gibbons, Fredric Hope	*The Merry Widow*
1935	Richard Day	*The Dark Angel*

1936	Richard Day	*Dodsworth*
1937	Stephen Goosson	*Lost Horizon*
1938	Carl J. Weyl	*The Adventures of Robin Hood*
1939	Lyle Wheeler	*Gone with the Wind*
1940	BLACK & WHITE, Cedric Gibbons, Paul Groesse	*Pride and Prejudice*
	COLOR, Vincent Korda	*The Thief of Bagdad*
1941	BLACK & WHITE, Richard Day, Nathan Juran; Interior Decoration: Thomas Little	*How Green Was My Valley*
	COLOR, Cedric Gibbons, Urie McCleary; Interior Decoration, Edwin B. Willis	*Blossoms in the Dust*
1942	BLACK & WHITE, Richard Day, Joseph Wright; Interior Decoration: Thomas Little	*This Above All*
	COLOR, Richard Day, Joseph Wright; Interior Decoration: Thomas Little	*My Gal Sal*
1943	BLACK & WHITE, James Basevi, William Darling; Interior Decoration: Thomas Little	*The Song of Bernadette*
	COLOR, John B. Goodman, Alexander Golitzen; Interior Decoration: Russell A. Gausman, Ira S. Webb	*Phantom of the Opera*
1944	BLACK & WHITE, Cedric Gibbons, William Ferrari; Interior Decoration: Edwin B. Willis, Paul Huldschinsky	*Gaslight*
	COLOR, Wiard Ihnen; Interior Decoration: Thomas Little	*Wilson*
1945	BLACK & WHITE, Wiard Ihnen; Interior Decoration: A. Roland Fields	*Blood on the Sun*
	COLOR, Hans Dreier, Ernst Fegte; Interior Decoration: Sam Comer	*Frenchman's Creek*
1946	BLACK & WHITE, Lyle Wheeler, William Darling; Interior Decoration: Thomas Little, Frank E. Hughes	*Anna and the King of Siam*
	COLOR, Cedric Gibbons, Paul Groesse; Interior Decoration: Edwin B. Willis	*The Yearling*
1947	BLACK & WHITE, John Bryan; Set Decoration: Wilfred Shingleton	*Great Expectations*
	COLOR, Alfred Junge; Set Decoration: Alfred Junge	*Black Narcissus*

1948	BLACK & WHITE, Roger K. Furse; Set Decoration: Carmen Dillon	*Hamlet*
	COLOR, Hein Heckroth; Set Decoration: Arthur Lawson	*The Red Shoes*
1949	BLACK & WHITE, Harry Horner, John Meehan; Set Decoration: Emile Kuri	*The Heiress*
	COLOR, Cedric Gibbons, Paul Groesse; Set Decoration: Edwin B. Willis, Jack D. Moore	*Little Women*
1950	BLACK & WHITE, Hans Dreier, John Meehan; Set Decoration: Sam Comer, Ray Moyer	*Sunset Blvd.*
	COLOR, Hans Dreier, Walter Tyler; Set Decoration: Sam Comer, Ray Moyer	*Samson and Delilah*
1951	BLACK & WHITE, Richard Day; Set Decoration: George James Hopkins	*A Streetcar Named Desire*
	COLOR, Cedric Gibbons, Preston Ames; Set Decoration: Edwin B. Willis, F. Keogh Gleason	*An American in Paris*
1952	BLACK & WHITE, Cedric Gibbons, Edward Carfagno; Set Decoration: Edin B. Willis, F. Keogh Gleason	*The Bad and the Beautiful*
	COLOR, Paul Sheriff; Set Decoration: Marcel Vertes	*Moulin Rouge*
1953	BLACK & WHITE, Cedric Gibbons, Edward Carfagno; Set Decoration: Edwin B. Willis, Hugh Hunt	*Julius Caesar*
	COLOR, Lyle Wheeler, George W. Davis; Set Decoration: Walter M. Scott, Paul S. Fox	*The Robe*
1954	BLACK & WHITE, Richard Day	*On the Waterfront*
	COLOR, John Meehan; Set Decoration: Emile Kuri	*20,000 Leagues under the Sea*
1955	BLACK & WHITE, Hal Pereira, Tambi Larsen; Set Decoration: Sam Comer, Arthur Krams	*Thê Rose Tattoo*
	COLOR, William Flannery, Jo Mielziner; Set Decoration: Robert Priestley	*Picnic*
1956	BLACK & WHITE, Cedric Gibbons, Malcolm F. Brown; Set Decoration: Edwin B. Willis, F. Keogh Gleason	*Somebody Up There Likes Me*
	COLOR, Lyle R. Wheeler, John DeCuir; Set Decoration: Walter M. Scott, Paul S. Fox	*The King and I*
1957	Ted Haworth; Set Decoration: Robert Priestley	*Sayonara*
1958	William A. Horning, Preston Ames; Set Decoration: Henry Grace, F. Keogh Gleason	*Gigi*

1959	BLACK & WHITE, Lyle R. Wheeler, George W. Davis; Set Decoration: Walter M. Scott, Stuart A. Reiss	*The Diary of Anne Frank*
	COLOR, William A. Horning, Edward Carfagno; Set Decoration: Hugh Hunt	*Ben-Hur*
1960	BLACK & WHITE, Alexander Trauner; Set Decoration: Edward G. Boyle	*The Apartment*
	COLOR, Alexander Golitzen, Eric Orbom; Set Decoration: Russell A. Gausman, Julia Heron	*Spartacus*
1961	BLACK & WHITE, Harry Horner; Set Decoration: Gene Callahan	*The Hustler*
	COLOR, Boris Leven; Set Decoration: Victor A. Gangelin	*West Side Story*
1962	BLACK & WHITE, Alexander Golitzen, Henry Bumstead; Set Decoration: Oliver Emrt	*To Kill a Mockingbird*
	COLOR, John Box, John Stoll; Set Decoration: Dario Simoni	*Lawrence of Arabia*
1963	BLACK & WHITE, Gene Callahan	*America America*
	COLOR, John DeCuir, Jack Martin Smith, Hilyard Brown, Herman Blumenthal, Elven Webb, Maurice Pelling, Boris Juraga; Set Decoration: Walter M. Scott, Paul S. Fox, Ray Moyer	*Cleopatra*
1964	BLACK & WHITE, Vassilis Fotopoulos	*Zorba the Greek*
	COLOR, Gene Allen, Cecil Beaton; Set Decoration: George James Hopkins	*My Fair Lady*
1965	BLACK & WHITE, Robert Clatworthy; Set Decoration: Joseph Kish	*Ship of Fools*
	COLOR, John Box, Terry Marsh; Set Decoration: Dario Simoni	*Doctor Zhivago*
1966	BLACK & WHITE, Richard Sylbert; Set Decoration: George James Hopkins	*Who's Afraid of Virginia Woolf?*
	COLOR, Jack Martin Smith, Dale Hennessey; Set Decoration: Walter M. Scott, Stuart A. Reiss	*Fantastic Voyage*
1967	John Truscott, Edward Carrere; Set Decoration: John W. Brown	*Camelot*
1968	John Box, Terence Marsh; Set Decoration: Vernon Dixon, Ken Muggleston	*Oliver!*

1969	John DeCuir, Jack Martin Smith, Herman Blumenthal; Set Decoration: Walter M. Scott, George Hopkins, Raphael Bretton	*Hello Dolly!*
1970	Urie McCleary, Gil Parrondo; Set Decoration: Antonio Mateos, Pierre-Louis Thevenet	*Patton*
1971	John Box, Ernest Archer, Jack Maxsted, Gil Parrondo; Set Decoration: Vernon Dixon	*Nicholas and Alexandra*
1972	Rolf Zehetbauer, Jurgen Kiebach; Set Decoration: Herbert Strabel	*Cabaret*
1973	Henry Bumstead; Set Decoration: James Payne	*The Sting*
1974	Dean Tavoularis, Angelo Graham; Set Decoration: George R. Nelson	*The Godfather Part II*
1975	Ken Adam, Roy Walker; Set Decoration: Vernon Dixon	*Barry Lyndon*
1976	George Jenkins; Set Decoration: George Gaines	*All the President's Men*
1977	John Barry, Norman Reynolds, Leslie Dilley; Set Decoration: Roger Christian	*Star Wars*
1978	Paul Sylbert, Edwin O'Donovan; Set Decoration: George Gaines	*Heaven Can Wait*
1979	Philip Rosenberg, Tony Walton; Set Decoration: Edward Stewart, Gary Brink	*All That Jazz*
1980	Pierre Guffroy, Jack Stephens	*Tess*
1981	Norman Reynolds, Leslie Dilley; Set Decoration: Michael Ford	*Raiders of the Lost Ark*
1982	Stuart Craig, Bob Laing; Set Decoration: Michael Seirton	*Gandhi*
1983	Anna Asp	*Fanny and Alexander*
1984	Patrizia Von Brandenstein; Set Decoration: Karel Cerny	*Amadeus*
1985	Stephen Grimes; Set Decoration: Josie MacAvin	*Out of Africa*
1986	Gianni Quaranta, Brian Ackland-Snow; Set Decoration: Brian Savegar, Elio Altamura	*A Room with a View*

1987	Ferdinando Scarfiotti; Set Decoration: Bruno Cesari, Osvaldo Desideri	*The Last Emperor*
1988	Stuart Craig; Set Decoration: Gerard James	*Dangerous Liaisons*
1989	Anton Furst; Set Decoration: Peter Young	*Batman*
1990	Richard Sylbert; Set Decoration: Rick Simpson	*Dick Tracy*
1991	Dennis Gassner; Set Decoration: Nancy Haigh	*Bugsy*
1992	Luciana Arrighi; Set Decoration: Ian Whittaker	*Howards End*
1993	Allan Starski; Set Decoration: Ewa Braun	*Schindler's List*
1994	Ken Adam; Set Decoration: Carolyn Scott	*The Madness of King George*
1995	Eugenio Zanetti	*Restoration*
1996	Stuart Craig; Set Decoration: Stephenie McMillan	*The English Patient*
1997	Peter Lamont; Set Decoration: Michael Ford	*Titanic*
1998	Martin Childs; Set Decoration: Jill Quertier	*Shakespeare in Love*
1999	Rick Heinrichs; Set Decoration: Peter Young	*Sleepy Hollow*
2000	Tim Yip	*Crouching Tiger, Hidden Dragon*
2001	Catherine Martin; Set Decoration: Brigitte Broch	*Moulin Rouge!*
2002	John Myhre; Set Decoration: Gordon Sim	*Chicago*
2003	Grant Major; Set Decoration: Dan Hennah, Alan Lee	*The Lord of the Rings: The Return of the King*
2004	Dante Ferretti; Set Decoration: Francesca Lo Schiavo	*The Aviator*
2005	John Myhre; Set Decoration: Gretchen Rau	*Memoirs of a Geisha*
2006	Eugenio Caballero; Set Decoration: Pilar Revuelta	*Pan's Labyrinth*
2007	Dante Ferretti; Set Decoration: Francesca Lo Schiavo	*Sweeney Todd: The Demon Barber of Fleet Street*

2008	Donald Graham Burt; Set Decoration: Victor J. Zolfo	*The Curious Case of Benjamin Button*
2009	Rick Carter and Robert Stromberg; Set Decoration: Kim Sinclair	*Avatar*
2010	Robert Stromberg; Set Decoration: Karen O'Hara	*Alice in Wonderland*
2011	Dante Ferretti; Set Decoration: Francesca Lo Schiavo	*Hugo*
2012	Rick Carter	*Lincoln*
2013	Catherine Martin; Set Decoration: Beverley Dunn	*The Great Gatsby*

NOTES

Introduction

1 Charles and Mirella Jona Affron, *Sets in Motion: Art Direction and Film Narrative* (New Brunswick, NJ: Rutgers University Press, 1995), 5.

2 Juan Antonio Ramirez, *Architecture for the Screen: A Critical Study of Set Design in Hollywood's Golden Age* (Jefferson, NC: McFarland, 2004), 5.

3 Cathy Whitlock, *Designs on Film: A Century of Hollywood Art Direction* (New York: HarperCollins, 2010), xi.

4 Affron and Affron, *Sets in Motion*, 11.

5 Jane Barnwell, *Production Design: Architects of the Screen* (London: Wallflower, 2003), 8.

6 Affron and Affron, *Sets in Motion*, 12.

7 Whitlock, *Designs on Film*, xi.

8 Leon Barsacq, *Caligari's Cabinet and Other Grand Illusions: A History of Film Design* (Boston: New York Graphic Society, 1976), 56.

9 Whitlock, *Designs on Film*, 9ff.

10 Ramirez, *Architecture for the Screen*, 26.

11 IMDb, http://www.imdb.com/title/tt0004972/fullcredits#cast/.

12 Charles Musser, *Before the Nickelodeon: Edwin Porter and the Edison Manufacturing Company* (Berkeley: University of California Press, 1991), 539.

13 Ibid., 426, quoting "Earmarks of the Makers," *New York Dramatic Mirror*, 14 November 1908.

14 Ramirez, *Architecture for the Screen*, 33.

15 Contemporary exceptions include Australian Catherine Martin, and, in the United States, Erin Muldoon Stetson, Anne Siebel, Polly Platt, Patrizia von Brandenstein, Jane Musky, and Kristi Zea.

16 Salmagundi Club: A Center for American Art Since 1871, http://www.salmagundi.org/history.htm. The fact that Cinemagundi was a variation on this is confirmed in Michael Baugh, "A Social Club for Art Directors?," *Perspective* (October-November 2007), 19.

17 Baugh, "A Social Club for Art Directors?," 19.

18 LADA Files, Parts 1 and 2 (Provided by Art Directors Guild), 19, 19–20.

19 Whitlock, *Designs on Film*, xii.

20 Ramirez, *Architecture for the Screen*, 14.

21 Ibid., 8.

22 Ibid., 9.

23 Theatre Historical Society of America, http://www.historictheatres.org/.

24 Ramirez, *Architecture for the Screen*, 81–89.

25 Turner Classic Movies, "The Magnificent Ambersons," http://www.tcm.com/tcmdb/title/683/The-Magnificent-Ambersons/articles.html, accessed 31 October 2013.

26 Ramirez, *Architecture for the Screen*, 84–85.

27 Ibid., 103.

28 Sony Pictures, "Sony Pictures a Greener World," *Sony Pictures*, http://www.sonypictures.com/green/act/corporate-operations/set-reuse.php/, accessed 28 December 2012.

29 "Environmentalist Makes Furniture from Reclaimed Movie Sets," *State Journal Register*, 24 September 1995, 39.

30 Andreas Fuchs, "Greening the Movie Set: Film Biz Recycling Gains Momentum," *Film Journal International* (September 2012): 28.

31 Gary Gentile, "Company Takes Off by Renting Film Sets," *Augusta Chronicle*, 23 December 2000, C09.

32 Barbara Cole, "Key Film Sets for Madiba Museum," *Pretoria News*, 21 July 2012, 7.

33 Whitlock, *Designs on Film*, 31.

34 Quoted in Vincent LoBrutto, *By Design: Interviews with Production Designers* (Westport, Conn.: Praeger, 1992), 191.

35 Joseph McBride, *Searching for John Ford* (Jackson: University Press of Mississippi, 2011), 288–289.

36 Ramirez, *Architecture for the Screen*, n.p.

37 See Lucy Fischer, *Designing Women: Cinema, Art Deco and the Female Form* (New York: Columbia University Press, 2003).

38 "Film Sets on Exhibit," *Los Angeles Times*, 12 October 1964, D17.

39 Damien Woolnough, "From Film Sets to Interiors," *Weekend Australian*, 6 October 2012, 9.

40 Bethany Seawright, "Cinema Style: 20 Unforgettable American Movie Interiors," *Apartment Therapy*, 3 August 2011, http://www.apartmenttherapy.com/cinema-style-am-152471/.

41 Colette McIntyre, "15 Apartments on Film That We Wish We Owned," *Flavorwire*, 24 December 2011, http://www.flavorwire.com/195413/15-apartments-on-film-that-we-wish-we-owned.

42 Ben Williams, "The 20 Houses from the Movies We'd Actually Want to Live In," *The Prodigal Guide*, 2 June 2011, http://www.theprodigalguide.com/2011/06/02/the-20-best-houses-in-the-movies/.

43 Barnwell, *Production Design*, 45–79.

44 Kirill Grouchnikov, "The Art Direction of *Unstoppable*—Interview with Drew Boughton," *Pushing Pixels*, 25 March 2011, http://www.pushing-pixels.org/2011/03/25/the-art-direction-of-unstoppable-interview-with-drew-boughton.html. Ann Jackman, "How to Be a . . . Production Designer," *New England Film.com*, 1 January 2003, http://www.newenglandfilm.com/news/archives/03january/pd.htm. Kirill Grouchnikov, "The Production of *Midnight in Paris*," *Pushing Pixels*, 18 November 2011, http://www.pushing-pixels.org/category/interviews/page/4.

45 Thehorrorchick, "Exclusive Video Interview: Production Designer Joe Alves Reflects on the Challengers and Triumphs of *Jaws*," *Dead Central*, 8 August 2012, http://www.dreadcentral.com/news/58072/exclusive-video-interview-production-designer-joe-alves-reflects-challenges-and-triumphs-.

46 LoBrutto, *By Design*, 161.

47 Avis Berman, "On the Set of Ron Howard's *Ransom*," *Architectural Digest* 53, no. 4 (April 1996): 36.

48 Barnwell, *Production Design*, 48.

49 Grouchnikov, "The Production of *Midnight in Paris*."

50 LoBrutto, *By Design*, 243.

51 Grouchnikov, "The Production of *Midnight in Paris*."

52 LoBrutto, *By Design*, 158.

53 Ibid., 219.

54 Berman,"On the Set of Ron Howard's *Ransom*," 36.

55 Laurent Bouzereau, *The Art of Bond: From Storyboard to Screen—The Creative Process Behind the James Bond Phenomenon* (New York: Abrams, 2006), 63.

56 Thehorrorchick, "Exclusive Video Interview."

57 LoBrutto, *By Design*, 186.

58 Steve Weintraub, "Production Designer Patrick Tatopoulos Talks Car Designs, Constructing New Cities, Product Placement and More on the Set of *Total Recall*," *Collider.com*, 12 June 2012, http://collider.com/patrick-tatopoulos-total-recall-interview/171658/.

59 LoBrutto, *By Design*, 252, 250.

60 Grouchnikov, "The Art Direction of *Unstoppable*."

61 LoBrutto, *By Design*, 159.

62 Grouchnikov, "The Production of *Midnight in Paris*."

63 Bouzereau, *The Art of Bond*, 93.

64 LoBrutto, *By Design*, 159.

65 Ibid., 187.

66 The Matrix.com. "Interview with Production Designer Owen Paterson," *Matrixfans.net*, http://www.matrixfans.net/movies/the-matrix/interview-with-production-designer-owen-paterson/.

67 Grouchnikov, "The Production of *Midnight in Paris*."

68 LoBrutto, *By Design*, 158, 184, 244.

69 Berman, "On the Set of Ron Howard's *Ransom*," 36.

70 LoBrutto, *By Design*, 246.

71 Peter Cook, "The 50 Greatest Matte Paintings of All Time," *Shadowlocked.com*, 27 May 2012, http://www.shadowlocked.com/201205272603/lists/the-fifty-greatest-matte-paintings-of-all-time/page-2-of-2.html.

72 Berman, "On the Set of Ron Howard's *Ransom*," 36.

73 LoBrutto, *By Design*, 157.

74 Ibid., 219.

75 Berman, "On the Set of Ron Howard's *Ransom*," 36.

76 Ibid.

77 Ibid.

78 Grouchnikov, "The Production of *Midnight in Paris*."

79 Bouzereau, *The Art of Bond*, 70–71.

80 Karl Shefelman, "Feature Films 2," *Shefelboards.com*, http://www.shefelboards.com/id3.html.

81 Tom and Heidi Lüdi, *Movie Worlds: Production Design in Film* (London: Edition Axel Menges, 2000), 22.

82 LoBrutto, *By Design*, 188, 217.

83 Bouzereau, *The Art of Bond*, 81, 85.

84 LoBrutto, *By Design*, 218.

85 Shefelman, "Feature Films 2."

86 "Between Film and Art: Storyboards from Hitchcock to Spielberg Exhibited in Berlin," *Art-daily.org*, 21 January 2013, http://www.artdaily.org/index.asp?int_sec=2&int_new=49874.

87 J. W. Rinzler, *Star Wars: The Blueprints* (Las Vegas: 47 North, 2013).

88 Ramirez, *Architecture for the Screen*, 51.

89 LoBrutto, *By Design*, 157.

90 Anthony Bond, "Harry Potter and the Film-Makers' Magic: Incredibly Detailed Model of Hogwarts Castle Used for Every Film in Blockbusting Series Is Revealed for the First Time," *Daily Mail*, 2 March 2012, http://www.dailymail.co.uk/news/article-2109071/Incredibly-detailed-model-Hogwarts-Castle-used-Harry-Potter-film-revealed-time.html, accessed 1 January 2013.

91 The Matrix.com, "Interview with Production Designer Owen Paterson."

92 Kirill Grouchnikov, "The Fine Craft of Set Decoration—Conversation with Katie Spencer," *Pushing Pixels*, 18 January 2012, http://www.pushing-pixels.org/2012/01/18/the-fine-craft-of-set-decoration-conversation-with-katie-spencer.html.

93 Berman, "On the Set of Ron Howard's *Ransom*," 36.

94 Thehorrorchick, "Exclusive Video Interview."

95 LoBrutto, *By Design*, 185.

96 The Matrix.com, "Interview with Production Designer Owen Paterson."

97 Jackman, "How to Be a . . . Production Designer."

98 Grouchnikov, "The Art Direction of *Unstoppable*."

1 The Silent Screen, 1895–1927

1 Brett Zonker, "Most U.S. Silent Films are Gone," *Pittsburgh Post Gazette*, 12 June 2013, B7.

2 Neither does the *AFI Catalog of Feature Films*.

3 Much of my information on the Black Maria comes from two Library of Congress websites. See http://memory.loc.gov/ammem/edhtml/edmvhist1.html; http://www.youtube.com/user/LibraryOfCongress/videos?query=black+maria.

4 Charles Musser, *Before the Nickelodeon: Edwin Porter and the Edison Manufacturing Company* (Berkeley: University of California Press, 1991), 32.

5 Charles Musser, ed., *Motion Picture Catalogs by American Producers and Distributors, 1894–1908: A Microfilm Edition* (Frederick, MD: University Publications of America, 1984–1985), n.p.

6 Musser, *Before the Nickelodeon*, 160.

7 Ibid., 339.

8 Marc Wanamaker, "Building the Movies: Tracing the Evolution of Set Design," *Architectural Digest* (April 1994): 106, 102, 104, 108.

9 Musser, *Before the Nickelodeon*, 161.

10 According to a MoMA print now on DVD.

11 IMDB lists Fleming as art director but the *AFI Catalog of Feature Films* does not.

12 Musser, *Before the Nickelodeon*, 182, 331, 342.

13 Ibid., 329.

14 Ibid., 240. According to the *AFI Catalog of Feature Films*, however, the first film for which he receives art direction credit is on *The Antics of Ann* (1917), a Famous Players film.

15 According to Musser (*Before the Nickelodeon,* 539–540n80), "Richard Murphy would later follow Porter to Rex and Famous Players. In 1919, when he went to the British Famous Players–Lasky Studio, he was accompanied by his assistant William Cameron Menzies."

16 "Earmarks of the Makers," *New York Dramatic Mirror*, 14 November 1908, 10 (reproduced in Musser, *Before the Nickelodeon*, 426).

17 "Edison Co.'s New Studio," *Film Index*, 28 November 1908, 4, quoted in Musser, *Before the Nickelodeon*, 387–388.

18 Musser, *Before the Nickelodeon*, 388–389.

19 Fionnuala Halligan, *Production Design* (Burlington, MA: Focal Press, 2013), 77.

20 Eileen Bowser, *The Transformation of Cinema, 1907–1915* (Berkeley: University of California Press, 1994), 24.

21 Quoted in Richard Koszarski, *Fort Lee: The Film Town* (Rome: John Libbey, 2004), 119.

22 Ibid., 120.

23 Joseph P. Eckhardt and Linda Kowall, *Peddler of Dreams: Siegmund Lubin and the Creation of the Motion Picture Industry, 1896–1916* (Philadelphia: National Museum of American Jewish History, 1984), 8.

24 Kalton Lahue, ed., *Motion Picture Pioneer: The Selig Polyscope Company* (New York: A. S. Barnes, 1973), 11–15.

25 James McQuade, "Making 'Selig' Pictures," in ibid., 59.

26 Bowser, *The Transformation of Cinema*, 157–158, 162.

27 Ibid., 159, 160.

28 Beverly Heisner, *Hollywood Art: Art Direction in the Days of the Great Studios* (Jefferson, NC: McFarland, 1990), 11, 13.

29 Nicholas Vardac, *Stage to Screen: Theatrical Method from Garrick to Griffith* (Cambridge, MA: Harvard University Press, 1949), 207; *AFI Catalog of Feature Films.*

30 Vachel Lindsay, *Art of the Moving Picture* (New York: Liverwright, 1970), 87.

31 Vardac, *Stage to Screen*, 207.

32 "Judith of Bethulia," Wikipedia, http://en.wikipedia.org/wiki/Judith_of_Bethulia.

33 Floyd W. Martin, "D. W. Griffith's *Intolerance*: A Note on Additional Visual Sources," *Art Journal* 43, no. 3 (Autumn 1983): 231. (Quotes of Griffith are from "How Moving Pictures Are Made," typescript from D. W. Griffith papers, MoMA.)

34 Promotional materials are reproduced as a special feature of the DVD.

35 Cathy Whitlock, *Designs on Film: A Century of Hollywood Art Direction* (New York: Harper-Collins, 2010), 42; Heisner, *Hollywood Art*, 12.

36 Heisner, *Hollywood Art*, 12, 11.

37 William Drew, *D. W. Griffith's Intolerance: Its Genesis and Its Vision* (Jefferson, NC: McFarland, 1986), 57, 61, 62.

38 Robert Sennett, *Setting the Scene: The Great Hollywood Art Directors* (New York: Harry N. Abrams, 1994), 26.

39 "The Lost City of DeMille," Guadalupe-Nipomo Dunes Center, http://dunescenter.org/visit-the-dunes/dunes-center/exhibits-and-activities-research/the-lost-city-of-demille/.

40 Whitlock, *Designs on Film*, 46; Sennett, *Setting the Scene*, 45.

41 George McAdam, "Our New Art for Export," *New York Times*, 13 April 1924.

42 Martha Greuning, *New York Times*, 31 October 1926.

43 Benjamin De Casseres, *New York Times*, 26 March 1922.

44 Arnie Bernstein, *"The Movies Are": Carl Sandburg's Film Reviews and Essays, 1920–1928* (Chicago: Lake Claremont Press, 2000), 242.

45 Louis Aragon, "On Décor," in *The Shadow and Its Shadows: Surrealist Writings on Film*, ed. Paul Hammond (London: BFI, 1978), 29 (*Aragon's emphasis*), 20.

46 William Cameron Menzies, "Pictorial Beauty in the Photoplay," in *Introduction to the Photoplay*, ed. John C. Tibbets (Shawnee Mission, KS: National Film Society, 1977), 163, 179.

47 "AFI's 10 Top 10–Fantasy," *AFI Catalog of Feature Films*, http://www.afi.com/10top10/category.aspx?cat=6.

48 Menzies, "Pictorial Beauty in the Photoplay," 174, 162.

49 Whitlock, *Designs on Film*, 46.

50 *The Art of Hollywood: A Thames Television Exhibition at the Victoria and Albert Museum* (London: Thames Television, 1979), 91.

51 Whitlock, *Designs on Film*, 46.

52 Sennett, *Setting the Scene*, 40. Other members of the Art Department included Park French, Harold Grieve, H. R. Hopps, Edward M. Langley, Irvin J. Martin, William Utwich, and Paul Youngblood. Paul Burns was property manager (uncredited).

53 *The Art of Hollywood*, 91.

54 Sennett, *Setting the Scene*, 40.

55 *The Art of Hollywood*, 93.

56 Ibid.

57 Juan Antonio Ramirez, *Architecture for the Screen: A Critical Study of Set Design in Hollywood's Golden Age* (Jefferson, NC: McFarland, 2004), 147.

58 Whitlock, *Designs on Film*, 46.

59 Ibid., 48.

60 Menzies, "Pictorial Beauty in the Photoplay," 170.

61 Sennett, *Setting the Scene*, 45.

62 Whitlock, *Designs on Film*, 48.

63 Menzies, "Pictorial Beauty in the Photoplay," 170.

64 Richard Koszarski, *Universal Pictures 65 Years* (New York: Museum of Modern Art, 1977), 7.

65 Phillip J. Riley, *The Making of The Phantom of the Opera* (Absecon, NJ: MagicImage Filmbooks, 1999), 55.

66 Koszarski, *Universal Pictures 65 Years*, 11.

67 Riley, *Making of the Phantom*, 37.

68 The film went through numerous rewrites (by a variety of scenarists including Raymond Schrock, Elliott J. Clawson, and Tom Reed) and reedits (including work by Lois Weber) based on test screenings and both a Los Angeles and San Francisco premiere before its official world premiere in New York City at the Astor Theater. Original director Rupert Julian was also eventually replaced by Edward Sedgwick.

69 *Frankenstein* (1910, J. Searle Dawley), *Life without Soul* (1915, Joseph Smiley), and *Il Mostro di Frankenstein* (1920, Eugenio Testa).

70 Riley, *Making of the Phantom*, 219, 221.

71 Ibid., 57.

72 *The Art of Hollywood*, 21–23.

73 Riley, *Making of the Phantom*, 58.

74 Scott MacQueen, "The 1926 *Phantom of the Opera*," *American Cinematographer* 70, no. 9 (September 1989): 37.

75 Riley, *Making of the Phantom*, 58.

76 MacQueen, "The 1926 *Phantom of the Opera*," 37.

77 Quoted in Bernstein, "*The Movies Are*," 286.

78 Ibid., 222.

79 Riley, *Making of the Phantom*, 218, 219, 230, 222; MacQueen, "The 1926 *Phantom of the Opera*," 36.

80 Riley, *Making of the Phantom*, 224, 229.

81 Ibid., 229.

82 Ibid., 230.

83 Ibid., 219.

84 George Perry, *The Complete Phantom of the Opera* (New York: Henry Holt, 1988), 48.

85 Riley, *Making of the Phantom*, 245, 230.

86 Ibid., 25.

87 Ibid., 224.

88 MacQueen, "The 1926 *Phantom of the Opera*," 37–38.

89 Perry, *The Complete Phantom*, 55.

90 MacQueen, audio commentary, *The Phantom of the Opera (1925): The Ultimate Edition* (Chatsworth, CA: Milestone/Image, 2003) (DVD).

91 The term "Freudian" was used on the following website: Stacia Kissick Jones, "Stage 28: *Phantom of the Opera* (1925) and the Universal Backlot," *She Blogged by Night*, 15 September 2012, http://shebloggedbynight.com/2012/stage-28-phantom-of-the-opera-and-the-universal-backlot/.

92 Kissick Jones, "Stage 28."

93 Riley, *Making of the Phantom*, 25.

94 Ibid., 24.

95 MacQueen, audio commentary.

96 Riley, *Making of the Phantom*, 224, 245, 222.

97 MacQueen, "The 1926 *Phantom of the Opera*," 38.

98 Ibid.

2 Classical Hollywood, 1928-1946

1 In the 1910s and 1920s, and to a lesser extent in the 1930s, New York City also had several large shooting stages producing historical films and others with large sets, such as at Astoria; but these stages and sets were relatively few in number and studio lots tended to be a lot smaller than in Los Angeles. See Richard Koszarski, *Hollywood on the Hudson: Film and Television in New York from Griffith to Sarnoff* (New Brunswick, NJ: Rutgers University Press, 2008), 34, 55, and 122.

2 "Billion Dollar Industry," *Los Angeles Times*, 2 January 1940, C7; Stephen Watts, *Behind the Screen: How the Films Are Made* (London: Arthur Barker Ltd., 1938), 49; and Tino Balio, *Grand Design: Hollywood as a Modern Business Enterprise, 1930–1939* (Berkeley: University of California Press, 1995), 98 and 102.

3 Balio, *Grand Design*, 147.

4 Brian Taves, "The B Film: Hollywood's Other Half," in Balio, *Grand Design*, 313; see also Table 6.3, "Budget Range of Studio Features," in Thomas Schatz, *Boom and Bust: American Cinema in the 1940s* (Berkeley: University of California Press, 1999), 174.

5 Thomas Schatz, *The Genius of the System: Hollywood Filmmaking in the Studio Era* (New York: Simon & Schuster, 1988), 164. See also Richard Koszarski, "Making Movies, 1915–28," in *The Classical Hollywood Reader*, ed. Steve Neale (New York: Routledge, 2012), 52.

6 "Cedric Gibbons," *Los Angeles Times*, 23 April 1929, C14.

7 James L. Davis, "Recent Film Outlay Totals $110,000,000," *Los Angeles Times*, 19 October 1930, D1, D3.

8 For an extensive discussion of Los Angeles movie studios and urban history, see my book *Hollywood Cinema and the Real Los Angeles* (London: Reaktion Books, 2012), 128–210.

9 "Mammoth Film Plant is Near Completion," *Los Angeles Times*, 9 January 1916, V1.

10 "Fox Erecting Large Plant," *Los Angeles Times*, 1 October 1928, A3.

11 "Contracts Given For Film Unit," *Los Angeles Times*, 10 November 1929, D1.

12 Edwin Schallert, "Studio Space Shortage Seen," *Los Angeles Times*, 6 March 1933, A5.

13 John L. Scott, "Film Sets Grow Larger," *Los Angeles Times*, 1 September 1929, 11.

14 Mary Corliss, "Designed for Film," *Film Comment* 14, no. 3 (May-June 1978): 49.

15 James W. Elliott, "Studios Spend Millions in Talkie Construction," *Los Angeles Times*, 5 August 1928, E1.

16 "Cedric Gibbons," *Los Angeles Times*, 23 April 1929, C14.

17 Homer G. Tasker, "Current Developments in Production Methods in Hollywood," *Journal of the Society of Motion Picture Engineers* 24 (January 1935): 4.

18 "Contracts Given For Film Unit," *Los Angeles Times*, 10 November 1929, D1.

19 David Bordwell, Janet Staiger, and Kristin Thompson, *The Classical Hollywood Cinema: Film Style and Mode of Production to 1960* (London: Routledge, 1985), 229.

20 Beverly Heisner, *Hollywood Art: Art Direction in the Days of the Great Studios* (London: St James Press, 1990), 189.

21 Cedric Gibbons, "The Art Director," in Watts, *Behind the Screen*, 43.

22 Ibid.

23 Watts, *Behind the Screen*, 40; Gibbons, "The Art Director," 50.

24 Scott MacQueen, "Midsummer Dream, Midwinter Nightmare: Max Reinhardt and Shakespeare versus the Warner Bros.," *The Moving Image: The Journal of the Association of Moving Image Archivists* 9, no. 2 (Fall 2009): 36, from "Murnau Gives Views of Film Art vs. Stage," *Washington Post*, 6 January 1929.

25 Arthur Millier, "Art Directors Would Show Films How to Save Money," *Los Angeles Times*, 2 July 1933, A3.

26 Ralph Flint, "Cinema's Art Directors," *New York Times*, 22 November 1931, 135.

27 Ibid.

28 Ellen Spiegel, "Fred and Ginger Meet Van Nest Polglase," *Velvet Light Trap* (Fall 1973): 18; Balio, *Grand Design*, 90.

29 See, for example, "Hollywood Styles Go to Europe," *Los Angeles Times*, 25 March 1936, A2.

30 "High Salaries Paid in Nation," *New York Times*, 8 April 1939, 8. Salaries for other more high-profile MGM employees: the character actor Basil Rathbone ($56,500), vice-president Irving Thalberg ($167,875), and box office sensation Joan Crawford ($302,307).

31 Watts, *Behind the Screen*, 40.

32 D.W.C., "Meet the Set Designer," *New York Times*, 16 August 1936, X4.

33 Gibbons, "The Art Director," 46.

34 Flint, "Cinema's Art Directors," *New York Times*, 22 November 1931, 135; see also Gibbons, "The Art Director," 45.

35 "Movie Making," *Life*, 8 January 1945, 70–71.

36 Ibid., 69.

37 "Pity the Film Architect," *New York Times*, 11 November 1934, X4.

38 Idwl Jones, "Archipenko on the Set," *New York Times*, 10 November 1935, X4.

39 "Drawings for Film Sets: Anton Grot," *Studio [An Illustrated Magazine of Fine and Applied Art]* 116, no. 549 (December 1938): 32. See also Donald Deschner, "Anton Grot: Warner Brothers Art Director," *Velvet Light Trap* (Fall 1975): 18–22.

40 Clarence W.D. Slifer, "Creating Visual Effects for G.W.T.W.," *American Cinematographer* 63, no. 8 (August 1982): 791; *Life*, 7 August 1944, 76–77.

41 Mark Morris, *Models: Architecture and the Miniature* (Chichester: Wiley-Academy Press, 2006).

42 *Life*, 7 August 1944, 78.

43 Edwin Schallert, "Film Studios Pinch Pennies," *Los Angeles Times*, 26 October 1930, B9.

44 Frederick James Smith, "Hollywood's Miracle Maker," *Los Angeles Times*, 13 February 1938, 17; Corliss, "Designed for Film," 40.

45 Laurence Irving, *Designing for the Movies: The Memoirs of Laurence Irving* (Lanham, MD: Scarecrow Press, 2005), 33.

46 Lucy Fischer, "City of Women: Busby Berkeley, Architecture, and Urban Space," *Cinema Journal* 49, no. 4 (Summer 2010), 116–117.

47 Irving, *Designing for the Movies*, 17.

48 "Glass No Longer Taboo in Studios," *Washington Post*, 31 August 1937, 10.

49 "Pity the Film Architect," *New York Times*, 11 November 1934, X4.

50 Irving, *Designing for the Movies*, 33.

51 David Harvey, *The Condition of Postmodernity* (New Malden, MA: Blackwell Publishing, 1989), 147.

52 Deschner, "Anton Grot," 21–22.

53 Corliss, "Designed for Film," 54.

54 MGM Art Department Collection, File #76, Academy of Motion Picture Arts and Sciences, Margaret Herrick Library, n.p.

55 Ibid.

56 Ibid.

57 Frances Fink, "Hollywood Stage Sets Sometimes Outshine the Brightest Star," *Washington Post*, 31 March 1935, F5; Schallert, "Studio Space Shortage Seen," *Los Angeles Times*, 6 March 1933, A5.

58 MGM Art Department Collection, File #76; D.W.C., "Meet the Set Designer," *New York Times*, 16 August 1936, X4.

59 Gibbons, "The Art Director," 48.

60 "Old Picture Sets Now Scattered Everywhere," *Los Angeles Times*, 16 June 1929, C14.

61 Fink, "Hollywood Stage Sets Sometimes Outshine the Brightest Star," *Washington Post*, 31 March 1935, F5.

62 Gibbons, "The Art Director," 41.

63 Quoted in Balio, *Grand Design*, 198, from Crowther, *The Lion's Share* (New York: Dutton, 1957). See also Crowther, "The Queen Was in Her Parlor – At the Waldorf," *New York Times*, 21 August 1938, X3, and Crowther, "Characters Out of History," *New York Times*, 13 April 1941, X5.

64 "Building Project," *New York Times*, 3 December 1944, X3.

65 Louis van den Ecker, "A Veteran's View of Hollywood Authenticity," *Hollywood Quarterly* 4, no. 4 (Summer 1950): 323–331. See also Fred Andersen, "The Warner Bros Research Department: Putting History to Work in the Classic Studio Era," *Public Historian* 17, no. 1 (Winter 1995): 51–69.

66 Hedda Hopper, "Hollywood Sets Would Fool Mother Nature," *Los Angeles Times*, 26 November 1939, C3.

67 Fink, "Hollywood Stage Sets Sometimes Outshine the Brightest Star," *Washington Post*, 31 March 1935, F5.

68 Frederick James Smith, "Hollywood's Miracle Maker," *Los Angeles Times*, 13 February 1938, 17.

69 Ibid.

70 Ibid.

71 MacQueen, "Midsummer Dream," 43, 90.

72 Frank S. Nugent, "The Screen," *New York Times*, 7 February 1936, 14.

73 *Life*, 7 August 1944, 72.

74 "All for Realism," *Los Angeles Times*, 18 May 1941, C1

75 Alma Whitaker, "Studios Sink Millions in Spectacular Sets," *Los Angeles Times*, 4 April 1937, C1.

76 James D. Herbert, *Paris 1937: Worlds on Exhibition* (Ithaca, NY: Cornell University Press, 1998).

77 Andrew Michael Shanken, *194X: Architecture, Planning, and Consumer Culture on the American Home Front* (Minneapolis: University of Minnesota Press, 2009); Stephen Ward, *Planning the Twentieth-Century City: The Advanced Capitalist World* (New York: Wiley, 2002).

78 On Los Angeles as a center of modernist architectural innovation, including modernist homes designed or commissioned by film industry personnel, see Thomas S. Hines, *Architecture of the Sun: Los Angeles Modernism, 1900–1970* (New York: Rizzoli, 2010), 382–392 and 414; "Cedric Gibbons and the MGM Style: Pioneering Art Director Who Brought Modernism to the Movies," *Architectural Digest* (April 1990): 100–112; Lucy Fischer, *Designing Women: Cinema, Art Deco and the Female Form* (New York: Columbia University Press, 2003); and Shiel, *Hollywood Cinema and the Real Los Angeles*. Soon after *Lost Horizon*, a near-replica of Goosson's Shangri-La was designed and built by the architect Raymond Harry Ervin as a private home for the Denver motion picture exhibitor Harry Huffman. See

James Bretz, *The Mansions of Denver: The Vintage Years* (Boulder, CO: Pruett Publishing Company, 2005), 171–172.

79 James Sanders, *Celluloid Skyline: New York and the Movies* (New York: Alfred A. Knopf, 2001), 44–84.

80 D.W.C., "Meet the Set Designer," *New York Times*, 16 August 1936, X4. See also Spiegel, "Fred and Ginger Meet Van Nest Polglase," 19.

81 Fink, "Hollywood Stage Sets Sometimes Outshine the Brightest Star," *Washington Post*, 31 March 1935, F5; Frank S. Nugent, "Property Man: New Style," *New York Times*, 25 November 1934, X5.

82 Whitaker, "Studios Sink Millions in Spectacular Sets," *Los Angeles Times*, 4 April 1937, C1.

83 "Stars Work in Open Air," *Los Angeles Times*, 4 January 1935, 19; see also Philip K. Scheuer, "California Towns Get Rich as Hollywood 'Locations,'" *Los Angeles Times*, 13 October 1935, A1.

84 D.W.C., "Meet the Set Designer," X4.

85 Gorham Kindem, "Hollywood's Conversion to Color: The Technological, Economic and Aesthetic Factors," *Journal of the University Film Association* 31, no. 2 (Spring 1979): 34; Fred E. Basten, *Glorious Technicolor: The Movies' Magic Rainbow* (New York: A. S. Barnes, 1980), 73.

86 Scott Higgins, "Technology and Aesthetics: Technicolor Cinematography and Design in the Late 1930s," *Film History* 11, no. 1 (1999): 56 and 65.

87 Frank S. Nugent, "The Screen," *New York Times*, 20 February 1936, 23.

88 Higgins, "Technology and Aesthetics," 70–72.

89 David O. Selznick, internal memo, 1 September 1937, quoted in Alan David Vertrees, "Reconstructing the 'Script in Sketch Form': An Analysis of the Narrative Construction and Production Design of the Fire Sequence in *Gone with the Wind*," *Film History* 3 (1989): 87–104.

90 Slifer, "Creating Visual Effects for G.W.T.W.," 836.

91 Frank S. Nugent, "Hollywood Counts the Pennies," *New York Times*, 30 August 1942, SM14.

92 Ted Gill, "$5000-a-Set Limit Stretches Movie Directors' Ingenuity," *Washington Post*, 31 May 1942, L2.

93 *Life*, 7 August 1944, 72.

94 Schatz, *Boom and Bust*, 223–240.

95 See Shiel, *Hollywood Cinema and the Real Los Angeles*, 243–272.

3 Postwar Hollywood, 1947-1967

Appreciation is extended to Barbara Hall and Faye Thompson at the Academy of Motion Picture Arts and Sciences, Beverly Hills, Ned Comstock at the Cinema and Television Library at the University of Southern California, Jonathan Auxier at the Warner Bros. Archives at the University of Southern California, and Rosemarie Knopka of the Art Directors Guild, Los Angeles.

1 Irving Bernstein, *Hollywood at the Crossroads: An Economic History of the Motion Picture Industry* (Los Angeles: Hollywood A.F.L. Film Council, 1957), 21–22.

2 Edward Carfagno, interviewed by Barbara Hall, Oral History Collection, December 1989, 8, Margaret Herrick Library, Academy of Motion Pictures Arts and Sciences, Beverly Hills (hereafter AMPAS). Carfagno and Gibbons won Academy Awards for Art Direction for *Ben-Hur* (William Wyler, 1959), *Julius Caesar* (Joseph Mankiewicz, 1953), and *The Bad and the Beautiful* (Vincente Minnelli, 1952). This is corroborated by designer Preston Ames,

who recalled that architect William Horning joined Gibbons at the helm of MGM's art department in the 1930s. Everything had to be presented to Gibbons through Horning; and "absolutely nothing went through unless Gibbons had Ok'd it." Preston Ames, in Patrick Downing, *The Art of Hollywood: A Thames Television Exhibition at the Victoria and Albert Museum* (London: Thames Television, 1979), 59. Two-time Academy Award winner Boris Leven had similar observations about the situation at Paramount under Hans Dreier, claiming that it was run like a military hierarchy, although the latter was more likely to accord secondary credit to his art directors than Gibbons. Boris Leven, in "Designed for Film: The Hollywood Art Director," *Film Comment* 14 (May-June 1978): 48. In *Production Design: Architects of the Screen* (New York: Wallflower, 2004), 54, Jane Barnwell claims that Dreier designed and shared credit with his team. However, the credits for many Twentieth Century–Fox films still give him primary credit.

3 Lyle Wheeler and Maurice Ransford, and special effects man Ray Kellogg, consulted experts at IBM for the computer set designs in the film *Desk Set* (Walter Lang, 1957, art dirs. Maurice Ransford and Lyle Wheeler). See chapter 4 in my *Skyscraper Cinema: Architecture and Gender in American Film* (Minneapolis: University of Minnesota Press, 2009).

4 John Belton, *Widescreen Cinema* (Cambridge, MA: Harvard University Press, 1992); Barry Salt, *Film Style and Technology* (London: Starwood, 1992)

5 David Rawnsley, "The Position of the Art Director in Modern Films," *Film Review* (1946): 18–29.

6 Mordecai Gorelik, "Hollywood's Art Machinery," *Hollywood Quarterly* 2 (January 1947): 153–160.

7 Ibid.

8 Ibid.

9 Daniel Cathcart, "Defendant's Answer in Which a Movie Art Director Replies to a Critic from the Theater," *New York Times*, 6 October 1946, 4X, clipping, Art Direction Files, AMPAS.

10 Cedric Gibbons Memo, MGM Art Department, E. J. Mannix, file 18, AMPAS, quoted in Charles Affron and Mirella Jona Affron, *Sets in Motion: Art Direction and Film Narrative* (New Brunswick, NJ: Rutgers University Press, 1995), 95.

11 Keogh Gleason, quoted in Donald Knox, *The Magic Factory: How MGM Made "An American in Paris"* (New York: Praeger, 1973), 151.

12 James Naremore, *The Films of Vincente Minnelli* (New York: Cambridge University Press, 1993); Angela Dalle Vacche, *Cinema and Painting: How Art Is Used in Film* (Austin: University of Texas Press, 1996); Vanessa Schwartz, *It's So French!: Hollywood, Paris, and the Making of Cosmopolitan Film Culture* (Chicago: University of Chicago Press, 2007); Joe McElhaney, ed., *Vincente Minnelli: The Art of Entertainment* (Detroit: Wayne State University Press, 2009); Mark Griffin, *A Hundred Years or More of Hidden Things: The Life and Films of Vincente Minnelli* (New York: Da Capo Press, 2010).

13 Although production design historian Michael Stephens acknowledged that Preston Ames, who worked with the director on ten films, had a "personal style," he questioned whether Minnelli's or Ames's influence on the design was more important and whether Ames's cinematic artistry was really a result of the influence of Minnelli. See Stephens, *Art Directors in Cinema: A Worldwide Dictionary* (Jefferson, NC: McFarland, 1998), 13.

14 Hugh Fordin, *MGM's Greatest Musicals: The Arthur Freed Unit* (New York: Da Capo Press, 1996), 314.

15 Preston Ames, "An American in Paris," *Production Design* I (October 1952): 6.

16 Ibid., 9. See also Preston Ames, "An American in Paris: The Ballet," *Production Design* 1 (November 1951): 6–8.

17 Vincente Minnelli, quoted in Knox, *The Magic Factory*, 132.

18 Gene Kelly, quoted in Knox, *The Magic Factory*, 142.

19 Vincente Minnelli, *I Remember It Well* (Garden City, NY: Doubleday, 1974), 122.

20 Leven, "Designed for Film," 48.

21 Robert F. Boyle, interviewed by George Turner, 1998, 4, 14, Oral History Collection, AMPAS.

22 Beverly Heisner, *Art Direction in the Days of the Great Studios* (Jefferson, NC: McFarland, 1990), 44, 66.

23 Janet Wasko, *Movies and Money* (Norwood, NJ: Ablex, 1982), 108, quoted in Peter Lev, "Independent Production," in *The Fifties Transforming the Screen 1950–1959* (Berkeley: University of California Press, 2003), 25; Bernstein, *Hollywood at the Crossroads*, 22. He asserted in 1957 that one of the main symptoms of the structural fragmentation of the studios was the rise in importance of the independent producer, who had become an important figure only in the last few years. Richard Griffith, in *Anatomy of a Motion Picture* (New York: St. Martin's Press, 1959), 7, a book on Preminger's *Anatomy of a Murder* (1959, art dir. Boris Leven), claimed that the studios were now entering into financial arrangements with powerful production companies and the savvy producer was now "the dominant figure on the Hollywood scene." Prior to that date, for example, Frank Capra anticipated the rise of the independent producer-director. In 1945, he, William Wyler, Samuel Briskin, and George Stevens established Liberty Pictures; however, it was a short-lived venture. Hitchcock formed Alfred Hitchcock Productions. For a more complete discussion of early postwar ventures, consult Denise Mann, *Hollywood Independents* (Minneapolis: University of Minnesota Press, 2008); Lev, "Independent Production," in *The Fifties*, 24–32; Janet Staiger, "Individualism Versus Collectivism," *Screen* 4–5 (July–October 1983): 68–79.

24 Alexander Golitzen, interview with Barbara Hall, 1992, Oral History Collection, 161, AMPAS. When referring to the "production man," Golitzen did not mean the production designer, who was Boris Leven.

25 Bernstein, *Hollywood at the Crossroads*, 1, 21.

26 Gerald Horne, *Class Struggle in Hollywood 1930–1950: Moguls, Mobsters, Stars, Reds, and Trade Unionists* (Austin: University of Texas Press, 2001), 52.

27 Michael Baugh, "A Social Club for Art Directors? A Brief History of the Art Directors Guild: The First 70 Years," *Perspective: The Journal of the Art Director's Guild & Scenic, Title and Graphic Artists*, no. 14 (October-November 2007): 22–27.

28 Horne, *Class Struggle in Hollywood*, 34.

29 *Production Design Bulletin of the Society of Motion Picture Art Directors* began publication in January of 1951 and ceased publication in 1953.

30 See notes 15 and 16.

31 Carl Milliken, "Research," *Production Design* 1 (August 1951): 14.

32 Herman Blumenthal," Cardboard Counterpart of the Motion Picture Setting," *Production Design* 2 (January 1952): 16–21. Blumenthal was perhaps giving too much credit to Lyle Wheeler and Twentieth Century–Fox for originality. In "Cedric Gibbons, The Art Director," in *Behind the Screen*, ed. Stephen Watts (London: Arthur Baker Ltd., 1938), 46, he also spoke of small-scale replicas or "built to a scale of about a quarter of an inch to the foot, would delight any child's heart." These would provide "suggestions or objections," which "could not possibly have been foreseen from the original drawings."

33 David O. Selznick, in Rudy Behlmer, ed., *Memo from David O. Selznick* (New York: Viking Press, 1972), 165–166.

34 See Will Schmenner and Corinne Granof, eds., *Casting a Shadow: Creating the Alfred Hitchcock Film* (Evanston, IL: Northwestern University Press, 2007), for a discussion of how Hitchcock himself in numerous interviews promoted the fictional notion that he visualized his films in their entirety before filming. As Schmenner writes: "He is more workman than

shaman, and with the consistent collaboration of his department heads, he is visualizing and revisualizing his films, synthesizing disparate thoughts, and incorporating suggestions into the project's original idea" (7). See also Scott Curtis, "The Last Word: Images in Hitchcock's Working Method," in Schmenner and Granof, *Casting a Shadow*, 15–27, who discusses the multiple ways in which storyboards were used in Hitchcock's films. For example, Robert Boyle is the one who first visualized *The Birds* (Alfred Hitchcock, 1963) after reading Daphne du Maurier's story.

35 Ken Adam, interview with Jennifer Peterson, 2008, 36, Oral History Collection, AMPAS. Adam achieved the designation of production designer in Robert Aldrich's *The Angry Hills* in 1959.

36 Christopher Frayling, *Ken Adam: The Art of Production Design* (London: Faber and Faber, 2007), 17–20. See also "Ken Adam Interviewed by James Delson," in *Film Comment* 18 (January-February 1982): 36–42; Tino Balio, *United Artists: The Company That Changed the Film Industry* (Madison: University of Wisconsin Press, 1987); Vincent LoBrutto, *By Design: Interviews with Film Production Designers* (New York: Praeger, 1992); David Sylvester, *Moonraker, Strangelove, and Other Celluloid Dreams: The Visionary Art of Ken Adam* (London: Serpentine Gallery, 1999); Donald Albrecht, "Dr. Caligari's Cabinets: The Set Design of Ken Adam," in *Architecture and Film*, ed. Mark Lamster (Princeton, NJ: Princeton University Press, 2000); Ken Adam and Christopher Frayling, *Ken Adam Designs the Movies: James Bond and Beyond* (New York: Thames and Hudson, 2008); Laurie N. Ede, *British Film Design* (New York: I. B. Tauris, 2010).

37 LoBrutto, *By Design*, 39.

38 C. S. Tashiro, *Pretty Pictures: Production Design and the History Film* (Austin: University of Texas Press, 1998).

39 Sylvester, *Moonraker, Strangelove, and Other Celluloid Dreams*, 8.

40 Howard Mandelbaum and Eric Myers, *Forties Screen Style* (New York: St. Martin's Press, 1989), 26–27.

41 Michael Abel to Darryl F. Zanuck, 4 March 1952, 1, interoffice correspondence, Twentieth Century–Fox Collection, *Niagara*, Cinema and Television Library, University of Southern California, Los Angeles, California.

42 Simon Schama, *Landscape and Memory* (New York: Alfred A. Knopf, 1995), 14. See also Walter Benjamin, *The Arcades Project*, trans. Howard Eiland and Kevin McLaughlin (Cambridge, MA: Belknap Press of Harvard University Press, 1999), for a discussion of the embedded character of architecture.

43 See my *Skyscraper Cinema*, xviii, and "Fatal Attractions: 'Place,' the Korean War, and Gender in Niagara (1953)," *Cinema Journal* 5 (Summer 2012): 26–43; Elena Gorfinkel and John David Rhodes, *Taking Place: Location and the Moving Image* (Minneapolis: University of Minnesota Press, 2011), x. These "codes" may operate on a variety of levels from the scopic to the haptic, as Giuliana Bruno views them, prompting an embodied spectator to traverse the space. C. S. Tashiro and Peter Wollen suggest that spectators create mental maps informed by memories by which they can travel in their imaginations. See Tim Bergfelder's discussion of these issues in *Film Architecture and the Transnational Imagination* (Amsterdam: Amsterdam University Press, 2007), 20–25.

44 Bernstein, *Hollywood at the Crossroads*, 46.

45 Greg Elmer and Mike Gasher, eds., *Contracting Out Hollywood: Runaway Productions and Location Shooting* (New York: Rowman & Littlefield, 2005), 7.

46 Schwartz, *It's So French*, 7.

47 Bernstein, *Hollywood at the Crossroads*, 39–42.

48 "Art Directors Prexy Again Hits 'Lunatic' Lensing of U.S. Pix Abroad," *Variety*, 10 December 1957, 3.

49 David Kamp, " *Cleopatra*," in Vanity Fair's *Tales of Hollywood: Rebels, Reds, and Graduates and the Wild Stories behind the Making of 15 Iconic Films*, ed. Graydon Carter (New York: Penguin Books, 2008), 144. Italian staff further padded the production bill, resulting in three million dollars for miscellaneous expenses alone. As the director Joseph Mankiewicz's son reported, "Once you start saying you need 10,000 soldiers' outfits—this is like an invitation." As Maria Wyke stated in *Projecting the Past: Ancient Rome, Cinema, and History* (London: Routledge, 1997), 101, "Shooting began in England in 1961, resulting in a loss of some five million dollars, change of director and serious illness for its big name star Elizabeth Taylor." Adding to the film's financial woes, when the studio deadline of June 1962 was not met, the film's producer was fired and the head of Fox resigned.

50 See Smyth and Bruce Petri, *A Theory of American Film: The Film and Techniques of George Stevens* (New York: Garland, 1987), 176–189, for good discussions of the myriad tensions that characterize the film.

51 J. E. Smyth, "Jim Crow, Jett Rink, and James Dean: Reconstructing Ferber's *Giant* (1952–1956)," *American Studies* 3 (Fall 2007): 17. See also chapter 6 in Smyth, *Edna Ferber's Hollywood: American Fictions of Gender, Race, and History* (Austin: University of Texas Press, 2010).

52 Wyke, *Projecting the Past*, 107.

53 Boris Leven in Freda Halwe, "Ferber's 'Giant' Is Striding across Plain of West Texas: Logistics of Film-Making on Location near Marfa Makes Instant Impression," *Beaumont Texas Enterprise*, 3 July 1955, File 681, George Stevens Papers (hereafter GSP), AMPAS.

54 Edna Ferber, *Giant* (Chicago: Sears Reader Club, 1952), 87.

55 Marilyn Ann Moss, *Giant: George Stevens, A Life on Film* (Madison: University of Wisconsin Press, 2004), 202.

56 Ibid., 206; according to Trevor Willsmer, *George Stevens' Giant: The Making of an Epic Motion Picture* (Los Angeles: Warner Bros., 1996), 10, "Stevens met Ginsberg in 1931 at the Hal Roach Studios. Ginsberg was Vice President and General Manager, Stevens, a cameraman and a gagman. Ginsberg moved to Selznick International and, in 1940, went over to Paramount as General Studio Manager. By 1948, Ginsberg had become studio production chief, but left in 1951 due to 'policy differences.'" For the dissolution of Giant Productions, see box 51, file 623 GSP, AMPAS.

57 Daily Production Progress Reports, *Giant* materials, file 403, Warner Bros. Archives, University of Southern California (hereafter WBA-USC), Los Angeles, California.

58 Boris Leven began requesting materials in January of 1954 that continued until May of 1955. See Research Record, *Giant* materials, File 1013, WBA-USC.

59 Daily Production Progress Reports, *Giant* materials, file 403, WBA-USC. Unfortunately, a journal describing some of these experiences while on the set, entitled "Leven Days in Texas," is no longer extant.

60 *Notes on "Giant," Giant* materials, file 2954, pp. 1–2, WBA-USC.

61 Dave McNair, "Giant Symbols: Belmont Manor Plays Its Part," 16 March 2006, http://www.readthehook.com/79070/architecture-igiant-isymbols-belmont-manor-plays-its-part, accessed 16 June 2013.

62 Fred Guiol and Ivan Moffatt, Final Script, 4/4/1955, box 38, file 480, GSP, AMPAS.

63 This was reported in "Location Daily," *Variety*, 13 December 1954, n.p., GSP box 54, file 678, AMPAS.

64 Carfagno, interviewed by Barbara Hall, 1989, p. 47, AMPAS.

65 See box 14, file 14, Boris Leven Collection (hereafter BLC), Film and Television Library (hereafter FTL), USC.

66 "Research Record," pp. 1–16, file 1013, *Giant* materials, WBA-USC. Leven made over fifty -five requests. For each of these daily requests, from early 1954 until mid-1955, there were multiple clippings provided to him on a variety of subjects.

67 "Stevens Unit Goes to Texas To Set Up 'Giant' Sites," *Hollywood Reporter*, 5 January 1955, n.p. box 54, file 679, GSP, AMPAS. Stevens was ultimately responsible for deciding on Valentine for the Mexican outpost of Vientecito, while Jett Rink's house was seven miles from Marfa. See Production Notes on George Stevens's Production *Giant*, eight-page manuscript, p. 5, Warner Bros. clipping files, AMPAS.

68 "Boris Leven (1908–1986)," Art Directors Guild website, http://www.adg.org/?art=hall_of_fame&VIEW=29268, accessed 3 June 2013.

69 Boris Leven and Editors, "A Portfolio of Drawings," *American Artist* 24 (March 1960): 17.

70 Ibid.; Denise Olsen, *Two Friends Two Artists: The Personal Watercolors of Production Designers Robert Boyle and Boris Leven*, 28 July 2012–8 September 2012, Gallery 800, Los Angeles, 8–9. Leven became an exhibiting visual artist.

71 Olsen, *Two Friends Two Artists*, 8–9

72 Trade Ad, c. 1965, Boris Leven Collection, FTL-USC.

73 Leven went on to work with Martin Scorsese on *New York*, New York (1977) and *The Color of Money* (1986) and Wise on *The Andromeda Strain* (1971).

74 Olsen, *Two Friends Two Artists*, 8.

75 Boris Leven, "What Is a Production Designer?," *Film Comment* 14 (May-June 1978): 136.

76 John Rosenfield, "Texas-Sized 'Giant,'" in Resident Arts column, *Southwest Review*, Southern Methodist University (Autumn 1956), http://smu.edu/smunews/giant/swreview.asp#top, accessed 15 May 2013.

77 *Hollywood Reporter*, 11 November 1955, n.p., box 54, file 677, GSP, AMPAS.

78 Production Breakdown Meeting, 23 December and 27 December 1954, box 53, file 670, 143, GSP, AMPAS.

79 Robert Boyle, obituary of Boris Leven, *Los Angeles Times*, 9 November 1986, http://articles.latimes.com/1986-11-09/entertainment/ca-24224_1_architecture, accessed 15 June 2013.

80 "Ten Days in Beautiful Texas" (29 November–8 December 1954), five-page manuscript, box 48, file 576, GSP, AMPAS.

81 "Location Party," *Variety*, 13 December 1954, box 54, file 678, GSP, AMPAS.

82 "Ten Days in Beautiful Texas," 1, GSP, AMPAS.

83 Ibid., 5.

84 Ibid., 2.

85 Ibid., 3.

86 Boris Leven to Henry Fuhrmann, 25 April 1955, box 49, file 601, GSP, AMPAS.

87 "Stevens Unit to Texas to Set Up 'Giant' Sites," *Hollywood Reporter*, 5 January 1955, box 54, file 679, GSP, AMPAS.

88 Eric Stacey to Col. J. L. Warner and Steve Trilling, interoffice memo, 21 February 1955, file 2954, *Giant* materials, WBA-USC. Stacey reported that the team would be leaving "tomorrow or Wednesday."

89 John Rosenfield, "'The Passing Show': Texas from the Inside Out," *Dallas Morning News*, 11 November 1954, box 54, file 678, GSP, AMPAS; Rosenfield, "Texas-Sized 'Giant,' Texas' Own 'Gone with the Wind,' George Stevens' Epic 'Giant,'" *Selvedge Yard*, 29 December 2010, 13.

90 Eric Stacey to Col. J. L. Warner and Steve Trilling, 21 February 1955, file 2954, *Giant* materials, WBA-USC.

91 Mel Dellar to Eric Stacey, interoffice memo, 22 February 1955, box 51, file 638, GSP, AMPAS; Arthur Rowan, "'Giant' Enhanced by Bold, Off-beat Photography," *American Cinematographer* 56 (March 1956): 158.

92 Notes on *Giant*, p. 1, file 2954, *Giant* materials, WBA-USC.

93 Ibid.

94 Publicity, 7 January 1955, file 631B, *Giant* materials, WBA-USC.

95 Ferber described the house as "ghostly" in *Giant* on p. 121. The watercolor is thirty by forty inches and located in the BLC at USC.

96 Ferber, *Giant*, 111.

97 Ibid., 348; Leven, "Designed for Film," 49.

98 http://www.wisehistory.com/waggoner_mansion.html, accessed 4 June 2013.

99 Leven, "Ten Days in Beautiful Texas," 5.

100 Robert Boyle noted that Dreier Academy members admired the painter's work and the adaptation of his imagery was referred to as the "Hopper Effect." Robert Boyle, in Daniel Raim, *Something's Gonna Live: Conversations with Six Great Hollywood Cinema Artists*, DVD, Adama Films, 2010.

101 Leven in "Designed for Film," 51.

102 Guiol and Moffatt, Final Script, 19, includes a brief description.

103 Many of these sketches are located in the BLC-USC.

104 Production Notes on George Stevens's Production *Giant*, eight-page manuscript, p. 4, Warner Bros. clipping files, AMPAS.

105 Notes on *Giant*, p. 1. See note 92.

106 Boris Leven to Patrick Downing, 3 August 1982, Boris Leven Correspondence, box 16, file 172, AMPAS.

107 Rowan, "'Giant' Enhanced by Bold Off-Beat Photography," 158.

108 Michel Foucault, *Of Other Spaces* (1967), "Heterotopias," http://foucault.info/documents/heterotopia/foucault.heterotopia.en.html, accessed 18 June 2013.

109 Several photographs of the Shafter Cemetery are in box 14, file 14 in the BLC-USC.

110 Ferber, *Giant*, 199.

111 Research Record, 5, *Giant* materials, WBA-USC.

112 Joseph Barry to Carl Benoit, 29 January 1955; William A. Mueller to Tom André, 22 July 1955, "'Giant' Bakersfield location," interoffice memos, box 51, file 638. The first memo states, "The best oil wells are located at Lost Hills, which is about ten miles from Black Wells Junction towards Bakersfield, on Highway #466."

113 *Giant* materials, File 631B, WBA-USC.

114 Vivian Sobchack, "'Surge and Splendor': A Phenomenology of the Hollywood Historical Epic," in *Film Genre Reader* II, ed. Barry Keith Grant (Austin: University of Texas Press, 1995), 286, 288, 290.

115 Production Notes on George Stevens's Production *Giant*, eight-page manuscript, p. 5, Warner Bros. clipping files, AMPAS.

116 *Giant* materials, file 631B, WBA-USC. The same type of material was reported in the trade press. See "Logistics Operation Set Up for 'Giant,'" *Hollywood Reporter*, 27 May 1955, n.p., box 54, file 680. GSP, AMPAS.

117 See Herb A. Lichtman and Richard Patterson, "*Blade Runner* Production Design and Photography," *American Cinematographer* 63 (July 1982): 715–723; Paul M. Sammon, *Future Noir: The Making of Blade Runner* (New York: HarperCollins, 1996); Ridley Scott in Andrew Abbott, prod., "On the Edge on Blade Runner" (London: Channel 4 Television Corporation, 2000), quoted in Jane Chi Hyun Park, *Yellow Future: Oriental Style in Hollywood Cinema* (Minneapolis: University of Minnesota Press, 2010), 58–59; Ridley Scott, "A Good Start Designing the Future," in *Dangerous Days: Making Blade Runner*, DVD, Warner Bros., 2007.

4 The Auteur Renaissance, 1968-1980

1 See François Truffaut, "A Certain Tendency in the French Cinema," in vol. 1 of *Movies and Methods: An Anthology*, ed. Bill Nichols (Berkeley: University of California Press, 1976), 224–237.

2 Andrew Sarris, "Notes on the Auteur Theory in 1962," in *Film Theory and Criticism: Introductory Readings*, ed. Gerald Mast and Marshall Cohen, 3rd ed. (New York: Oxford University Press, 1985), 527–541.

3 "Sarris does some pretty fast shuffling with Huston and Bergman; why doesn't he just come out and admit that writer-directors are disqualified by his third premise? They can't arrive at that 'interior meaning, the ultimate glory of the cinema' because a writer-director has no tension between his personality and his material." Pauline Kael, "Circles and Squares," in *Film Theory and Criticism: Introductory Readings*, ed. Mast and Cohen, 550.

4 As far as I know, there is no written policy statement from any of the major film programs that would support this assertion, but I can testify to personal experience of it at UCLA in the late seventies and early eighties.

5 David Thomson, "The Art of the Art Director: Designing the Film," *American Film* (February 1977): 12–21.

6 See also Mary Corliss and Carlos Clarens, "Designed for Film," *Film Comment* (May-June 1978): 25–58, for a brief overview of the role of the art director in the classical era.

7 Axel Madsen, *The New Hollywood: American Movies in the '70s* (New York: Thomas Y. Crowell Company, 1975), 74.

8 "Dialogue on Film: Harry Horner," *American Film* (February 1977): 33–48.

9 For an elaborated discussion of the need to convince that a film object or space could exist in reality, see Charles Tashiro, *Pretty Pictures: Production Design and the History Film* (Austin: University of Texas Press, 1998), particularly chapter 1.

10 Jonathan Kirshner, *Hollywood's Last Golden Age: Politics, Society and the Seventies Film in America* (Ithaca, NY: Cornell University Press, 2012), 21.

11 Ibid., 21–22.

12 Léon Barsacq, *Caligari's Cabinet and Other Grand Illusions: A History of Film Design*, rev. and ed. by Elliott Stein (New York: New American Library, 1970, 1976), 56.

13 For a discussion about Kubrick and *Barry Lyndon*, see Michel Ciment, *Kubrick* (New York: Holt, Rinehart and Winston, 1980), 166–179. See also Vincent Dowd, "Kubrick Recalled by Influential Set Designer Sir Ken Adam," *BBC News*, 15 August 2013, http://www.bbc.co.uk/news/entertainment-arts-23698181, accessed 16 August 2013.

14 See "Ready or Not, Here Comes Gatsby," *Time*, 18 March 1974, 82–91.

15 Peter Lev, *American Films of the 70s: Conflicting Visions* (Austin: University of Texas Press, 2000), 59.

16 Beverly Heisner, *Production Design in the Contemporary American Film: A Critical Study of 23 Movies and Their Designers* (Jefferson, NC: McFarland, 1997), 148.

17 Kirshner, *Hollywood's Last Golden Age*, 41.

18 Heisner, *Production Design*, 149.

19 Pauline Kael, "Alchemy," in *Deeper into Movies* (Boston: Little, Brown, 1972), 421.

20 Quoted in Cathy Whitlock and the Art Directors Guild, *Designs on Film: A Century of Hollywood Art Direction* (New York: HarperCollins, 2010), 192. Originally from Maria Katsounaki, "The Magician of Hollywood to Show Paintings in Greece," *Kathimerini* (English ed.) (7 November 2005), http://www.ekathimerini.co/4dcgi/_w_articles_civ_1_07/11/2005_62741.

21 Kael, "Alchemy," 424–425.

22 Quoted in Whitlock, *Designs on Film*, 190. Originally from Harlan Lebo, *The Godfather Legacy* (New York: Simon & Schuster, 1997), 68.

23 See "Show Business: Playing the End Game," *Time*, 30 July 1979, 55–57.

5 The New Hollywood, 1981-1999

1 Patrizia von Brandenstein, in Vincent LoBrutto, *By Design: Interviews with Film Production Designers* (Westport, CT: Praeger, 1992), 179–191, 181.

2 Deborah Nadoolman Landis and Pat Kirkham, "Designing Hollywood: Women Costume and Production Designers," in *Women Designers in the USA 1900–2000: Diversity and Difference*, ed. Pat Kirkham (New Haven, CT: Yale University Press, 2000), 247–267, 263–264.

3 Charles Affron and Mirella Jona Affron, *Sets in Motion: Art Direction and Film Narrative* (New Brunswick, NJ: Rutgers University Press, 1995), 36.

4 Ibid., 184, 194.

5 One solution that I do not pursue here would be to attempt for production design what David Bordwell, Janet Staiger, and Kristin Thompson sought to do for classical Hollywood—generate a large, but neutral, sample of films to serve as the basis for statistical experiment (controlled in any number of ways). The aim here would be to approximate the design unconscious of the period—to find those baseline procedures accepted unknowingly by practitioners. My sense is that the Affrons' typology is not rigorous enough to support such distinctions.

6 Richard Sylbert and Sylvia Townsend, with Sharmagne Leland-St. John-Sylbert, *Designing Movies: Portrait of a Hollywood Artist* (Westport, CT: Praeger, 2006), 148. Townsend took up the project after Sylbert's death in 2002; the chapters I am principally concerned with are less memoir and more historical than his contributions.

7 Ibid., 149.

8 Ibid., 153.

9 Max Horkheimer and Theodor Adorno, *Dialectic of Enlightenment*, trans. Edmund Jephcott (Palo Alto, CA: Stanford University Press, 2002), 133 (slightly modified).

10 Michael Atkinson, "Thunder Roads," *Sight & Sound* (August 2009): 32–34, 34.

11 *Amadeus: Director's Cut* (DVD), "The Making of Amadeus."

12 Every national experience was, of course, different. Collections of case studies include Sibelan Forrester, Magdalena J. Zaborowska, and Elena Gapova, eds., *Over the Wall/After the Fall: Post-Communist Cultures through an East-West Gaze* (Bloomington: Indiana University Press, 2004); Peter Gross and Karol Jakubowicz, eds., *Media Transformations in the Post-Communist World: Eastern Europe's Tortured Path to Change* (Lanham, MD: Lexington Books, 2013); Lars Kristensen, ed., *Postcommunist Film—Russia, Eastern Europe and World Culture: Moving Images of Postcommunism* (New York: Routledge, 2012).

13 LoBrutto, *By Design*, 186, 187.

14 Justin Wyatt, *High Concept: Movies and Marketing in Hollywood* (Austin: University of Texas Press, 1994), 17. I have more to say about marketing extraction below.

15 Ibid., 26.

16 *St. Elmo's Fire*, DVD Commentary.

17 Ibid.

18 By this I mean that it won the award for films from 1989; the ceremony, as usual, was held the next year.

19 Townsend, *Designing Movies*, 179.

20 Ibid., 183.

21 Sylbert, quoted in ibid., 177.

22 Julie Salamon, *The Devil's Candy: "The Bonfire of the Vanities" Goes to Hollywood* (Boston. Houghton Mifflin, 1991), 298.

23 Vivian Sobchack, "'Surge and Splendor': A Phenomenology of the Hollywood Historical Epic," *Representations* 29 (Winter 1990): 24–49.

24 Carol Titelman, ed., *The Art of "Star Wars"* (New York: Ballantine, 1979); David Michael Petrou, *The Making of "Superman, the Movie"* (New York: Warner Books, 1978); Carl Macek, *The Art of "Heavy Metal," the Movie: Animation for the Eighties* (New York: Zoetrope, 1981); Brian Froud, *The World of "The Dark Crystal"* (New York: Knopf, 1982); Michael Bonifer, *The Art of "Tron"* (New York: Little Simon, 1982). (The last is a children's book, but its illustrations are in keeping with the "Art of" practice.)

25 John Thornton Caldwell, *Production Culture: Industrial Reflexivity and Critical Practice in Film and Television* (Durham, NC: Duke University Press, 2008).

26 For an insider's discussion of the decision to price videotapes for sell-through, see Michael Eisner with Tony Schwartz, *Work in Progress: Risking Failure, Surviving Success* (New York: Hyperion, 1999), 185–192; for a broader overview, see Stephen Prince, *A New Pot of Gold: Hollywood under the Electronic Rainbow, 1980–89* (Berkeley: University of California Press, 2000), chap. 3.

27 Laura J. Miller, *Reluctant Capitalists* (Chicago: University of Chicago Press, 2006), esp. chap. 5 "Serving the Entertained Consumer: The Multifunction Bookstore"; Jim Collins, *Bring on the Books for Everybody* (Durham, NC: Duke University Press, 2010).

28 Data available in Joseph Sunra Copeland, "The State of Publishing," 7 February 2011, http://www.mcsweeneys.net/articles/us-book-production.

29 James Bates, "Steven Spielberg Enjoys Rich Deal with Universal," *Orlando Sentinel*, 24 June 2003, http://articles.orlandosentinel.com/2003-06-24/news/0306240172_1_steven-spielberg-theme-park-universal-studios.

30 See Eisner, *Work in Progress*. Additionally, Disney produced the landmark entry into the "Art of" industry with Robert D. Field, *The Art of Walt Disney* (New York: Macmillan, 1942).

31 Tad Friend, "Waiter, There's a Bankable Star in My Soup," *Esquire*, September 1991, 152–162, 152.

32 Ibid., 152, 161.

33 Ibid., 161.

34 Rick Carter, *Filmscapes: A Journey with Steven Spielberg and Bob Zemeckis* (n.p., 2007), 41, 43.

35 Townsend, *Designing Movies*, 180.

36 *The Truman Show* (DVD), "Faux Finishing."

37 In the 1970s alone there were twenty contemporary nominees and three winners (*All the President's Men* [Alan Pakula, 1976, art dir. George Jenkins, Warner Bros.], *Heaven Can Wait* [Warren Beatty, Buck Henry, 1978, art dirs. Paul Sylbert, Edwin O'Donovan, Paramount], and *All That Jazz* [Bob Fosse, 1979, art dirs. Philip Rosenberg, Tony Walton, Columbia/Twentieth Century–Fox]). Information for the films in the list above that have not yet been mentioned: *William Shakespeare's Romeo + Juliet* (Baz Luhrmann, 1996, art dir. Catherine Martin, Twentieth Century–Fox), *How the Grinch Stole Christmas* (Ron Howard, 2000, art dir. Michael Corenblith, Universal), *The Birdcage* (Mike Nichols, 1996, art dir. Bo Welch, MGM/United Artists), *Babe* (Chris Noonan, 1995, art dir. Roger Ford, Universal), *Hook* (Spielberg, 1991, art dir. Norman Garwood, TriStar), *Men in Black* (Barry Sonnenfeld, 1997, art dir. Bo Welch, Columbia), *What Dreams May Come* (Vincent Ward, 1998, art dir. Eugenio Zanetti, PolyGram), *Toys* (Barry Levinson, 1992, art dir. Ferdinando Scarfiotti, Twentieth Century–Fox),

Interview with the Vampire (Neil Jordan, 1994, art dir. Dante Ferretti, Geffen/Warner Bros.), *Titanic* (James Cameron, 1997, art dir. Peter Lamont, Twentieth Century–Fox/Paramount).

38 All Academy Awards data is taken from oscars.org.

39 Jack Da Govia, *Trace* 1, no. 1 (March 1997): 2. I would like to thank Rosemarie Knopka and the terrific staff of the ADG for their help during my visit.

40 Ann Champion, "The Night at the Round Table," *Trace* 1, no. 4 (June 1997): 4. "There was lively and constructive conversation about the sudden revitalization of our Society with its new leadership. The event's main topic was 'How do we go about restoring prestige and respect for our position on a production?'"

41 Jack Da Govia, interview with Scott Roth, *Trace* 1, no. 6 (September 1997): 4–5.

42 All ADG data is taken from adg.org.

43 Tom T. Taylor, *Trace* 1, no. 4 (June 1997): 4.

44 Personal communication, 9 September 2013.

6 Hollywood's Digital Backlot, 2000–Present

1 "Ben Affleck: *Argo*," Set Décor Online, http://www.setdecorators.org/incEngine/?art=directors_chair_features&SHOW=1052161310.

2 "*Appaloosa:* A Conversation with Actor/Director Ed Harris," *Set Décor* (Summer/Fall 2008): 34.

3 "*The Curious Case of Benjamin Button:* A Conversation with Director David Fincher," *Set Décor* (Summer/Fall 2008): 63.

4 "The Craft of Art Direction—Conversation with Sarah Horton," *Pushing Pixels*, http://www.pushing-pixels.org/2011/08/16/the-craft-of-art-direction-conversation-with-sarah-horton.html.

5 "The Art and Craft of Production Design—Conversation with Sarah Greenwood," *Pushing Pixels*, http://www.pushing-pixels.org/2012/11/15/the-art-and-craft-of-production-design-conversation-with-sarah-greenwood.html.

6 "Film Décor: *The Help*," Set Décor Online, http://www.setdecorators.org/incEngine/?content=admin&&art=film_decor_features&article_id=1052160983&SHOW=1052161243.

7 "Film Décor: *Star Trek Into Darkness*," Set Décor Online, http://www.setdecorators.org/incEngine/?content=admin&&art=film_decor_features&article_id=1052160983&SHOW=1052161331.

8 Ibid.

9 "Sarah Greenwood," *Pushing Pixels*.

10 Ibid.

11 Kristen Whissel, "The Digital Multitude," *Cinema Journal* 49, no. 4 (Summer 2010): 90–110.

12 "Sarah Horton," *Pushing Pixels*.

13 Charles Affron and Mirella Jona Affron, *Sets in Motion: Art Direction and Film Narrative* (New Brunswick, NJ: Rutgers University Press, 1995), 24.

14 Barbara Robertson, "Painting the Town," *Computer Graphics World* 26, no. 9 (September 2003).

15 Jody Duncan, "*Anonymous*," *Cinefex* 127 (October 2011): 49.

16 Jody Duncan, "Rough around the Edges," *Cinefex* 134 (July 2013): 24.

17 See Jody Duncan, "*Les Miserables*," *Cinefex* 133 (April 2013): 12–27.

18 Rachael K. Bosley, "Creative Conspiracies," *American Cinematographer* (November 2012): 56.

19 Vincent LoBrutto, *By Design: Interviews with Film Production Designers* (Westport, CT: Praeger, 1972), 85.

20 I develop this point extensively in my book, *Digital Visual Effects in Cinema: The Seduction of Reality* (New Brunswick, NJ: Rutgers University Press, 2012).

21 Quoted in Nick Wrigley, "Stanley Kubrick, Cinephile," http://www.bfi.org.uk/news-opinion/sight-sound-magazine/polls-surveys/stanley-kubrick-cinephile.

SELECTED BIBLIOGRAPHY

Affron, Charles, and Mirella Jona Affron. *Sets in Motion: Art Direction and Film Narrative.* New Brunswick, NJ: Rutgers University Press, 1995.

Albrecht, Donald. *Designing Dreams: Modern Architecture in the Movies.* New York: Harper & Row, 1986.

The Art of Hollywood: A Thames Television Exhibition at the Victoria and Albert Museum. London: Thames Television, 1979.

Barnwell, Jane. *Production Design: Architects of the Screen.* London: Wallflower, 2004.

Barsacq, Léon. *Caligari's Cabinet and Other Grand Illusions: A History of Film Design.* Rev. and ed. Elliott Stein. New York: New American Library, 1970, 1976.

Baugh, Michael. "*A Social Club for Art Directors?* A Brief History of the Art Director's Guild The First 70 Years." *Perspective: The Journal of the Art Director's Guild & Scenic, Title, and Graphic Artists*, no. 14 (October-November 2007): 22–27.

Bergfelder, Tim, Sue Harris, and Sarah Street. *Film Architecture and the Transnational Imagination: Set Design in 1930s European Cinema.* Amsterdam: Amsterdam University Press, 2007.

Ettedgui, Peter. *Production Design and Art Direction.* Burlington, VT: Focal Press, 2000.

Fischer, Lucy. *Designing Women: Cinema, Art Deco, and the Female Form.* New York: Columbia University Press, 2003.

Halligan, Fionnuala. *Production Design.* Burlington, MA: Focal Press, 2013.

Heisner, Beverly. *Hollywood Art: Art Direction in the Days of the Great Studios.* Jefferson, NC: McFarland, 1990.

Lamster, Mark, ed. *Architecture and Film.* New York: Princeton Architectural Press, 2000.

LoBrutto, Vincent. *By Design: Interviews with Film Production Designers.* London: Praeger, 1992.

———. *The Filmmaker's Guide to Production Design.* New York: Allworth Press, 2002.

Lüdi, Tom, and Heidi Lüdi. *Movie Worlds: Production Design in Film.* London: Edition Axel Menges, 2000.

Mandelbaum, Howard, and Eric Myers. *Forties Screen Style: A Celebration of High Pastiche in Hollywood.* Santa Monica, CA: Hennessy & Ingalls, 2001.

———. *Screen Deco: A Celebration of High Style in Hollywood.* Santa Monica, CA: Hennessy & Ingalls, 2001.

Preston, Ward. *What an Art Director Does: An Introduction to Motion Picture Production Design.* Beverly Hills, CA: Silman-James Press, 1994.

Ramirez, Juan Antonio. *Architecture for the Screen: A Critical Study of Set Design in Hollywood's Golden Age.* Jefferson, NC: McFarland, 2004.

Rhodes, John David. *Taking Place: Location and the Moving Image.* Minneapolis: University of Minnesota Press, 2011.

Rizzo, Michael. *The Art Direction Handbook for Film.* Burlington, VT: Focal Press, 2005.

Schleier, Merrill. *Skyscraper Cinema: Architecture and Gender in American Film.* Minneapolis: University of Minnesota Press, 2009.

Sennett, Robert S. *Setting the Scene: The Great Hollywood Art Directors.* New York: Harry N. Abrams, 1994.

Stephens, Michael L. *Art Directors in Cinema: A Worldwide Dictionary.* Jefferson, NC: McFarland, 1998.

Sylbert, Richard, and Sylvia Townsend, with Sharmagne Leland-St. John-Sylbert. *Designing Movies: Portrait of a Hollywood Artist.* Westport, CT: Praeger, 2006.

Tashiro, C. S. *Pretty Pictures: Production Design and the History Film.* Austin: University of Texas Press, 1998.

Wanamaker, Marc. "Building the Movies: Tracing the Evolution of Set Design." *Architectural Digest* (April 1994): 102–108.

Whitlock, Cathy. *Designs on Film: A Century of Hollywood Art Direction.* New York: HarperCollins, 2010.

NOTES ON CONTRIBUTORS

J. D. Connor is an assistant professor of History of Art and Film Studies at Yale. He is the author of *The Studios after the Studios: Neoclassical Hollywood, 1970–2010* (forthcoming). He has written about tax credits and Tony Scott's *Déjà Vu* in the volume *Reading Capitalist Realism*; the discourse of independence in the *Blackwell History of American Cinema*; and *Super 8* for *Media Fields Journal*. He is currently at work on a history of tape recording from World War II to Watergate. He is a steering committee member of Post45, a group of scholars of American postwar literature and culture.

Lucy Fischer is a Distinguished Professor of English and Film Studies at the University of Pittsburgh, where she directed the Film Studies Program for thirty years. She is the author or editor of ten books: *Jacques Tati* (1983), *Shot/Countershot: Film Tradition and Women's Cinema* (1989), *Imitation of Life* (1991), *Cinematernity: Film, Motherhood, Genre* (1996), *Sunrise* (1998), *Designing Women: Art Deco, Cinema, and the Female Form* (2003), *Stars: The Film Reader* (co-edited with Marcia Landy, 2004), *American Cinema of the 1920s: Themes and Variations* (2009), *Teaching Film* (co-edited with Patrice Petro,

2012), and *Body Double: The Author Incarnate in the Cinema* (2013). She has held curatorial positions at the Museum of Modern Art (New York City) and the Carnegie Museum of Art (Pittsburgh), and has been the recipient of both a National Endowment for the Arts Art Critics Fellowship and a National Endowment for the Humanities Fellowship for University Professors. She has served as president of the Society for Cinema and Media Studies (2001–2003) and in 2008 received its Distinguished Service Award

Stephen Prince is a professor of cinema at Virginia Tech and an honorary professor at the University of Copenhagen. He is a past president of the Society for Cinema and Media Studies and the author of numerous books, including *Movies and Meaning: An Introduction to Film* (2013), *Digital Visual Effects in Cinema: The Seduction of Reality* (2012), *Firestorm: American Film in the Age of Terrorism* (2009), *The Warrior's Camera: The Cinema of Akira Kurosawa* (1999), and *Savage Cinema: Sam Peckinpah and the Rise of Ultraviolent Movies* (1998).

Merrill Schleier is a professor of art and architectural history and film studies at the University of the Pacific. Her books include *Skyscraper Cinema: Architecture and Gender in American Film* (2009) and *The Skyscraper in American Art, 1890–1931* (1990). She has published in the *Journal of the Society of Architectural Historians, Film Studies, Mosaic,* the *Journal of Architecture, QRFV,* and *Cinema Journal.* Her chapter "'A Place of No Return': Frank Lloyd Wright's Undomestic Ennis House in Film" recently appeared in *Archipop,* edited by Medina Lasansky (2014). She is currently working on a book on Frank Lloyd Wright and the cinema program at Taliesin and a chapter on cinematic penthouses for Pamela Robertson Wojcik's forthcoming volume *The Apartment Plot Reader* (2016).

Mark Shiel is Reader in Film Studies and Urbanism at King's College London. He is the author of *Hollywood Cinema and the Real Los Angeles* (2012) and *Italian Neorealism: Rebuilding the Cinematic City* (2005), and the co-editor of *Screening the City* (2003) and *Cinema and the City* (2001). He is currently working on editing and contributing to a new book, *Architectures of Revolt: The Cinematic City circa 1968.*

Charles Tashiro is an independent filmmaker and scholar. His critical writing has appeared in such publications as *Film Quarterly, Screen, Cineaste,* and *Cinema Journal.* His book *Pretty Pictures: Production Design and the History Film* is acknowledged as one of the leading texts on the sub-discipline of production design, and is particularly notable for its concentration on design's contribution to a single genre.

INDEX